The Finances of the European Union

Brigid Laffan

First published 1997 by
MACMILLAN PRESS LTD
Houndmills, Basingstoke, Hampshire RG21 6XS
and London
Companies and representatives
throughout the world

ISBN 0–333–60985–9 hardcover
ISBN 0–333–60986–7 paperback

A catalogue record for this book is available
from the British Library.

This book is printed on paper suitable for recycling and
made from fully managed and sustained forest sources.

10   9   8   7   6   5   4   3   2   1
06   05   04   03   02   01 00   99   98   97

Typeset by EXPO Holdings, Malaysia

Printed in Hong Kong

Published in the United States of America 1997 by
ST. MARTIN'S PRESS, INC.,
Scholarly and Reference Division
175 Fifth Avenue, New York, N.Y. 10010

ISBN 0–312–17294–X

THE EUROPEAN UNION SERIES

General Editors: Neill Nugent, William E. Paterson, Vincent Wright

The European Union Series is designed to provide
on the European Union ranging from general
definitive assessments of key institutions and actors, and policy
processes, and the role of member states.

Books in the series are written by leading scholars in their fields and reflect
the most up-to-date research and debate. Particular attention is paid to
accessibility and clear presentation for a wide audience of students,
practitioners and interested general readers.

The series consists of four major strands:

- general textbooks
- the major institutions and actors
- the main areas of policy
- the member states and the Union

Published titles

Desmond Dinan
**Ever Closer Union? An Introduction
to the European Community**

Wyn Grant
The Common Agricultural Policy

Justin Greenwood
**Representing Interests in the
European Union**

Fiona Hayes-Renshaw and
Hellen Wallace
The Council of Ministers

Simon Hix and Christopher Lord
**Political Parties in the European
Union**

Brigid Laffan
The Finances of the European Union

Janne Haaland Matláry
**Energy Policy in the European
Union**

Neill Nugent
**The Government and Politics of the
European Union** (Third Edition)

For Michael

Le Mór Ghrá

Contents

List of Boxes, Figures and Tables

Boxes

Figures

Tables

Preface

This volume was researched and largely written while I was on sabbatical in the Netherlands during the academic year 1994/95. I very much appreciated the opportunity to work on the book in a consistent manner over eight months without the diversions of my home university. I carry warm memories of my attic study in a farmhouse in the Dutch countryside. Proximity to Brussels and Luxembourg was a great help in interviewing MEPs, auditors, Commission officials and bankers. My thanks to Professor Tom Garvin, who released me from the day-to-day routines of teaching and administration and to Professor Peter Mair who welcomed me in Leiden.

I must thank many others who provided the material on which this volume is based. Numerous MEPs, EP officials, Commission officials, members of the Council's Budget Committee, members and officials of the Court of Auditors, officials in the EIB, the EBRD, the EIF, representatives of Brussels-based regional offices and umbrella groups of one kind or another gave me insights into the Byzantine world of EU finances. Special thanks are due to Mr A. Bletsas (DG 20), Mr Jean-Pierre Bache (DG19), Mr H. Oksanen in the Liikanen Cabinet, Mr Peters in UCLAF, Mr P. Zangel in DG5, Mr James Elles MEP, Mr John Tomlinson MEP, Mr Tillich MEP, Mr Brinkhorst MEP, Mr P. Dankert MEP, Mr James Spence EP Budget Committee, Ms Clare Wells EP Budgetary Control Committee, Mr Bernhard Freiedmann Member Court of Auditors, Mr John Wiggins Member Court of Auditors, Mr Barry Desmond Member Court of Auditors, Mr Hubert Weber Member Court of Auditors, Mr Chris Kok Chef de Cabinet, Court of Auditors and numerous other officials in the Court, Mr Peter Brennan Irish Business Bureau, and Ms Mary Sutton Trocaire.

I very much appreciated the assistance given by Michael Shackleton of the European Parliament's DG for Relations with Parliaments of the Member States. Mike spent many years servicing the Parliament's Budget Committee, where he observed at first hand the dramas of the annual budgetary cycle. He shared this experience with the scholarly community in his many books and articles on the budget. He was unfailingly helpful and generous with his time. A shorter piece co-authored with him on the Budget provided me with the impetus I needed to embark on a longer study of EU finances.

I owe special thanks to Maura Adshead, who did the initial library search for material, my colleague Anna Murphy, who provided material on East Central Europe, Chris and Eileen, who helped with producing the text, Jonathan Williams for his red pen, and my family for putting up with the inevitable last-minute pressures of completing a book.

University College Dublin   Brigid Laffan

List of Acronyms, Abbreviations and Glossary of Terms

ACP African, Caribbean and Pacific states linked to the EU by the Lomé Convention.

Acquis Communautaire Term used to describe the corpus of Community legislation and policy commitments among the member states arising from the Treaties, subsequent legislation and policy developments.

Action Jean Monnet Financial instrument to support teaching on European Integration in universities.

ADAPT New Community initiative to promote industrial change.

ADAR Audit Development and Reports.

ALA Asia and Latin American States.

Budgetary Authority Council and the European Parliament.

CAP Common Agricultural Policy.

CFSP Common Foreign and Security Policy.

Cohesion Fund Financial instrument provided for in the Treaty on European Union.

COMECON Council for Mutual Economic Assistance.

Community Initiative EU funding under the structural funds outside the Community Support Framework.

COREPER Committee of Permanent Representatives.

CSF (Community Support Framework) statement of financial support from the structural funds.

CEEC Central-East European Countries.

Delors I Budgetary Agreement 1988–92.

Delors II Budgetary Agreement 1993–99.

DG Directorate General name of departments within the Commission.

Dirigisme Term used to describe an interventionalist economic policy.

EAGGF European Agricultural Guidance and Guarantee Fund.

EBRD European Bank for Reconstruction and Development founded in 1990.

EC European Community.

ECHO European Community Humanitarian Office.

ECOFIN EC Economic and Finance Council.

ECSC European Coal and Steel Community.

ECU European currency unit – basket of 15 EC currencies used in all matters relating to the budget.

EDF European Development Fund for aid to ACP states.

EEA European Economic Area Agreement between EU and EFTA states minus Switzerland.

EFTA European Free Trade Association.

EFTA Cohesion Fund Financial mechanism established as part of EEA Agreement.

EIB European Investment Bank.

EIF European Investment Fund.

EMS European Monetary System.

EMU Economic and Monetary Union.

EP European Parliament.

EPC European Political Co-operation.

Erasmus Mobility scheme for third-level students.

ERDF European Regional Development Fund.

ERM Exchange Rate Mechanism.

ESF European Social Fund.

ESPRIT European Strategic Programme for Research and Development.

EUA European Unit of Account Basket of Member State Currencies used from 1975 in the European Development Fund, later replaced by the ECU.

EU European Union

FIFG Financial Instrument for Fisheries Guidance.

Financial Perspective Agreement on budgetary resources over a number of years. The current agreement runs from 1993 to 1990.

Framework Programme Financial programmes to support R&D.

G24 Group or Twenty-Four Industralised Countries.

GATT General Agreement on Tariffs and Trade.

GDP   Gross Domestic Product.

GNP   Gross National Product.

HORIZON   Community initiative for the handicapped.

IGC   Intergovernmental Conference/formal conference to negotiate Treaty change.

IIA   Interinstitutional Agreement.

IMP   Integrated Mediterranean Programmes.

INTERREG   Community initiative for border regions.

Inter-institutional Agreements   Agreements between the two arms of the Budgetary Authority on the conduct of the budgetary process and on substantive policy issues.

KONVER   Community initiative to help regions faced with a decline in defence spending.

LEADER   Community initiative for rural development.

LEONARDO   Framework programme for vocational training.

LIFE   Financial instrument for environmental measures.

LINGUA   Teaching and learning of foreign languages in the EU.

Lomé   Convention between EU and 69 ACP states.

Med-Campus   Co-operation between EU universities and those in the Mediterranean.

Med-Invest   Co-operation to encourage links between EU and Mediterranean companies.

MED-URBS   EU-Mediterranean programme for local authorities.

MEP   Member European Parliament.

NATO   North Atlantic Treaty Organisation.

NGO   Non-Governmental Organisation.

NOW   Community initiative for Women.

Own resources   Sources of finance for the Community budget.

PDB   Preliminary Draft Budget.

Phare   Programme for economic reconstruction in Eastern Europe.

RECHAR   Community initiative for coal mining regions.

REGIS   Programme for the Union's outermost regions.

SEA   Single European Act.

SINCOM   The Commission's computer system for budgetary management.

SOCRATES   Co-operation in education.

STABEX   System for the Stabilisation of Export Earnings in the Lomé Convention.

Structural Funds The guidance section of the EAGGF, the ESF and ERDF.

SYSMIN Mineral products in Lomé Convention.

TACIS Technical assistance for the CIS states.

TEMPUS TransEuropean Mobility Programme for Eastern Europe.

TENs TransEuropean Networks.

TEU Treaty on European Union.

UCLAF Unité de Coordination pour la Lutte Antifraude.

URBAN Community initiative for urban regions.

Youth for Europe Civic and social education of young people.

WEU Western European Union.

1

Introduction

The central thrust of the European project is both economic and political: to promote the integration of markets, the integration of states and the integration of peoples. The public finances of the European Union (EU) have played a central, albeit rarely acknowledged, role in supporting market consolidation, constitution-building and in the internal politics of the Union. The purpose of this volume is to provide a comprehensive but non-technical analysis of the evolution of EU finances and the political processes that have generated the range of financial instruments at the disposal of the Union. Most writing on the EU budget is done by those working on budgetary matters in the institutions, largely because the complexities of the financial regulation and the annual budgetary cycle tend to act as a barrier to engagement. The finances of the Union do, however, repay scrutiny because an analysis of the politics of budgetary matters provides powerful insights into the tensions between market creation and political integration, and between the EU and the national levels of public policy-making. It highlights the possibilities and limits of integration as the Union's political process grapples with issues of distribution and redistribution, for so long confined to politics within states.

The development of EU finances: an overview

EU finances developed from rather modest beginnings into a medley of different policy instruments which together endow the Union with considerable policy reach. Policy integration has taken place against a backdrop of legal and institutional change which together frame the Union's financial constitution, a constitution that has been shaped as much by political forces as by economics. Seven major compelling forces, highlighted again and again in this volume, moulded the development of the Union's financial system. First, the system is characterised by a gradual but definite expansion in the range of financial instruments available to the Union. The *Europeanisation* of public policy inevitably gives rise to pressures for further expenditure at a European level, despite the predominance of regulation in EU governance (see Figure 1.1). Second, the EU level of governance has struggled to secure a measure of financial autonomy from the member states. The decision to create a system of 'own resources' constitutes an important federal element in the Union's evolving political structures. Third, the deployment of financial resources has been central to *every* major development in economic integration – the customs union and the Common Agricultural Policies (CAP), Delors I and single market, and Delors II and Economic and Monetary Union (EMU). Fourth, EU institutions, notably the Commission, deploy EU finances to strengthen their hand in dealing with member state governments and to mobilise subnational and non-state participants in transnational networks around joint problem-solving strategies. Fifth, there has been a continual search for a stable and non-contentious budgetary process. Endemic conflict between the Council and the European Parliament characterised the budgetary process for many years. Sixth, the Commission and the European Parliament have striven to transform a disparate set of instruments into a coherent financial strategy that can be used to deepen integration. Seventh, *each* enlargement of the Union has shifted the political and economic context of EU finances, sometimes in a radical fashion (Shackleton, 1990; Strasser, 1992; Wallace, 1980).

1952–70: the foundation stones of a financial constitution

The 1951 Paris Treaty, which led to the establishment of the European Coal and Steel Community (ECSC), gave the new Community substantial financial scope. Its provisions allowed the High Authority to impose levies on the coal and steel industries to finance its activities and to raise loans. ECSC finance was used to tackle the social costs of structural change in these two industries

FIGURE 1.1

Community expenditure from 1958 to 1995 (at current prices and 1994 prices)

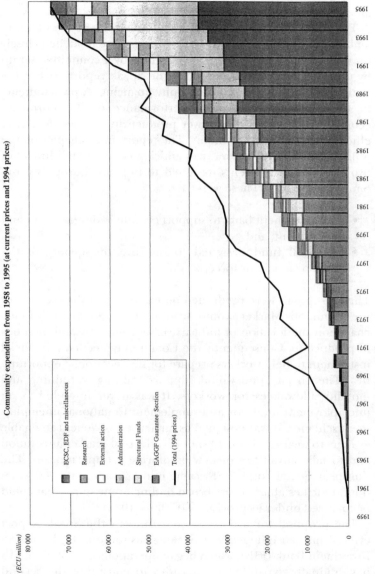

Source: European Commission (1994) *The Community Budget: The Facts in Figures*, Sec (94) 1100, p. 29.

by financing the building of subsidised housing for coal and steel workers, and by providing mobility and resettlement grants to workers who had lost their jobs in either industry. Thus market integration was accompanied by interventionist social policies, albeit of a limited nature, from the outset.

The Rome Treaty marked a further milestone in the financial ambition of the Community. Its provisions were modelled closely on the Spaak Report which was produced by a committee set up by the 1955 Messina Conference. The Spaak report set out the initial views of the Six on Community financing. A pivotal theme in the report was the weak performance of the European economy, characterised by lower productivity and less technical efficiency than the US economy. The report, in its chapter on the utilisation of Europe's resources, anticipated the establishment of two financial instruments designed to improve Europe's economic performance. These were:

- An investment bank to support economic development and adjustment; and
- A social fund designed to improve the quality of the European labour force.

These proposals were predicated on the view that the creation of the Common Market would lead to considerable economic change in the location of industry, labour mobility and methods of production. Consequently the Community needed a financial instrument to help workers prepare for new economic opportunities. The Social Fund would support training, retraining and mobility allowances for workers. It was never intended as an unemployment fund nor as a supplement to national unemployment schemes. It was designed as an active instrument to enable workers to weather the 'cold shower' effects of market integration and to take advantage of new employment opportunities. The European Social Fund (ESF) came into operation in 1960 when the Council established the broad outline of measures that could be financed under its provisions (Collins, 1983).

The proposal for a development fund in the Spaak Report evolved into an independent banking institution, the European Investment Bank (EIB), which began operations in 1958. The EIB has gradually expanded its activities to constitute the second financial arm of the Union. It represented a scaled down version of what had been proposed by Spaak since it was limited to raising money on the international capital markets.

The inclusion of agriculture in the Rome Treaty was one of the essential bargains between France and Germany that facilitated agreement on the Common Market. France saw free trade in agriculture as a counterbalance to free trade in industrial goods, which would benefit Germany. Farming provided a livelihood for 25 per cent of the workforce in the Six and represented 10 per cent of gross national product. Moreover, national governments intervened extensively in the agricultural sector to support farm incomes. For these reasons, the inclusion of agriculture implied a transfer from national support for agriculture to a Community system of support, which in turn implied a means of financing the support mechanisms. Article 39 of the Rome Treaty set out five objectives for the Common Agricultural Policy:

- Increased agricultural productivity;
- A fair standard of living for the farming community;
- Stable markets;
- Security of supplies; and
- Reasonable prices for consumers.

In reality, farm incomes, security of supplies and increased productivity have tended to overshadow the commitment to Europe's consumer. In the first half of the 1960s, a series of marathon Council meetings established the framework of the CAP across the range of agricultural products.

In addition to agriculture, France wanted to ensure that provision was made in the Rome Treaty for its overseas territories and colonies. This it achieved with Part 4 of the Treaty covering 'Association of the overseas countries and territories' that provided for a European Development Fund (EDF) to finance development activities in these territories. The first EDF came into operation in 1959 and lasted until 1964 when its was replaced by the second EDF which formed part of the first Yaoundé Convention (1964–70). Furthermore, Articles 136 and 238 which provided for agreements between the Community and developing countries formed the legal basis for other development expenditure (see Box 1.1).

```
┌─────────────────────────────────────────────────────────────┐
│                         BOX 1.1                              │
│            Principal developments in EU finances             │
│                                                              │
│                    Revenue              Expenditure          │
│  ECSC (1951)     Automatic levis      Housing, Mobility,     │
│                                       Restructuring          │
│  EEC (1958)      National Contributions  European Social Fund│
│  EDF             National Contributions  Development Co-     │
│                                          operation           │
│  EIB             Borrowing             Lending               │
│  EAGGF (1963)    EEC Budget            Agricultural Support   │
│  Budget treaties Own resources         All Budget            │
│  (1970/75)                             Expenditure           │
└─────────────────────────────────────────────────────────────┘
```

The pattern of EU finances that developed during the foundation period was dependent on the integration bargains struck between the member states, particularly Germany and France, and on the expectation of economic change as a result of market integration. Thus basic choices about economic integration implied the development of a financial capacity in the Community. The decision to replace national agricultural support mechanisms with open agricultural markets and price support led to common funding of market intervention. This ensured that financing agriculture would be a central and recurring theme in the budgetary politics of the Union. The Treaty articles on association and provision for a European Development Fund (EDF) laid the groundwork for the expansion of the international role of the Union, particularly in North–South relations. Provision for an independent financial institution, the European Investment Bank (EIB), and the European Social Fund (ESF) formed the basis for later consideration of uneven development and the social consequences of economic integration. The recognition that mechanisms to aid adjustment to market integration were desirable was built on in later years.

1970–86: development and crisis

The main budgetary development of this period was the granting of budgetary autonomy to the Union in the Budget Treaties of

1970 and 1975 which together underpin the current budgetary system. The Treaties established two main features of EU finances:

- An autonomous resource base for the budget; and
- A novel budgetary decision-making process.

The Rome Treaty envisaged that national contributions to the EC budget would be replaced by a system of 'own resources' which in Euro parlance was taken to mean a revenue base that was automatic in nature and not dependent on the will of the national authorities. The 1970 Treaty allocated three different resources to the EC's general budget from 1971: all customs duties collected on extra-EC trade, agricultural levies and a proportion of the VAT (1%) base in the member states. The Treaty made provision for a transitional period during which national contributions were phased out and replaced by the Community system.

The most significant constitutional development in the Budget Treaties was granting the of 'power of the purse' to the European Parliament (EP). The 1970 Treaty gave the Parliament the power to adopt the budget together with the Council. These powers were greatly enhanced in the 1975 Treaty which made the EP the second arm of a joint Budgetary Authority. The Parliament was given the final say on items in the budget defined as 'non-compulsory' expenditure, the right to reject the budget in its entirety and the sole right to discharge the budget. The sharing of budgetary power between the Council and the Parliament inevitably led to serious contention, taken up in Chapter 4, on issues of substance and procedure. The EP wanted to maximise its influence in the budgetary cycle and sought to use the budget to gain influence on substantive policy issues. The Council, on the other hand, in an attempt to protect its autonomy, sought to minimise and contain the Parliament's influence in the policy-making process.

Institutional conflict at EU level was mirrored by protracted conflict between the member states about the financial resources of the budget and its spending priorities. The 1970 budgetary deal was struck before the UK joined the Community in 1973. The deal was designed to present the incoming British with a *fait accompli*. However, enlargement disturbed the cosy budgetary compact between the Six by highlighting problems of equity and the regressive nature of the budget.

By 1978, the Commission concluded that the budget faced a resource problem and might not be able to fulfil its expenditure commitments. In 1982 the VAT rate reached 0.92 per cent and was almost breached the next year. The pattern and structure of expenditure exacerbated the resource problem because of the predominance of agricultural expenditure. CAP price support began to eat up the lion's share of the budget, accounting for 70 per cent of total spending in 1979. The automatic nature of the price support mechanisms made it impossible to plan and control agricultural spending.

The predominance of agriculture exacerbated what became known as the 'British problem' which dominated EU politics between 1979 and 1984. The structure of EU expenditure and its resource base did not suit Britain because of its small farming community and the pattern of its trade. The prospect that the UK would end up as a major contributor to the budget, despite being one of the less prosperous states, was apparent from the time of accession. The British had to battle to get the budgetary issue onto the agenda and to ensure that the distributional consequences of the budget would be taken seriously. Britain demanded a system of structured rebates and structural reform of the budget. These interlinked budgetary problems came to a head at the Fontainebleau European Council in June 1984 when France held the Presidency of the Community. President Mitterrand, who had decided to adopt an active European role in 1983, wanted to get the contentious budgetary dispute off the agenda. This he achieved with agreement from the member states to raise the VAT level from 1 per cent to 1.4 per cent in 1986 and to establish a complex mechanism of rebates for the UK. The Fontainebleau agreement tamed the budgetary conflict in the Union but did not solve the resource problem; by 1986 the limits of the VAT increase had been already reached. The accession of Greece in 1981 and the two Iberian states (Spain and Portugal) in 1986 intensified the budget's resource problems. The normalisation of the budgetary process and fundamental change in the budget had to wait the resurgence of formal integration underlined by agreement to the Single European Act.

Notwithstanding the tortuous nature of budgetary politics in this period, there was a considerable diversification of the Community's financial instruments. First, in 1975 the Community established the European Regional Development Fund (ERDF) as an active instrument to redress economic divergence in the Community. This was the beginning of a shift from agricultural spending. Second, new policy areas, notably fisheries, environment, and research and development, generated a host of new spending programmes. Third, the agreement to a European Monetary System (EMS) in 1979 was accompanied by the provision of soft loans to the two less-prosperous states participating in the mechanism, Ireland and Italy. Fourth, the Community's relations with developing countries were transformed in 1975 with the signing of the first Lomé Convention and a better endowed European Development Fund (EDF). Fifth, the borrowing and lending capacity of the Community and especially the European Investment Bank, expanded greatly.

Delors I: the turning point for EU finances

The Single European Act (SEA) (1987) marked a decisive turning point in the development of EU finances. Renewed confidence in the Community and the commitment to the 1992 programme heralded a relaunch of integration after the Euro-sclerosis of the early 1980s. Although the SEA appeared to have no direct implications for EU finances, the new article on 'economic and social cohesion' (Article 130) provided a powerful peg for the Commission's budgetary ambitions (Shackleton, 1990). The Commission, and particularly its President Jacques Delors, made a clear connection between the internal market and the budget when it launched two influential documents setting out a strategy for budgetary reform: *Making a Success of the Single Act* and *Report on the Financing of the Community Budget* (see European Commission, 1987, 1987a).

The changed political environment in the Community and the political cement provided by the shared goal of an internal market enabled the Commission to adopt a radical and comprehensive approach to the reform of EU finances. The Commission's proposals formed the basis for a major financial settlement which became known as Delors I. The settlement, which was agreed in February 1988 after seven months of tough and tense negotiations, allowed for a sizeable increase in the financial resources of the budget, an expansion of the monies going to the lesser-developed parts of the Community, and budgetary discipline to contain expenditure on agriculture (see Table 1.1). The thrust of the reform was supplemented by detailed proposals on the structural funds, budgetary discipline, additional own resources and amendments to the financial regulations. Delors I was a major negotiating success for the Commission president; the Commission announced that it had got 90 per cent of what it wanted, a claim that cannot often be made in EC negotiations. In addition, the deal was followed by an inter-institutional agreement between the three EC institutions that heralded a normalisation of the budgetary process after the struggles of the 1980s.

Debtors II: financial cement for the Treaty on European Union

The link between constitution-building in the Union and a budgetary settlement was once again evident after the signing of the Treaty on European Union (TEU) in 1992. The Delors

TABLE 1.1
Delors I – financial perspective, 1988–92, million ECU at 1988 prices

| Expenditure | Commitment appropriations | | | | |
	1988	1989	1990	1991	1992
EAGGF	27 500	27 700	28 400	29 000	29 600
Structural	7 790	9 200	10 600	12 100	13 450
Multiannual policies	1 210	1 650	1 900	2 150	2 400
Other	2 103	2 385	2 500	2 700	2 800
Repayments	5 700	4 950	4 500	4 000	3 550
Monetary reserve	1 000	1 000	1 000	1 000	1 000
Total	45 303	46 885	48 900	50 950	52 800
Own resources % GNP	1.15	1.17	1.18	1.19	1.20
Actual own resources used 1988–92	1.12	1.02	0.99	1.09	1.13

Source: European Commission (1995) *European Union Public Finance*, pp. 23–27.

Commission published its budgetary proposals just five days after the signing of the TEU in February 1992, in a document with the ringing title *From the Single Act to Maastricht and Beyond: The Means to Match Our Ambitions.* The Commission adopted a formula similar to Delors I by proposing a five-year budgetary strategy organised around six categories of expenditure. Budgetary increases were earmarked for structural expenditure, further strengthening the redistributive aspect of EU finances, and for external expenditure, reflecting the growing international demands on the Union. The negotiations were just as controversial and tense as the negotiations on Delors I; the member states were establishing the framework for EU finances to the end of the decade.

Moreover, the negotiations on Delors II were taking place in the aftermath of the Danish 'no' vote on the TEU and the September 1992 Exchange Rate Mechanism (ERM) crisis (Shackleton, 1993). Unlike the euphoria of 1987/88, the political atmosphere in 1992 was one of turbulence and a loss of confidence about the European project. The negotiations on Delors II were in the hands of the UK presidency which was reeling from the forced departure of sterling from the ERM and the protracted TEU ratification crisis in Westminster. Although the Union was not faced with a financial crisis in 1992, failure to agree to Delors II would have heightened the political crisis in the Union, hence the willingness of the participants at the European Council to come up with the elements of an agreement. The Commission was less successful during this round of negotiations in getting the member states to agree to their budgetary proposals. It failed to get the budgetary increases it sought; its proposal for revenue, amounting to a ceiling of 1.37 per cent of GNP over five years (1997), was reduced to 1.27 per cent of GNP over a longer timescale of seven years. The cohesion countries once again succeeded in getting a sizeable increase in financial transfers to the poorer parts of the Union and in getting agreement to a new policy instrument, the Cohesion Fund. Apart from structural spending, the Commission failed to get increases for additional internal expenditure. The member states were unwilling to countenance large increases in expenditure for research and development, transport networks and telecommunications. External expenditure, however, was another matter; there the member states endorsed an effective doubling of EU finance during the seven-year period.

The shadow of the future

The financial perspective agreed to in Edinburgh (1992) has already been adjusted to take account of the enlargement of the Union in January 1995 to include Austria, Finland and Sweden (see Table 1.2). The prospect that the European Free Trade Association (EFTA) states would be net contributors to the EC budget was undoubtedly one of the main attractions of an EFTA enlargement. Already under the European Economic Area (EEA) agreement the EFTA states had agreed to contribute to a Cohesion Fund, not to be confused with the TEU Cohesion Fund. Spain, in particular, was determined that the richer EFTA states should not have free access to the internal market without contributing towards cohesion. Thus, the cohesion issue spilled

TABLE 1.2
Delors II – financial perspective, 1995–6, with adjustment for enlargement, million ECU at 1995 prices

	Commitment appropriations				
Expenditure	1995	1996	1997	1998	1999
CAP	37 944	39 546	40 267	41 006	41 764
Structural operations	26 329	27 710	29 375	31 164	32 956
Internal policies	5 060	5 233	5 449	5 677	5 894
External action	4 895	5 162	5 468	5 865	6 340
Administrative expenditure	4 022	4 110	4 232	4 295	4 359
Reserves	1 146	1 140	1 140	1 140	1 140
Compensation	1 547	701	212	99	0
Total	80 943	83 602	86 143	89 246	92 453
Own resources as a % GNP	1.21	1.22	1.24	1.26	1.27

Source: European Commission (1995) p. 37, and European Commission (1994b).

over into the Community's negotiations with third countries. During the enlargement negotiations, regional policy, agricultural policy and budgetary payments became intertwined. Finland and Sweden successfully pressed for the development of a new budget line (objective 6) for Arctic areas with a population density of less than six inhabitants per kilometre. Moreover, the EFTA states got agreement for a generous system of budgetary compensation, amounting to 2559 (ECU million) over the period 1995 to 1999, which enabled them to phase in the financial consequences of membership.

The prospect of an enlargement of the Union to the east and south raises the financial stakes for the Union in an unprecedented manner. At Copenhagen in June 1993, the European Council accepted the principle of an eastwards enlargement as a Union goal. The process was intensified at the Essen Summit (December 1994) when the member states agreed to adopt a strategic approach towards preparing the associated states for membership.

Enlargement will undermine the existing bargains and will necessitate considerable changes in the *acquis communautaire*. The contributors to the budget and the winners from existing bargains face difficult choices about budgetary reform. All the remaining prospective applicants are poorer and more agricultural than the present member states. The existing financial resources cannot be stretched to accommodate the future enlargements without a major restructuring and increase in the total pool of resources. EU institutions and the existing member states are engaged in the process of calculating the likely financial costs. These are set to severely test the Union's decision-making capacity and the values, notably cohesion, that have come to play an important role in the existing Union. The development of Union finances is part of a wider search for structures that can accommodate the continent as a whole. The problem was succinctly put in the draft Interim Report from the Reflection Group set up to prepare the 1996 Intergovernmental Conference. It stated that some members of the group wanted to know 'who will be paying for what before going ahead not only with enlargement but also with ratification of the Conference itself' (European Union, 1995, p. 39). Money is once more becoming an issue of high politics in the Union.

The plan of this volume

Chapter 2 analyses the importance of the budget in the dynamic of integration in terms of market integration, constitution building and the internal politics of the Union. It attempts to tease out the relationship between economic and political integration and between market integration and the flanking policies that must accompany it. The chapter includes a discussion of theoretical lenses that are useful in analysing the development of the Union's financial capacity.

Chapter 3 begins with an assessment of the financial resources that are available to finance policy integration. The development of 'own resources' remains one of the major turning points in the Union's constitutional development. However, the regressive nature of the Union's resource base led to fierce conflict about contributions to the budget and the balance between payments and receipts. Chapter 4 analyses the historic budgetary decisions, the annual budgetary cycle and the growing mobilisation of national and transnational groups around the Budget.

Chapters 5 and 6 analyse in turn the use of financial instruments to build the Union internally and to project the influence of the Union in the international system. Chapter 7 turns to the management of EU finances and the nature of the control and accountability that governs EU expenditure. Particular attention is paid to the European Court of Auditors as the Union's external audit institution and to UCLAF, the Commission's anti-fraud unit.

Chapter 8 examines the quiet but inexorable growth of the Union's borrowing and lending activities. Diversification of budgetary instruments has been mirrored by an important diversification of lending instruments. The chapter analyses the European Investment Bank, the newly created European Investment Fund and the European Bank for Reconstruction and Development. Although the latter is not a Union body, the Community and its members states are the major shareholders of the Bank. Chapter 9 looks into a crystal ball to assess the major issues that will influence the Union's finances beyond 1999 when the current financial perspective runs its course.

2

Public Finance and European Integration

The central objective of the European Union is to create a union of states and an integrated market area. European integration has evolved in a gradual, incremental and cyclical manner since the end of World War II – highs and lows, fits and starts. Episodic periods of treaty change, policy innovation and institutional deepening have been punctuated by periods of stagnation, institutional stasis and political stalemate. The continental model of integration subscribed to by the original six member states has always involved an interplay between economic and political integration. The relationship between market integration and political union is fluid, complex and multilayered. Although the core of the Rome Treaty was devoted to provisions on economic integration, the common market was regarded as a route to political integration by the political élite who established it. Economic integration carried the burden of building a polity.

Market integration was and remains one of the pivotal means of binding the economies and societies of Europe together. On its own, however, it will neither create nor sustain the conditions for political union. Moreover, market integration, if it is to be robust, must rest on a degree of political cohesion. The public finances of the Union lie at the borderline between politics and economics, between market integration, wider economic integration and political union. Financial resources play an important role in complementing market integration and in providing sufficient cohesion to sustain economic and political integration. There is thus an important link between the finances of the Union and the process of political and economic integration.

Why analyse EU finances?

Although budgets are important instruments of economic governance, the making and managing of public budgets is inherently
political. Historically budgets have played a major role in the development of the modern state and in the extension of the public
sphere. The great struggles between parliaments and executives
about the 'power of the purse' involved conflicts about control
over the acquisition and distribution of public monies. The
modern states' capacity to intervene extensively in national
economies and societies rests to a considerable extent on the size
of the public purse and its capacity to tax. The search for social
cohesion within states is lubricated by the willingness to redis-
tribute from the 'winners' in the process of economic modernisation to the 'losers'. The traditional Laswellian questions of
politics, 'Who gets what, where and how?', are partly answered
through the mobilisation and distribution of public monies.

A study of EU public finances provides us with an important
lens through which to analyse the political and economic capacity
and potential of the Union. It casts light not just on where the
Union has come from, but on where it may be going, both as a
union of states and as an integrated market. Questions about the
purposes of EU finances and the principles that should govern
the distribution of European monies are bound up with deeper
questions about the nature of the Union as a polity and as an
economic space. The EU budget is a *horizontal* measure touching
in one form or another on all major policy domains. It is used not
only to foster policy integration but to expand the reach of the
Union as an international actor.

The history of budgetary politics in the Union highlights just
how difficult it is for the member states and EU institutions to
decide on who should get what from EU finances and why they
should get it. Highly contentious political battles are fought over
the minutiae of budgetary lines and about who should control the
dispersal of EU resources. Notwithstanding the small amounts of
money involved in the enormous struggles about EU finances, the
budget touches on a range of highly sensitive issues about distribution and redistribution between different regions and states.
To a large extent *solidarity* in contemporary Europe is limited to interregional and interpersonal transfers within the societal boundaries established by states. Obligations on the wealthy to help the

poor have evolved with the deepening of the sense of political community within states. It is no wonder then that the Union has struggled to deal with the distributional issues on its agenda and to push the bonds of solidarity beyond states. Jean-Pierre Cot, former chairman of the Parliament's Budget Committee, argues that:

> The quarrel over the Community Budget is the natural translation of deep political disagreements: do we want a Community or a free trade zone? An external agricultural policy or social management of a sector in decline? Regional solidarity or brutal liberalism? (Cot, 1989, p. 229)

Budgetary battles are fought on the basis of differing visions of integration, differing attitudes towards the use of public finance and differing interests expressed in the balance between budgetary receipts and contributions. The development of EU finances is influenced both by the logic of interests in this domain and the logic of ideas about the role of public finance in furthering integration.

At a more prosaic level, the study of EU finances allows us to unravel an important subsystem of the Union's decision-making process. The evolution of the Union's budgetary process provides insight into the Union's evolving institutional landscape and the role of relatively young institutions such as the Court of Auditors and the European Investment Fund (EIF). Many of the great institutional disputes in the EU have been fought on budgetary matters. Highly obscure distinctions between 'compulsory' and 'non-compulsory' expenditure, or innocuous references to 'amounts deemed necessary' in EC legislation, are the stuff of tough battles between the Council and the European Parliament. In recent years, attention has moved from a concentration on the formal budgetary process to the management of EU finances and questions of 'value for money'. It is no longer a question of how much money should flow through the EU budget but how the money is spent. The growing emphasis on evaluation is particularly noteworthy. Judgements about the effectiveness of various financial instruments have an impact on the willingness of the 'paymasters' to expand the financial resources of the Union. The ability of the Commission to manage the policy instruments it currently has influences the member states in their assessment of what tasks the Union should be granted in the future.

A focus on EU finances brings us into the nooks and crannies of the member states where different regions, social groups, public and private agencies battle for a slice of the Brussels pie. Budgetary flows to the member states are highly visible and can be calculated more easily than the costs and benefits of market integration. Although budgetary flows do not in any way give a true picture of the costs and benefits of integration to a particular member state or region, calculations of budgetary flows make 'winners' and 'losers' highly visible. National treasuries keep a watchful eye on their position in the budgetary league table. When, as was the case for the UK in the 1970s and 1980s, a state is structurally disadvantaged with respect to EU finance, it will attempt to use political pressure to alter the balance of expenditure and revenue.

Grantsmanship is an important sub-process of the Union's policy process. National politicians want to be seen to 'bring home the bacon' in the form of grants and loans from the Union. Brussels funds may have an impact on electoral politics within states as Governments seek to manipulate budgetary flows for political advantage. Different regions vie for a share of Union largesse and in the process territorial politics within states may be disturbed. The growing size of the budget and the expansion of programmes financed by the Union have greatly increased the number of organisations and individuals affected by budgetary decisions. The extension of EIB banking activities and its international remit add to the reach of the Union's financial instruments. This has spawned a flourishing consultancy business on how to avail of grants, loans and contracts from the Union.

The development of EU finances must be set in the context of the Union as an increasingly integrated economic space and as an emerging polity. The political and economic context within which EU finances function has changed greatly since the mid-1980s.

From policy-making arena to polity?

The European Union has gradually and tentatively evolved from an arena of public policy-making into a part-formed or semi-developed regional polity with some state-like characteristics.

Since the mid-1980s the Union has engaged in an intense period of constitution-building that has altered its governance structures and capacity profoundly. The Union has extensive law-making powers, an embryonic constitution, a widening policy remit, a strong judicial arm and a directly-elected parliament. The Union is not, however, a traditional political hierarchy with strong central political institutions, although this remains the goal of committed federalists. Rather, the Union may be described as a multi-leveled but unstable governance structure stretching from the local to EU level with a complex division of shared competencies between the national and EU levels of governance. The Union's capacity for public management is based on the enmeshing of the national and European levels of governance into a set of discrete policy communities which are bound together by the intense participation of national and European-level politicians, officials, para-governmental agencies, and representatives of interest groups in a process of formal and informal collaboration. European integration has fostered a gradual but definite 'Europeanisation' of the West European nation-state.

Almost all facets of public policy-making in the members states now have a European dimension. National policy networks and policy communities are being reshaped by their involvement in the EU. EU finances are part of this process of 'Europeanisation' although the participation of a growing number of national actors in transnational governance should not be reduced simply to seeking additional financial resources. The role of the EU budget in the process of integration is more complex and nuanced than mere grantsmanship and money from Brussels.

There is continuing tension and conflict about the division of power between the national and European levels of governance and within the EU level between the various EU institutions. There is also enduring conflict about the policy remit of the Union and its reach as a governance structure. Underlying all of this is a continuing political debate and struggle about the goal of political union and the pattern of governance that is and should be fostered by European integration. The Union makes policy not just to solve policy problems but as part of a process of building a polity.

Member state governments, political parties, social groups within the member states, Europe's regions and EU institutions have very different views about the role of public finance in the Union's economic and political order. Their views are shaped by objective economic and social conditions, their institutional position and their belief systems about the appropriate model of integration and European governance. There is endemic conflict about the kind of polity and economic order that is considered both feasible and desirable. EU finances have thus evolved in a highly contested political environment. The budget was not constructed as a federal budget for Western Europe but as an instrument for financing a number of policies that the member states could agree on (Denton, 1981, p. 80). Those who promote integration as state-building advocate a strong financial capacity for the Union, whereas those who wish to restrict political integration to the minimum necessary to sustain market integration advocate a restrictive view of EU finances. Ideas have played an important role in the political debate on EU finances. Insights drawn from a vast economics literature, particularly on the role of public finance in federal systems and the economics of integration, are used to provide a rationale for the development of the Union's financial capacity. As always, disputes among different schools of thought are deployed in political argument about the fiscal implications of economic integration. Moreover, shifts in economic doctrine and in the dominant 'economic paradigm' have a major influence on the intellectual climate within which EU public finances evolve.

The link between economic entity and polity

The foundation Treaties of the Union provided a framework for the emergence among the member states of an increasingly integrated market and a common economic space. The objective of integration was to generate economic benefits to enhance the *efficiency* with which resources were allocated in the national economies of the member states and thereby to enhance the material well-being of Western Europe. The founding fathers envisaged a level of economic integration that went beyond a free trade area or customs union by including provisions for a common market in the Rome Treaty. The creation of a common market implied the free flow of goods, services, capital and workers. Hence, the Treaty provided for the liberalisation and if necessary the elimination of national laws that discriminated against the goods, services or workers of the partner states.

Much of the Rome Treaty was predicated on the view that market integration primarily involved what Pinder has defined as negative integration, notably the removal of tariffs, quotas and national regulations that were barriers to trade, investment and the mobility of labour (Pinder, 1972). It quickly became apparent that market integration might also require considerable positive integration in the form of common policies because modern governments intervene in the mixed economy in a myriad of ways which affect competitive conditions within this borders. However, the Union's constitutional order favoured negative integration from the outset. Negative integration was promoted through regulation and the jurisprudence of the Court of Justice. Positive integration, on the other hand, required the agreement of national governments in the Council of Ministers which was not always forthcoming. The tough battles over the Union budget, a small budget, point to the difficulty of getting the member states to agree to common policies and an EU capacity for economic intervention. There has always been disagreement in the Union about the instruments of public intervention that are required to complete market integration.

Given the ambitious nature of the common market project, it is not surprising that the attainment of a truly unified internal market proved elusive; trade liberalisation in goods proceeded apace but exporters were continually confronted with the survival of a multiplicity of non-tariff barriers which impeded the free flow of goods. The liberalisation of capital movements, the free movement of people and a single market for services were even more problematic with the result that by the 1980s, more than 20 years after the signing of the Rome Treaty, it was possible to talk of the 'uncommon market' and 'non-Europe'. In response to growing competitive pressures from the world economy and the failure of the West European economies to adapt to the end of the golden era of growth, the Community launched a renewed effort to complete the internal market which became known in popular parlance as the 1992 project. The internal market project was in tune with the ascendance of neo-liberal economic doctrines that emphasised deregulation, market solutions and a change in the public/private balance.

The internal market programme highlighted one of the most noteworthy features of EU governance, namely the centrality of *regulation* which is the predominant instrument of public power in the Union (Majone, 1993). EU governance, when viewed from a regulatory perspective, represents 'strong government with a slender purse' because it allows the Union to have an economic presence without a large budget (Ludlow, 1989). The main policy instrument used in regulatory politics is *law*, rather than money or personnel. 'Integration through law' is a prominent characteristic of the Union's governance system. Legal instruments, buttressed by an active Court of Justice, has been largely instrumental in the establishment of an integrated economic space.

The primacy of regulation has two main consequences for public finance and European integration. First, the costs of the regulatory programmes 'are borne directly by the firms and individuals who have to comply with them' (Majone, 1993, p. 18). Second, the cost of implementing and enforcing regulations falls in large measure to the member states. Regulatory instruments do not require enormous central budgetary resources. According to Majone, 'regulation offers the only solution to the problem of maximising the influence of EC policy-makers' because they are severely constrained in budgetary terms (Majone, 1993, p. 18). The EU if seen as essentially a 'regulatory state' implies that the European polity need not be bolstered by significant fiscal resources in the future because the member states will continue to be primarily responsible for the welfare state and large spending programmes.

However, the evolution of the EU as an economic space has raised important issues of public finance that go well beyond *regulation* and questions of *efficiency*. From the very beginning, agreement on a common market was accompanied by the Common Agricultural Policy, a distributive mechanism. Moreover during the 1970s, the economic consequences of market integration and the enlargement of the Union to include a number of less-prosperous states forced further distributional issues, and hence issues of public finance, onto the agenda. Therefore although regulation and efficiency criteria have loomed large, distributive issues hover over all considerations of economic integration and the model of economic integration being pursued in the Union.

The economic system that evolved from the Rome Treaty left all the major instruments of macro-economic policy in the hands of the member governments. The choice of a common market as the major vehicle of integration reflected the boom economic conditions of the late 1950s when the countries of Western Europe were experiencing annual growth rates of over six per cent in very stable monetary conditions. The authors of the Spaak report, who drew up the blueprint for the Rome Treaty, were very influenced by the analogy of the large US market with its concomitant economies of scale; the founding fathers were more concerned with growth than with the distributional consequences of integration. They did not 'anticipate that long-term disruptions and imbalances would emerge from the creation of a customs union; on the contrary, all would ultimately benefit from a unified, free and competitive market' (Hodges, 1981, p. 15). Thus the commitment to 'harmonious development by diminishing both the disparities between the various regions and the backwardness of the less favoured regions' is found in the preamble to the Treaty which lacked any active instrument of regional policy (EEC Treaty, Preamble). That said, the Treaty allowed for derogations from the competition rules governing the common market and made provision for two policy instruments which were intended to deal with regional inequality. The gradual enlargement of the union after 1973 to the poorer parts of the European continent and the awareness that the benefits of market integration are felt unevenly meant that the issue of cohesion and uneven development had to be taken seriously in the Union. The Commission strove to get the cohesion issue onto the agenda from the early 1960s onwards and did so with increasing success after 1973.

The goal of a single currency, Economic and Monetary Union, has always been portrayed by committed federalists as the key to the final stages of integration and the creation of a truly integrated economic and political space. The renewed emphasis on market integration in the 1980s and the relative success of the EMS, led member states and the Commission to look again at Economic and Monetary Union (EMU). There were two main reasons for the renewed attention to EMU. First, the liberalisation of capital markets as part of the 1992 programme required either the abandonment of fixed exchanged rates or greater co-ordination of monetary policy. Second, it was felt that a genuine common market, the goal of the 1992 project, needed a single currency to ensure that the benefits of the single market would accrue (O'Donnell, 1991, p. 9). In 1988 the European Council asked the Commission President, Jacques Delors, to chair a committee of central bankers to draft proposals on EMU. The Delors report on EMU, published in 1989, formed the basis for negotiations in an Intergovernmental Conference on EMU which, together with parallel work on political union, emerged as the Treaty on European Union (TEU), signed in 1991 and ratified with some difficulty by November 1993. The TEU commits the member states to a three-stage approach to EMU:

- Stage one was designed to consolidate the exchange rate mechanism (ERM) and remove all exchange controls as part of the single market process.
- Stage two began on 1 January 1994 with the establishment of the European Monetary Institute (EMI) responsible for preparing for a single currency.
- Stage three which involved the European Council in deciding before 1996 whether or not the majority of member states fulfil the necessary conditions for the adoption of a single currency and, if so, that a date be set for stage three. If not, the final stage will begin on 1 January 1999 with the involvement of those states that are eligible to participate.

Developments since the ratification of the TEU mean that 1999 is now the target date for the beginning of the final stage of the EMU. At the Madrid European Council (15/16 December 1995), Europe's leaders concluded that the decision on which countries will participate in EMU should be taken in early 1998.

The principle, in the Delors Report, that there should be parallel development between the economic and monetary aspects of the system are not borne out in practice. The Treaty is far more prescriptive about what constitutes a monetary union than it is on economic union. What the Treaty certainly does not provide for is a 'fiscal union' which remains largely the responsibility of the national level of governance. Nearly all federal systems and monetary unions are also fiscal unions, with tax and expenditure mechanisms to maintain interregional cohesion. Yet the Treaty proposes a monetary union without a fiscal union. This again reflects a limited view of the role of public finance in integration and the limits to political integration in the Union. The underlying dilemma concerning the link between economic and political union is aptly summed up by Goodhart:

> The establishment of a successful monetary union may well require support from a strong, centralised, or at least inter-regionally co-ordinated, fiscal (and regional) policy to ease the complications of regional adjustment. Yet it is difficult to establish a centralised fiscal authority unless there is monetary union, a single currency. It seems unlikely then that a fixed exchange-rate system can be maintained until political harmony and social agreement allow the division of burdens within the area and the direction of policy in each major part of the system to be decided by an accepted central political authority. (Goodhart, 1989)

The Community's economic order and the nature of economic governance in the Community is bound up with the nature and potential of the EU as a polity and vice versa. EU finances have developed in a complex and uneasy relationship to the overall development of the EU as an economic and political space. Both the nature of the Union as a polity and as an economic order are highly contested; different member states, social, economic and political forces within Europe, and EU institutions have very different views about the desirable political and economic order that should be fostered by European integration. Hence EU finances represent the outcome of various struggles about the integration process itself rather than an optimum blueprint of the role of public finance in integration.

Useful theoretical lenses

This volume draws on two sets of literature to help unravel the labyrinthine processes of EU finances and to identify the main factors that shape the principles and purposes which lie behind EU finances. Evolving ideas about the role of public finance in integration are themselves part of the political process to be used by different interested coalitions. The first strand of literature draws primarily on fiscal federalism, sometimes described as constitutional economics. The second finds inspiration in the growing body of policy-oriented research on the Union's governance structure and policy communities.

Fiscal federalism

Ideas about the role of public finance in integration and the assignment of public functions in multi-tiered systems draw on the insights of a branch of political economy known as fiscal federalism. The focus in this literature is on budgeting and task allocation in multi-leveled polities. Budgetary issues are intrinsically linked to questions about the assignment of different public functions to different levels of government, a critical issue in the EU given the current emphasis on subsidiarity. Much of the literature deals with fiscal arrangements in well-established mature federations and thus has limited applicability and certainly does not provide a blueprint for the evolution of the Union's financial constitution (European Commission, 1993b). We must be mindly that 'Theory provides no prefabricated models for the structure of unions in general or of the Community in particular...empirical evidence shows that federations function with widely-varying degrees of expenditure-and-revenue-centralisation. Much depends on the political process embracing the constitutional foundations of the union, the rules of co-operation between levels of government, the characteristics of the democratic system and the sharing of power between executive and legislative branches of government' (Reichenbach, 1994, p. 196). The design of a financial system owes as much to the political conflict as to the aspiration for an efficient and equitable deployment of resources. Because the EU is not a stable polity, the process of assigning policy responsibility to different levels of government is highly politicised. However some of its major themes in this literature highlight the challenges facing the Union as it grapples with the problem of public assignment and the design of an appropriate financial framework for its activities.

Questions of *efficiency*, on the one hand, and *equity* on the other form the core of the fiscal federalist literature. Support for the assignment of public functions to a particular level of government rest on arguments about the efficiency of resource allocation and issues of distribution (Helm and Smith, 1989). The principle of equity implies that a system of public finance should be progressive on both its revenue side and its expenditure side. A progressive financial system, in simple words, means that the wealthy pay more and the poor least, and that the less prosperous benefit from redistributive transfers from the rich. Reichenbach refers to this as the resource flow principle, i.e. the resources must flow, in net terms, from richer regions of the Union to poorer ones (Reichenbach, 1989, p. 201).

Discussions of public assignment usually begin with the Musgravian triptych that distinguishes between:

- *allocative* policies that strive for an efficient allocation of resources;
- *distributive* and *redistributive* policies of an interpersonal and interregional character;
- *stabilisation* policies to iron out troughs in the business cycle. (Musgrave and Musgrave, 1989, pp. 3–17)

It could be argued that *external policies*, although allocative in nature, deserve separate treatment because they involve the deployment of instruments of public power outside the polity (Costello, 1995, p. 12). Arguments that support either *decentralised* or *centralised* provision form the core of the fiscal federalist literature (Costello, 1995; Biehl, 1994; Musgrave and Musgrave, 1980). Economic theory begins from a general presumption that a decentralisation of economic policy-making is most efficient (Helm and Smith, 1989, p. 3). The inclusion of the principle of subsidiarity in the TEU which stipulates that the Community shall take action only if national action will not suffice embodies a presumption of decentralisation (Smith, 1992, p. 107). Hence, subsidiarity implies that the burden of proof lies with those proposing to centralise public functions in the Union (Reichenbach, 1994, p. 197).

What follows is an attempt to distill the most important principles that should influence the assignment of public finance responsibilities to one or other level of government; some of these principles support decentralisation, others centralisation.

- Oates argues that in any budgetary decision-making system there should be a *correspondence* between those who benefit from public expenditure and the taxpayers who fund the budget. If beneficiaries predominate, the budget will be too high; if the taxpayers predominate the budget will be too low (Oates, 1977; Biehl, 1994).
- The principle of *voter preference* supports the view that lower levels of government are better able to respond to the expressed needs of citizens. Higher levels of government may impose too high a degree of uniformity and not pay adequate attention to the diversity of needs and interests (Costello, 1995).
- *Democratic accountability* is best assured by lower-level units of government where voters can monitor public provision and its costs. This avoids the problems of 'fiscal illusion', the illusion that there are no budgetary costs.
- According to some writers, innovation and efficiency are fostered by competition between jurisdictions (Costello, 1995).

The main arguments in favour of centralised provision rely on the following:

- Centralised provision responds to problems of *spillover* between different jurisdictions and allows the higher level of government to benefit from *economies of scale*. The ability of the higher tier of government to manage spillovers or the externalities arising from policies is one of the most frequently cited arguments in favour of the assignment of public functions to the higher tier of government.
- Centralisation fosters uniformity of public provision and allows the higher level of government to subsidise the pro-vision of goods.
- Centralisation allows the higher level of government to equalise fiscal conditions (fair fiscal equalisation) in the lower level units so as to provide a minimum level of public services throughout a jurisdication. This draws on what Helm and Smith define as the rights of positive freedom which suggests that 'by virtue of membership of the EC, each citizen is entitled to a common minimum standard of

living' (Helm and Smith, 1989, p. 4). Underlying this principle is the need for fiscal transfers from richer to poorer regions.

* Centralisation allows the higher level of government to stabilise economic conditions during economic downturns. The stabilisation function is always seen as belonging to the upper tier in a federal system of public finance.

Underlying the arguments in favour of centralisation or decentralisation is a concern with efficiency and equity and the tension between these two principles. EU finances are predominantly directed towards allocation, with a limited distributional capacity and no role in stabilisation. The small size of EU finances, 1.28 per cent of Union GDP in 1994 and 2.5 per cent of public expenditure in the member states, militates against a role for the Union in stabilising economic activity. The figure of 2.5 per cent must be seen against the proportion of gross national product (between 30 per cent and 50 per cent of GNP) that flows through national coffers as public expenditure. Issues of redistribution and fair burden-sharing were prominent on the EC budgetary agenda from the mid-1970s onwards and have hovered over all budgetary negotiations since then. Moreover, agreement to move to a single currency by the end of the 1990s raises unresolved issues about the budget and the EMU.

The Commission has looked to theoretical and empirical analyses based on fiscal federalism to provide it with intellectual arguments for the development of the public finances of the Union (see Box 2.1). In 1974 it commissioned the MacDougall Report (A study group on the role of public finance in European integration) to analyse the public finance needs of an integrated economic space. The study group, which is widely acknowledged to have broken new theoretical ground, published its report in 1977 having examined public finance in five federal states and three unitary ones to assess financial arrangements between different levels of government and the effects of public finance on different regions. It based its assessment of development of EU finances on the principles of *economies of scale* and *spillover*. It devoted considerable attention to the *redistributive* function of EU public finances and argued strongly for the promotion of a redistributive capacity at EU level. The group concluded that a small public

---

BOX 2.1
Reports on the role of public finance in European integration

1977   The MacDougall Report
Attempt to apply the principles of fiscal federalism to EU finance.
Comparison with existing federations and unitary states. Key criteria were externalities and spill-over, but main conclusions focused
on the distributive role of EU public finances. Made a strong case
in favour of redistribution from the richer to the poorer member
states, largely through grants, but did see a possible place for a
federal equilisation mechanism.

1987   The Padoa-Schioppa Report
Analysis of the Community's economic system in general and not
just is public finances. Devoted considerable attention to the
Community budget and was concerned with the role of the
budget in the politics of integration. The report argued that
because the Community was a political entity with a narrow range
of policy instruments it had to be concerned with the broad
balance of economic advantages that it offered the member states.
Made the case for redistribution of a limited nature (more limited
than MacDougall) and supported a progressive revenue base of
the budget.

1993   Sound Money: Stable Finances
The report is an assessment by DG 2 and an independent group
of economists of the role of public finance in integration in the
context of EMU and enlargement. The report differs markedly
from MacDougall with the emphasis on decentralisation and subsidiarity. The reports concludes that a small budget of 2 per cent
of GDP is adequate for an EMU.

---

sector federation, with a budget of between 5 and 7 per cent of
GDP (more if defence was included) would facilitate monetary
union, although the authors were very sceptical about the
prospects of monetary union in 1977. The report also advocated a
'pre-federal' budget of between 2 and 2.5 per cent of GDP, which
it argued would achieve considerable interregional redistribution.
The predominant view in the report was that economic integration disproportionately benefited the richer parts of the
Community and that the Union had to take distributional issues
into account. Although the MacDougall proposals were modest,
the prospects for the implementation of even a 'pre-pre federal

budget' remained poor until the mid-1980s. The proposals foundered on the weakness of 'political homogeneity' in the Community, a criterion which surfaces in the report.

MacDougall was followed by the Padoa-Schioppa Report of 1987, entitled *Efficiency, Stability and Equity*, which was given the brief of looking at the Union's economic system as a whole and not just its financial constitution. In a very lucid overview of the different dimensions of the Union's economic system, the report reached a number of conclusions about the Union budget. It made a strong case for strengthening the Union's regional policy on the grounds that 'any extrapolation of "invisible hand" ideas into the real world of regional economics in the process of market-opening measures would be unwarranted in the light of economic history and theory' (Padoa-Schioppa, 1987, p. 10). Hence the group supported a substantial increase in the size of the structural funds and highlighted the need to tackle the CAP budget. The report also favoured conditionality when it argued that substantial transfers should be accompanied by agreement over macro-economic policy strategy. It was particularly concerned that the Union should establish budgetary arrangements that reduced distributive conflict and provided incentives for sound policy-making. The budgetary fatigue occasioned by the *ad hoc* treatment of the UK budgetary problem was largely instrumental in this prescription.

The Commission itself published a report, *Stable Money: Sound Finances* (European Commission, 1993b) which was a distilled version of a voluminous tone (630 pages), *The Economics of Community Public Finance* (European Commission, 1993a) drafted by a group of external experts and the Commission's staff in DG 2 (Directorate General, Economic and Financial Affairs). The endeavour was essentially to review public assignment in the EU in the light of theoretical developments in fiscal federalism and in economics since MacDougall. The exercise was not universally favoured in the Commission; DG 19 (Budgetary Affairs) while engaged in the process of negotiating the Delors II package did not want interference from another DG. Nor did it want policy prescriptions or unrealistic options that might not find favour in the Council hovering over the debate. The tradition in DG 2 of producing the big report (Cecchini/single market, One Market: One Money/EMU) to justify and highlight the benefits of major policy developments in economic integration is apparent (European Commission, 1988 and 1990). After EMU and in the context of the Delors II negotiations, the Union's fiscal constitution was the next major issue that needed tackling. The inclusion of the principle of subsidiarity in the TEU was a very major concern in the report. The analysis began with an assessment of different categories of policies (allocation, distribution, stabilisation and external) in the EU and the budgetary means that would be required to carry out these functions.

The tone of the 1993 report differed markedly from the earlier MacDougall Report in that it did not argue for a substantial increase in the size of the budget underlined by two headings which state 'Beware of centralisation' and 'A small budget will do'. The report contains five main recommendations. First, while accepting the principle of subsidiarity, it concluded that there was an economic rationale for additional Community expenditure on environmental protection, infrastructure, research and development, and to a lesser extent on higher education. Second, it endorsed the growth of external aid and concluded that an increasing proportion of third-country assistance should flow from the Union budget. Third, the report emphasised the principle of budgetary fairness whereby interregional transfers should flow from the richer to the poorer areas of the Union. The report, however, did warn of the inherent dangers of 'grantsmanship' and the building of 'cathedrals in the desert'. Fourth, the report concluded that the EU budget should assist member states to deal with specific external shocks in an EMU, but that a small budget would achieve this. Fifth, the report looked at the budgetary implications of further deepening and widening (European Commission, 1993b, pp. 1–9). The conclusions of the report on EMU and enlargement are discussed in Chapter 9.

Policy analysis

Our analysis aims to examine the 'process' elements of EU finances to unravel how financial instruments are derived, reformed and managed. EU finances emerge from a process that begins with constitutional decisions such as the Budget Treaties and the 'big decisions' on medium-term financing. It includes an annual budgetary cycle which provides a cyclical framework for

well-established and routinised exchanges between the Union's
institutions. Tagged on are the processes that govern non-budget
items and EIB lending and borrowing. Once money is committed
and priorities decided on among different forms of expenditure,
budgets must be managed and implemented by the Commission
and the member states. Management involves an internal audit
function in each institution and external auditing by the Court of
Auditors. Audits necessarily go beyond accountability to questions
of 'value for money' and sound financial management. A large
number and variety of public and private agencies, across numerous levels of government, are involved in managing EU monies.
This rather truncated synopsis of the 'process' dimensions of EU
finances suggests that we need to trawl the literature on public
policy-making, particularly relating to the EU's policy process, for
insight (Wallace and Wallace, eds, 1996; Mazey and Richardson,
1993; Peterson, 1995). The following themes prominent in this
literature are particularly helpful for our purposes:

- The iterative nature of the policy process suggests that we
  need to take seriously the *time* dimension and the possibility
  of *policy-oriental learning* in the system (Sabatier and Jenkins-
  Smith, 1993). By adopting a reasonably long-term view of
  EU finances, it is possible to chart changes in priorities,
  interests and influences.
- The process of *agenda-setting* on budgetary matters is particularly important because major changes in the agenda were
  apparent between 1973 and 1995 (Peters, 1994).
- The congested nature of the policy space means that particular attention must be paid to distinguishing the central
  players and those who are less central to focusing not just
  on *formal* budgetary politics but also on the *informal* dimension of budgetary politics.
- The multi-leveled model, dominant in the literature, of the
  Union's governance structures, draws attention to the *nested
  games* that different actors play in different decision-making
  arenas (Tsebelis, 1990).
- A prevailing theme in many policy-making studies of the EU
  process is the role of the Commission as *policy entrepreneur*
  and *policy innovator* (Majone, 1993; Cram, 1994; Sandholtz,
  1992). How important have EU finances been to the

Commission as a policy entrepreneur? How has it used financial resources to further its policy aims and as leverage *vis-à-vis* the member states?

- The importance of *advocacy coalitions* has been highlighted in the public policy literature (Sabatier and Jenkins-Smith, 1993). Budgetary politics offers an important lens with which to analyse the mobilisation of advocacy coalitions in the Union.

- Linked to the notion of *advocacy coalitions* is the suggestion that the Union, and the Commission in particular, can foster joint problem-solving strategies, and hence integration may become an agent of change in the member states. The availability of financial resources is important to the Commission in this endeavour (Jachenfuchs and Kohler-Koch, 1995; Laffan, 1995).

- *Regional mobilisation* and the Europeanisation of *social movements* are an important dynamic in European integration in the 1980s (Hooghe, 1996). The importance of EU send money and the lure of Brussels money in mobilisation must be analysed. Lobbying is an increasingly important part of EU budgetary politics.

- Insights drawn from *public management* and the literature on *evaluation* and *implementation* are important because of the renewed emphasis on financial management, delivery of programmes, monitoring and combating fraud (Metcalfe, 1992).

Conclusions

There are very significant differences between the role of public finance and budgets in the EU and in the member states. National budgets are a major instrument of public power representing a high proportion of the domestic product of all EU states. The 'night watchman' state of the nineteenth century gave way to the spending state of the twentieth century as the state became increasingly active in economic management, education and the provision of welfare services. Although the advent of neo-liberalism in the 1980s dented the activism of the state and heralded a shift in the public/private balance, government expenditure continues to eat up a sizeable proportion of the national product throughout Western Europe.

In contrast, the EU budget has meagre resources at its disposal. The major instrument of public power in the Union is regulation rather than common policies or positive integration. The Union budget is not based on the key tenets of fiscal federalism although the fiscal federalist literature has been deployed in political argument about EU finances. The Union has managed to develop as an economic space without a large budget because it is built largely on market liberalisation. Notwithstanding this, issues of distribution and redistribution have been on the EU agenda from the beginning and the Union has had to develop a range of policies to respond to demands for a more active EU budget. The expansion of the budget has been accompanied by considerable struggle over the principles that should govern EU expenditure and the purposes to which it should be put. This is set to continue as the political purpose of the Union is highly-contested and the balance between national and European policy competencies unsettled.

3

Budget Rules and Where the Money Comes From

The search for financial autonomy in the Union and the development of a set of financial instruments separated from national public finances were central to the evolution of the Union as a part-formed political system rather than a traditional international organisation. It mattered a great deal to the Union that it achieved financial autonomy from the member states. The budget, however small, represents one of the central supranational features of European integration. Hence, financial autonomy forms part of the Union's embryonic constitution. The purpose of this chapter is to trace the development of the Union's financial constitution, and to analyse its resources and the impact of the financial rules on member state contributions.

Budgetary rules

The budgetary rules governing the Union's public finances are based on provisions in the original Treaties, the 1970 and 1975 Budget Treaties, the financial regulation and decision on the resource base of the budget. See Box 3.1 for a outline of the main budgetary rules, only the most significant of which are discussed below.

The search for budgetary unity

The Union's financial system evolved from a series of distinct financial provisions in the Treaties establishing the European Coal and Steel Community (ECSC), Euratom and the European

---

BOX 3.1
Budgetary rules in the European Union

The rule of unity	Article 199.
The rule of universality	Budgetary revenue may not be assigned to particular items of expenditure and no adjustments may be made between revenue and expenditure.
The rule of annuality	Budget operations related to a specific budget year – detailed rules about automatic and non-automatic carry overs.
The rule of equilibrium	Budget revenue must be equal to budget expenditure; no borrowing to balance budget.
The rule of specification	Each appropriation must be given a purpose and assigned to a specific objective.

Source: European Commission (1989) *Community Public Finance* (Luxembourg: Official Publications).

Economic Community. The nature of the constitutional framework meant that EU finances were originally fragmented into operating and administrative budgets for both the ECSC and Euratom and the EC budget (see Box 3.2). The concept of budgetary unity was enshrined in Article 199 of the EEC Treaty which specified that 'all items of revenue and expenditure ... shall be included in estimates to be drawn up for each financial year and shall be shown in the budget' (Article 199, EEC Treaty). The separate administrative budgets of the ECSC and Euratom were incorporated into the Community's general budget by the Merger Treaty (1965) and in 1970 the Euratom research and investment budget was also brought into the general budget. A number of the Union's financial instruments do not, however, constitute part of the general budget and therefore limit the unity of the Union's financial constitution:

1. The ECSC, which expires in 2002, continues to have a separate operating budget which is financed by a special levy with the Commission as the role budgetary authority.

BOX 3.2
The evolution of own resources

Own Resource System 1970	1. Customs levies and duties
	2. Agricultural levies and sugar levies
	3. VAT contribution up to a ceiling to 1 per cent
Fontainebleau 1984	1. and 2. as above
	3. VAT call-up rate raised to 1.4 per cent
Delors I 1988–92	1. and 2. as above
	3. Maximum VAT rate maintained at 1.4 per cent but capped at 55 per cent of GNP for all member states
	4. Topping up resources calculated on the basis of GNP
	5. Revenue limited to ceiling of 1.2 per cent of EC GNP
Delors II 1993–99	1. and 2. as above
	3. Maximum VAT rate reduced to 1 per cent and capped at 50 per cent for cohesion states from 1996.
	4. Topping up based on GNP
	5. Revenue limited to 1.27 EC GNP

---

2. The European Development Fund (EDF) for aid to third countries has never been part of the general budget. The Fund is financed by national contributions and managed by the EDF Steering Committee. The EDF is regarded by the Parliament as the main hindrance to budgetary unity.
3. The borrowing and lending activities of the Community analysed in Chapter 8 do not appear in the budget, despite repeated attempts by the EP to have them included.

Although the search for unity has led to a less fragmented set of financial instruments, complete unity of all of the Union's financial instruments has not been achieved.

Annuality and a balanced budget

The principle that the budget should be an *annual* one leads to a yearly budgetary cycle in which expenditure is authorised for one financial year. Annuality is reconciled with the need for multi-annual programmes by a distinction between what are called:

- Commitment appropriations – the pool of money available for authorising expenditure which may be carried out over a period of several years; and
- Payment appropriations – which cover the payment of commitments from previous years and commitments entered into during the financial year that are due for payment in the same year.

In essence, the general budget is divided between a commitments budget and a payments budget. The implementation of the budget inevitably involves a time lag between the commitment of financial resources and payments which in the past led to problems of financial management if the payments budget did not have sufficient resources to meet past commitments or if commitments that had been entered into lay dormant. The Commission conducted a purge of dormant commitments in 1986 and 1987 in an attempt to clean up the budget (European Commission, 1995, p. 62). Since then, revisions of the financial regulation are designed to ensure that the 'costs of the past' are duly considered in the annual budgetary process. In principle, commitment appropriations and payment appropriations will lapse if they have not been used by the end of the year for which they were entered in the budget. Rules about carrying over commitment and payment appropriations from one year to the next are tighter than in the past. The principle of annuality leads to a flurry of spending activity in the last quarter of the budget year as Commission officials scramble to commit their authorised appropriations. When asked about the principle of annuality, one senior Commission bureaucrat claimed that 'the two cardinal sins of a Commission official were one, not to spend a budget line and two, to lose the money'.

The rule of *equilibrium* is a very important principle in the Union's financial constitution because, unlike the member states, the EU budget cannot run a deficit, nor can it borrow to cover expenditure. The revenue estimates contained in the budget must be equal to the payment appropriations for that year. Any shortfall between the forecasts for revenue and actual revenue must be made up by a supplementary or amending budget. The principle of a balanced budget means that the financial limits contained in the 'own resources' decisions form the outer limits of EU expenditure.

The 1970 and the 1975 Budget Treaties

The Budget Treaties of 1970 and 1975 constitute the central core of the Union's financial constitution because they established *financial autonomy* for the Union and, as a corollary, the European Parliament joined the Council as the second arm of a joint budgetary authority. The two Treaties fundamentally altered the resource base of the budget and decision-making on budgetary matters. Financial autonomy was underlined by a move away from national contributions to the budget, to what is known as the system of 'own resources'. The granting of autonomous financial resources activated Article 201 of the EEC Treaty which envisaged that financial contributions from the member states eventually would be replaced by 'own resources'. The constitutional nature of Article 201 is underlined by the provision that agreement to an independent financial regime required ratification by the member states according to their respective constitutional provisions. In other words, national parliaments had to endorse a move to 'own resources' (Ehlermann, 1982, p. 571). All subsequent changes in own resources required passage through the national parliaments of the member states. Any one member state can effectively block an increase in the Union's financial resources. Because national parliaments were in effect losing control over some public monies with the agreement to own resources, the European Parliament was given the 'power of the purse' to compensate for the loss of power by national parliaments. The evolution of relations between the two arms of the budgetary authority are analysed in Chapter 4.

Own resources

The political debate on own resources in the Community concerns the size of the budget and the resources that should make up its revenue base. Questions of equity, fairness, and 'ability to

pay' hovered over 'own resources' negotiations from the beginning, but were not universally accepted as part of the budgetary
aquis until the mid-1980s. The UK budgetary problem, discussed
below, forced distributional issues onto the agenda and led to a
consideration of fair burden-sharing in the Union. The
Commission has gradually sought to alleviate the most regressive
attributes of the revenue pattern as part of the wider budgetary
deals of 1988 and 1992.

The milestone decision in 1970 to replace national contributions with the Communities' own resources made provision for
three sources of revenue:

- Levies on agricultural and sugar trade (transferred
  immediately);
- Customs duties on trade with third countries (transferred
  progressively between 1970 and 1975);
- Resources accruing from a proportion of VAT (not more
  than 1 per cent) on the basis of a uniform VAT base
  throughout the Community (European Communities, 1970)

Agricultural levies and customs duties are regarded as traditional
'own resources' because they arise from Community policy instruments – the Common Agricultural Policy and the common
commercial tariff. Because it was recognised that these sources of
revenue would not on their own be sufficient to finance
Community expenditure, an additional source of revenue – up to
1 per cent of VAT – was required. By 1975 the traditional 'own resources' were fully transferred to the Community but it took until
1979 to get agreement on a harmonised VAT base. From the
beginning, there was a distinct difference in political perceptions
at domestic level between traditional 'own resources' and VAT.
The Commission itself concluded that 'The traditional own
resources (customs duties, agricultural levies and sugar levies) do
seem to be accepted as genuine own resources in the sense that
they are not seen as a national contribution towards the
Community budget'. However, the VAT resource and the addition of a new fourth resource, discussed below, are 'generally
perceived by governments and by national parliaments as mere
budgetary contributions from the Member States' (European
Commission, 1992, p. 44). Although all budgetary resources are

regarded as the same under Community law, the sense that traditional own resources belong to the Community and that the other revenue sources constitute a transfer from domestic coffers to the EU level has continued salience in the budgetary politics of the Union.

Two important trends can be identified in the evolution of 'own resources' and the balance between different budgetary resources. First, the principle of a balanced budget discussed above and the legal limit on available resources meant that as demands on the budget grew with the expansion of policies and the addition of new member states, the budget was bedevilled by a shortage of resources. Second, traditional 'own resources' are inflexible and do not constitute a buoyant source of revenue. They have declined dramatically as a proportion of total resources because successive trade negotiations reduced world tariffs, and the yield from agricultural and sugar levies depends on world prices. The share of traditional 'own resources' in EU revenue declined from 49 per cent of the budget in 1979, to 37 per cent in 1985, and to just 20 per cent in 1993 (European Commission, 1994, p. 39). The Community has had to rely more and more on other sources of revenue. See Figure 3.1 for an analysis of the composition of own resources in 1995 and Figure 3.2 for an analysis of the changing composition of 'own resources'.

The prospect of a serious revenue problem in the Community was identified by the Commission in 1978 with its paper on *Financing the Community Budget: The Way Ahead* (European

FIGURE 3.1

Composition of 'own resources' in the 1995 budget

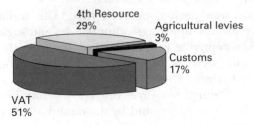

Source: European Commission (1995a) *General Budget for 1995*, Sec(95), 10 January 1995, p. 20.

FIGURE 3.2

Changing composition of 'own resources'

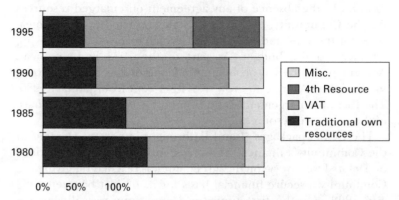

Source: European Commission (1994) *The Community Budget: The Facts in Figures,* Sec(94)1100, pp. 38–9 and European Commission (1995a) *General Budget of the EU, 1995*, Sec(95), 10 January 1995.

Commission, 1978) which anticipated that the 1 per cent VAT rate might be exceeded by 1981. The Commission, having gained the breakthrough with 'own resources', opposed any return to national contributions. The report examined a number of different forms of taxation, both indirect and direct, to see which might be appropriate to a Community resource. The study concluded that there were in the short term only three possibilities:

1. A simple increase in the VAT rate;
2. The transfer to the Community of part of the taxes on cigarettes;
3. The transfer of part of the taxes on petrol (EU Commission, 1978).

In the medium term, it might be possible to have a tax on energy consumption or the transfer in part of taxes on alcohol (European Commission, 1978).

This largely academic exercise conducted by the Commission was lost in the continuing conflict about UK contributions to the budget and the controversy attached to all budgetary issues at this time. It took longer than the Commission anticipated for the 1 per cent limit to be reached. It was not until 1983/84 that the

Community was faced with a really serious resource problem: the 1983 budget was balanced only by the artificial device of delaying some agricultural payments until 1984 when the VAT base finally ran out. In the absence of any agreement on enlarged resources for the Community, the member states resorted to *ad hoc* measures for the 1984 and 1985 budgets which involved them making advances to the budget. As part of the 1984 Fontainebleau Agreement on the UK problem, the heads of government agreed to allow the VAT rate to grow to 1.4 per cent from January 1986. The Iberian enlargement was destined to eat up the lion's share of the increased resources.

The Delors packages (I and II) brought important changes in the Community's financial resources. Although the negotiations on Delors I were very tough, agreement was reached on giving the Community a secure financial basis for its budget between 1988 and 1992. For the first time the Community was allocated a ceiling of 1.3 per cent of total Community GNP for commitment appropriations, and 1.2 per cent of total GNP for payment appropriations. The Brussels European Council 1988 anticipated an orderly progression of commitment appropriations to not more than 1.3 per cent of GNP by 1992. The resources accorded to the budget in Delors I included:

- Traditional own resources (agricultural levies, sugar levies and CCT customs duties);
- Up to 1.4 per cent of VAT calculated on a uniform basis for the member states. The assessment basis for VAT would not exceed 55 per cent of the GNP of any member state;
- A new *fourth resource* based on a topping up of the revenue available from the other resources and related to GNP. The rate for this resource is determined each year during the budgetary procedure in the light of the total amount available from all other sources of revenue related to the total GNP of all the member states.

Agreement on a *fourth* resource provided the Community with a budgetary buffer each year and did away with the need for *ad hoc* budgetary contributions. The decision to create a new resource rather than rely on a higher VAT call-in rate was an attempt to deal with the regressive nature of the VAT resource. VAT tends to form a far higher proportion of the GNP of the poorer states of the Community, and any system of contributions based on VAT as an indication of wealth inevitably overstates the ability of the poorer member states to pay (Groutage and Zangel, 1991, p. 2). In addition, capping the proportion of VAT for calculations on the uniform base at 55 per cent represented a search for more equitable burden-sharing in the budget. The conclusions of the European Council of June 1987 stipulated that the new financial system would take 'greater account of the proportionality of con-tributions in accordance with the relative prosperity of Member States' (European Council, June 1987). The fourth resource was less successful than anticipated in making the budget more equi-table because economic growth was higher than forecast, which meant that VAT returns were also higher and thus contributed a higher proportion of the budget than the GNP resource. The Commission's report on 'own resources' concluded that the less-prosperous states, Greece, Spain, Ireland and Portugal all had rel-atively high VAT bases and thus were disadvantaged under the 1988 system, even with capping (European Commission, 1992).

By 1992 when negotiations on a second medium-term financial package began, the Community was not in fact using the full GNP ceiling available to it. The negotiations on the 'own resources' element of the second Delors package took place within the context of a protocol agreed at the Maastricht European Council and appended to the Treaty on European Union. The Commission and the member states declared their willingness to take greater account of the contributive capacity of individual member states in the system of 'own resources' and to examine ways of correcting the regressive elements of the 1988 system (European Commission, 1992). The Report was quite blunt in identifying the regressive nature of the existing 'own resources' system because it gave advantages to member states with a low VAT base and penalised those, generally the poorer states, with a high VAT base (*ibid.*). The capping introduced in 1988 had not in itself adequately tackled the central issue of fairness and equitable burden-sharing.

The Commission, in its proposals to the member states, advo-cated a number of changes to the system of 'own resources'. First, Commission proposals included a reduction in the importance of the VAT resource by reducing the call rate on the VAT resource from 1.4 per cent to 1 per cent. Second, it proposed that the capping of the VAT base should be further reduced from 55 per cent to 50 per cent. These proposals were designed to reduce the importance of the VAT resource to the budget and to lessen the burden of payments on the poorer member states. These proposals were likely to shift the financial burden to Belgium, Italy and the Netherlands whose GNP share exceeded their VAT share. The Commission also advocated a new *fifth resource* to supplement the existing four resources, but did not specify what this resource might be. The fifth resource was not central to the Delors II negotiations.

The negotiations on Delors II, discussed extensively in Chapter 4, led to two important decisions for the financial basis of the budget. The Commission was unsuccessful in its attempt to get an increase in the size of the budget of 1.37 per cent of GNP by 1997. The absence of a resource crisis, this time round, and the growing number of net contributors weakened the Commission's case considerably. It had to be content with an increase to a ceiling of 1.27 per cent over a longer time period to 1999. The Commission had more success with its proposal on contributive capacity or 'ability to pay'. Agreement was reached at Edinburgh to reduce the VAT call-in rate from 1.4 per cent to 1.0 per cent between 1993 and 1999. The VAT rate would be capped for the four cohesion states (Spain, Ireland, Portugal and Greece) at 50 per cent from 1995, and this level would be phased-in for the other member states between 1995 and 1999. As a consequence, the proportion of resources from VAT is set to decline so that, by 1999, the GNP resource should finance over half the budget (Zangel, 1993).

During the implementation of the Delors I financial perspective from 1988 to 1992, the pool of 'own resources' was more than adequate to deal with growing external demands on the budget because economic growth was higher than anticipated when the financial perspective was agreed to. The implementation of the Delors II package has not progressed in such a benign economic climate. Recession between 1992 and 1994 meant that available monies were considerably lower than anticipated when the Edinburgh agreement was put in place. The revenue shortfall amounted to ECU two billion in 1992 and ECU six and a half billion in 1993 (European Commission, 1995, p. 34) The Commission had to resort to very tight financial management to ensure that the shortfalls did not turn into a tax on the future by reducing the pool of resources available for subsequent years. The economic recovery in late 1994 helped to alleviate a growing resource problem for the budget.

The thorny question of net contributions

Contributions to the Community budget have proved to be one of the most explosive and passionately debated issues on the financial agenda since the 1970s. Tortuous debates on the benefits and costs of Community membership nearly always begin from an assessment of the balance sheet on budgetary contributions because of their visibility to national politicians and the national media. National parliaments and politicians tend to think of contributions to the EU budget as their money – a transfer from their taxpayers to the Community despite the system of 'own resources' and the principle that EU finances are autonomous. The French lay considerable stress on the automatic character of 'own resources' as a central element of the *acquis* from the outset, in order to protect agricultural expenditure. The 1970 Decision can be interpreted as an attempt to fix the budgetary rules before British accession. The question of budgetary contributions became an issue when Britain joined the Community in 1973 – it quickly became apparent that it would pay a disproportionate amount to the Community's coffers. With great difficulty, and in the teeth of considerable resistance, successive UK governments insisted that the issue of net contributions be taken seriously by the other member states and the Commission. The Commission, with reluctance, published calculations of budgetary contributions and accepted the principle of national contributions under protest. The following two arguments are deployed against the notion of a balance sheet:

1. Calculating national contributions poses considerable methodological difficulties in relation to traditional 'own resources' because the point of collection is not necessarily the point of consumption. This is evident in relation to what is called the 'Rotterdam effect' where goods are imported through one country and consumed in another.

The collection of customs duties and payment to the Community budget takes place in one country while the economic burden is carried elsewhere (EU Commission, 1992). Payments from customs duties and levies should not in the Commission's view be taken into account because these payments are the direct results of Community policies on agriculture and trade.

2. The Commission has always been concerned that the distribution of budgetary receipts and benefits across the member states gives a restricted and partial view of the true costs and benefits of Community membership. A narrow focus on budgetary transactions does not take into consideration the indirect effects of economic integration, notably increased productivity, improved competitiveness and access to the large market.

From the Commission's perspective, an overemphasis on net contributions carries the danger of *juste retour* – that each member state would seek to get out of the Community budget more or less what it paid in which would fundamentally undermine the budget's financial autonomy. That said, fair burden sharing is a *sine qua non* of an equitable system of taxation. Member states which feel themselves inequitably treated in the budgetary process can and will marshal political leverage in favour of budgetary reform.

Before analysing the UK problem, a number of more general points about the balance between contributions to and benefits from the Budget are worth making. A central principle of the system of 'own resources' at the outset was that the rules would apply to all member states, regardless of wealth and ability to pay. In other words, issues of equity and fairness were not automatically accepted as principles of the budgetary *acquis*. Rather, budgetary payments depended on the structure of the national economy and receipts were determined by the focus of the main spending policies, notably agriculture. The Union's financial system was not designed as a response to a series of sound budgetary principles; it evolved from decisions about the common financing of a limited number of policies.

Notwithstanding the difficulty of calculating the national incidence of the Community budget, such calculations have been undertaken by economists and governments interested in their position in the budgetary league table. Even when the Union was unwilling to acknowledge the existence of national costs and benefits resulting from the budget, national governments attempted to assess them and such assessments influenced their policies on budgetary matters (Ardy, 1988). In a piece published in 1988, Ardy undertook a detailed analysis of the budget's financial consequences for the member states. He described the net benefits of the CAP as *eccentric* since there was no consistent relationship between benefits as a percentage of GDP or per capita; the highest relative benefits were enjoyed by Ireland, a member state with a lower per capita income, whereas the second highest relative benefits were experienced by Denmark, a country with one of the highest per capita incomes. Ardy concluded that there was a 'haphazard and even chaotic national incidence of the EC budget', and that the EC has a budget 'which derives revenue and distributes benefits in a manner entirely unrelated to levels of national wealth' (Ardy, 1988, p. 425) In 1992, Bowles and Jones analysed the EC budget to see whether fiscal redistribution via the budget could be perceived as equitable. Their analysis of payments from the budget, 'own resources', and GDP per capita between 1985 and 1989 showed that two low-income countries, Spain and Portugal, received modest net payments, and two high-income countries, the Netherlands and Denmark, received generous payments during this period (Bowles and Jones, 1992, p. 91). The central conclusion of the Bowles and Jones analysis was that some member countries were treated more favourably than others and that the budget was neither neutral nor straightforwardly progressive in its impact. Relative wealth played some role but not a crucial one in the flow of resources from the budget.

Analysis of the system of 'own resources' shows that the largest contributor to the revenue pool of the Union is Germany (33.3 per cent in 1994), followed by France (19.6 per cent), Italy (12.1 per cent) and the UK (10.0 per cent). These four states contributed three-quarters of the Community's 'own resources' in 1994. Among the other member states, Spain, the Netherlands and Belgium contributed a further 18.4 per cent with the other states making up the balance (see Table 3.1 which provides details of national contributions as a proportion of total 'own resources' between 1990 and 1994). The balance between contributions and actual payments shows that Germany, the UK, Italy, France and

TABLE 3.1
'Own resources' by member state, 1990 and 1994, ECU million

	Financial year			
	1990	%	1994	%
Belgium	17 63.7	(4.3%)	2822.1	(4.4%)
Denmark	775.1	(1.9%)	1296.2	(2.0%)
Germany	10 357.5	(25%)	21 366.3	(33.3%)
Greece	563.6	(1.4%)	992.3	(1.5%)
Spain	3671.4	(8.9%)	4718.1	(7.4%)
France	8089.5	(19.5%)	12 550.9	(19.6%)
Ireland	368.2	(0.9%)	638.9	(1.0%)
Italy	6097.7	(14.7%)	7759.6	(12.1%)
Luxembourg	74.5	(0.2%)	165.4	(0.3%)
Netherlands	2615.2	(6.3%)	4245.9	(6.6%)
Portugal	502.4	(1.2%)	1215.6	(1.9%)
UK	6534.3	(15.8%)	6417.4	(10.0%)
Total	41 413.1	(100%)	64 188.8	(100%)

Source: European Court of Auditors (1995) *Annual Report 1994* (C303),
14 November.

the Netherlands are net contributors whereas relatively wealthy
states such as Denmark, Luxembourg and Belgium continue to
benefit from financial transfers. The struggle for equity in the
Community budget is far from over, although the reform of the
CAP and the increase in structural funding introduced greater
fairness to the pattern of net contributions.

The absence of distributional conflict in the early 1970s owes
much to the fact that the budget was small. Moreover, there was a
very cosy financial compact between the 'inner six' – all member
states, apart from Germany, were net beneficiaries. Britain,
however, was structurally disadvantaged *vis-à-vis* the budget and
was thus intent on modifying this situation. The tortuous process
of finding agreement to the British problem in the 1980s led to
pressures by the end of the decade for stable budgetary relations
and a medium-term financial perspective. The growing volume of
budgetary resources as a consequence of Delors I and the reform
of the Common Agricultural Policy, however, increased
significantly the number of net contributors to the budget.

This has altered the dynamics of budgetary politics in a
very fundamental manner. The German government has put its

partners on notice that it will not provide an open-ended financial commitment to the budget. Moreover, the Netherlands, for long a beneficiary from the budget, is preparing itself for a tough battle on a new budgetary deal for 1999. The Netherlands found itself joining the contributors' club in 1990. Hence its reluctance to ratify the Edinburgh Agreement of 1992, only ratifying it in the spring of 1996.

The UK problem

It was recognised during the accession negotiations that an 'unacceptable situation' might arise for Britain in relation to the budget, but because it was impossible to calculate budgetary contributions with any accuracy the problem was shelved for future consideration (Ardy, 1988). UK negotiators argued that Britain would pay a disproportionate amount into the Community budget because of its structure of trade and particularly the high level of imports from non-Community states. On the expenditure side, the UK was unlikely to benefit greatly from the Common Agricultural Policy. The Commission argued at the time that 'should an unacceptable situation arise within the present Community or an enlarged community, the very survival of the Community would demand that the Institutions find equitable solutions' (quoted in Emerson and Scott, 1977, p. 210). Whoever penned that remark could not have predicted just how difficult it would be for the Community to find a solution to the British budgetary problem. The British budgetary conflict worked its way through the Community's decision-making system in three phases: the phoney war 1973–78, 'our money back' 1979–84, and a structural solution at Fontainebleau in 1984.

The phoney war

When the Labour government took over from the Conservatives in March 1973, it very quickly informed its partners that it was seeking a renegotiation of the terms of British entry into the Community and would hold a referendum on the question of membership. The key complaint of the Wilson government was that its budgetary contributions would become excessive and unfair once the transitional period ran out. The goal of the British government was to negotiate a more equitable method of financing the budget so as to reduce the financial burden on the UK (Ostrom, 1982, p. 79).

The other member states, in an attempt to prolong the issue, agreed that the Commission would examine the economic and financial situation in the Community so that discussion of the British case could proceed on the basis of an agreed analysis. The Commission paper concluded that the UK was likely to pay a disproportionate contribution to the budget based on relative wealth. The 1974 Paris Summit asked the Council and the Commission to devise a 'corrective mechanism' that could be brought into play if the budgetary contributions from any member state were too high. There was considerable reluctance in the Commission and in a number of member states to treat any one state as a special case. Agreement was reached on a financial mechanism at the subsequent Dublin Summit (1975) which largely fulfilled the political requirements of the Wilson government facing into a referendum on Europe. The mechanism was extremely complex and would come into operation only if three preconditions were met, relative GNP, GNP growth and the level of budgetary contributions. It would have been extremely difficult for any member state to fulfil the preconditions necessary to trigger the mechanism (Dodsworth, 1975; Emerson and Scott, 1977).

'Our money back'

The tone and intensity of the budgetary dispute altered when Margaret Thatcher took over as British Prime Minister in 1979. Elected on an austerity platform, attacks on the Community budget and slogans of 'we want our money back' made good sense politically. Moreover, the end of the transitional period meant that the UK was about to assume the full burden of budgetary contributions. In 1978 Jim Callaghan, the then British Prime Minister, already signalled that by 1980 the UK would become the single largest contributor to the budget, with a net contribution of some EUA (European Unit of Account) 1.4 billion, according to British estimates. The 1975 corrective mechanism was ineffective because, as the 1970s progressed, the main problem arose from agriculture which meant that the UK received limited receipts from the budget; the issue was one of net receipts rather than gross contribution.

The British budgetary problem moved to centre-stage on the Community's agenda and dominated it until 1984 when a longer-term solution was found. One of the first difficulties was to reach broad agreement about the extent of the problem. In 1979, the Commission, with great reluctance, began to study the relative positions of the member states *vis-à-vis* the budget. The results of the study showed that there was indeed a UK problem with the country's deficit worsening rapidly between 1977 and 1980. Although there was continuing dispute about the reasons for the UK problem, the other member states were forced to accept that an 'unacceptable situation' was emerging.

The focus then moved to strategies for dealing with the issue and debate about the volume of resources that should be re-turned to the UK. A medley of proposals, such as 'special windows' in the Regional Fund, automatic receipts to a certain level, and a ceiling on British budgetary contributions, were all canvassed by the Commission, the UK and a number of other member states. At this stage the budgetary dispute became entan-gled with other issues, notably the annual CAP price review. By May 1980, all member states wanted to solve the problem, albeit in an *ad hoc* and unsatisfactory manner, because the overall agricultural package was held up. A marathon General Affairs Council under the Italian presidency in May, led to agreement on *ad hoc* shadow spending programmes from 1980 to 1982 which were designed significantly to reduce the British contribution (Jenkins, 1980). The money was earmarked for special pro-grammes in particular regions, inner cities and for a number of energy projects. The longer-term problem of structural reform of EU public finances was heralded in the Commission's May Mandate Report.

The road to Fontainebleau

Ad hoc solutions to the UK problem in 1980 did little to satisfy the British Government, which by this stage was intent on structural reform of the budget. Relations between the UK and its partners deteriorated over the next years with continuing acrimony about the budget and the effective linkage by the British of its budgetary contribution with the future financing of the Community. The resource crisis of the budget meant that the British had sufficient leverage to extract longer-term concessions from their partners. When France took over the presidency of the Community in 1984, President Mitterrand was intent on getting agreement on all the outstanding budgetary issues – a higher VAT ceiling, a permanent formula for the UK rebate, and budgetary discipline for agriculture – so that he could concentrate on the relaunch of the European project.

The central element of the Fontainebleau Agreement was an acceptance that the UK contribution would be limited to a percentage of its net contribution. The UK accepted a refund of ECU 1 billion for 1984 and then 66 per cent of the difference between receipts and VAT contributions in 1985 and subsequent years. The calculation of the rebate on VAT only was a major concession made by the British because it implied that the traditional 'own resources' should not be calculated as part of a net contribution. Mrs Thatcher succeeded in getting the other member states to accept the essence of her case based on considerations of equity but did so in a manner that copperfastened the perception of the UK as *non-communautaire*, argumentative and difficult. Officials working on the budgetary issue talk of the poisoned atmosphere in the Community at this time. An agreement largely along the lines of Fontainebleau was on offer at a much earlier stage of the negotiations, but Mrs Thatcher was unwilling to compromise. The UK rebate was formalised in the Delors I negotiations although many member states wished to see it abolished during the negotiations on Delors II.

A German problem?

Successive German governments have accepted that Germany is a substantial net contributor to the Community budget, but have always been concerned lest this is read as an open-ended financial commitment to finance the Community. With agreement to *ad hoc* spending programmes in the UK, Germany found itself shouldering an increasing financial burden. As a result of the UK measures, German net contributions were calculated to rise in 1980 from some MEUA (million EUAs) 1200 to nearly 1650 MEUA (Jenkins, 1980). During the continuing negotiations on the UK budgetary problem, German bureaucrats constantly stressed the growing financial burden on themselves. This was recognised at Fontainebleau when German contributions to the UK rebate were limited to two-thirds of its VAT share. In other words, other member states had to shoulder a higher proportion of the UK rebate.

Although always concerned by the financial burden of the EU budget, the predilection towards austerity in the German Economics Ministry did not prevent Chancellor Kohl from digging into German coffers to support the significant increase in EU spending as part of Delors I. As a consequence, Germany's net contribution rose sharply during the life of Delors I when contributions rose from DM 20 million in 1987 to 36 million in 1992 – an increase in net contributions from DM10.5 million in 1987 to DM 22 million in 1992 (Bundesbank, 1993, p. 62). Germany contributes more to the budget than Britain and France combined.

Since Edinburgh, where once again Germany helped to secure a medium-term budgetary deal, there has been growing criticism in Germany of contributions to the budget. During the European Parliament election campaign in June 1994, many on the hustings raised the matter. Chancellor Kohl warned that the German contribution 'has reached its furthest limit' (*European Report*, 1994). Theo Waigel, Finance Minister, claimed that a 'one-sided and exaggerated burden for one member state is no longer acceptable' (*Financial Times*, 6 April 1995). Although statements of this kind have been heard from German politicians in the past, there is reason to believe that they will prove more serious this time. Three concerns dominate German considerations:

1. Up to 1990, Germany had the second highest per capita income in the Community; it fell to sixth place in the prosperity league following the incorporation of the new *Länder*, yet Germany remains the highest contributor to the EU, both in volume terms and on a per capita basis.
2. German public finances are under considerable pressure because of the continuing needs of the new *Länder*.

3. Germany is bearing a considerable burden of financial aid
   to the former Soviet bloc. It has undertaken to pay Russia
   a total of ECU 41.9 billion by 1996 and is channelling
   similar amounts into the countries of East Central Europe.
   (Friedmann, 1995, p. 58)

Already in Council, German Ministers together with the British
and Dutch are adopting a position of austerity on all of the discre-
tionary elements of the Delors II package in an effort to restrict
the size of the annual budget. Moreover, although politically committed to the broad outlines of the financial perspective in Delors
II up to 1999, its attitude towards the financing of the Union
following enlargement are less clear. The tone of German pronouncements since Edinburgh suggests that it is looking to other
member states to bear their share of the burden in future.
Germany in 1998/99 will be confronted with the dilemma faced
by all large powers – the leading power in any region always pays
more than its neighbours because in the end it has the highest
stake in regional stability (Wallace, 1995). German politicians will
have to reconcile their desire for regional stability, on the one
hand, with their reluctance to shoulder a heavier financial burden
in the Union, on the other. Germany will look to the other large
states in the Union to carry more of the budgetary burden.

A Dutch problem?

The emerging debate in the Netherlands on the EU budget
illustrates the changing mood among the net contributors and
the perception among national parliamentarians that transfers to
the Community budget represent national contributions. The
Netherlands, although wealthy by EU standards, was for many
years a net beneficiary from the budget because of flows from the
Common Agricultural Policy. With the agreement on Delors I,
there was a dramatic change as the Netherlands was transformed
from a beneficiary to a contributor which in turn led to a political
reaction in Dutch domestic politics. The Netherlands went from
being a net beneficiary in 1988 to a net contributor in 1993
(Brouwer, 1995). In 1993, Germany was the only larger net contributor in relative terms (as a a percentage of GNP) to the EU. In

response to the politicisation of the budgetary issue, the Dutch Finance Ministry prepared a major memorandum for the Dutch Parliament, setting out the net position *vis-à-vis* the budget. A central argument in the Dutch paper is that the volume of Dutch contributions increased each year from 1990. The debate is fuelled in Holland by the leader of the Dutch Liberal Party (VVD) who is an avowed sceptic on European matters. The Dutch debate on the 1996 Intergovernmental Conference (IGC) is largely focused on the prospect that the Netherlands will emerge as the largest per capita net contributor in the years to come (Belmont, 1995, p. 8).

The Government was forced to deal with the issue by preparing analytical documents for the Dutch Parliament setting out the financial position of the Netherlands in relation to the budget. The document, which was transmitted to the Parliament in February 1995, consists of two parts, a background paper putting financial flows in the context of EC membership and a detailed statistical section setting out the financial relationship between the Netherlands and the EC. There is a discernible difference in tone between the two parts of the document; the first part strives to put the issue of financial flows in a broad political and econ-omic context whereas the statistical section seeks to make the best possible case for the Netherlands (Netherlands 1995). The first part of the report, although penned by the Finance Ministry, was heavily influenced by observations from the Ministry of Foreign Affairs while the latter part is vintage Finance Ministry material. This points to conflict within the contributing states between the zeal for austerity in Finance Ministries and the remit of Foreign Affairs with a commitment to the political goals of the European project.

The paper has as its main element a presentation of the Dutch financial position in the Union. The change in the Dutch position from recipient to contributor during the life of Delors I arises because:

- The MacSharry reforms of the Common Agricultural Policy (CAP) had a very significant impact on the Dutch receipts from the budget. Because the Netherlands has a relatively small share of production of the main sectors covered by the reform (cereals/beef) only a tiny proportion of the income support measures benefit Dutch farmers. The Netherlands receives only 1.1 per cent of MacSharry monies (hectare support, ewe premiums, bull premiums and suckling animal premiums). In 1988, the Netherlands received over 2.5 billion guilders from the CAP; this amount shrunk to 400 guilders by 1992 and in 1995 the Netherlands became a net contributor to the CAP budget. Historically, the Netherlands has been one of the main beneficiaries of the Common Agricultural Policy. The share of Dutch receipts from the CAP will decline even further as the MacSharry support schemes become a larger part of the overall policy (Netherlands, 1995, p. 8).

- The significant increases in the volume of aid devoted to structural measures, inevitably affects the Dutch net position because it is one of the wealthier member states and thus would not expect to benefit from large-scale transfers. However, the Dutch argue that the structural funds benefit other wealthier states even more. According to the Dutch analysis, the Netherlands receives the smallest per capita transfer from the structural funds and that even the three new member states, which are wealthier, receive even more.

The most contentious part of the Dutch argument relates to the 'own resources' dimension of the paper. The Ministry of Finance bases its assessment of payments to the budget and the Dutch net position on all resources including the traditional 'own resources'. The Netherlands' relatively large payments to the budget are partly based on customs duties. For example in 1993 the Netherlands collected ECU 1.44 billion in customs duties when the French figure was ECU 1.48 billion. The importance of customs duties is usually attributed to the so-called Rotterdam effect because of the amount of transit traffic through the port of Rotterdam. The Dutch Report refutes this claim by arguing that 90 per cent of the customs duties paid by the Netherlands relate to the Dutch economy since much of the non-Dutch trade is in sealed transit (Netherlands, 1995). Further analysis is necessary before the validity of the argument on gross payments can be substantiated.

The importance of the Dutch report lies not in the technical details it contains concerning the net Dutch position in relation

to the budget, but as a signal of how the debate on the future
financing of the Union is likely to develop in the run-up to 1999.
The fact that many more states are now net contributors to the
budget changes the dynamics of budgetary politics in a very fundamental way. Politicians, rooted in their domestic support-base,
are sensitive to the impact on domestic resources of transfers via
the Union budget. The Dutch report makes the point that 'it
remains a matter of concern that a very restrictive policy must be
pursued with regard to national expenditure at a time when payments to the European Union are rising sharply' (Netherlands,
1995, p. 5). Moreover, the enhanced volume of money flowing
through the EU budget increases the political significance of the
budget in all member states. The Dutch report seeks to mobilise
the issue of equity by pointing out that there are major differences in the benefits and burdens of the budget not only between
the 'poor' and the 'rich' member states but also among the rich
member states themselves.

The Dutch Government has committed itself to working with
like-minded partners to ensure that there is a policy of restraint
on future expenditure. The government is committed to keeping
the budget as low as possible between 1995 and 1999 by regarding
the financial perspective as a ceiling and not a target. It will endeavour to ensure that there is maximum restraint in setting the
level of expenditure and that fraud will be combated more
actively. In the longer term, the government is preparing for the
battles ahead on the financial perspective post-1999. Pressure may
well grow within the contributors club for some inbuilt limit on
the size of contributions to the budget.

A net limiter

The UK, and to a lesser extent Germany, have a ceiling placed on
their payments to the budget in the form of the UK rebate and
Germany's reduced payments for the UK refund. With the
growing number of net contributors, other member states might
seek to have a system of net limiters included in the financial
framework. The Dutch government is already devoting considerable attention to the concept of an in-built mechanism which
would limit the net contribution of an individual member state in

relation to GNP. The Padoa-Schioppa report (1987) drew up a blueprint for an 'equity safeguard mechanism' which was designed to correct inequitable situations arising from the budget. The proposed system would allow for a broad range of budgetary outcomes by country but such that a certain standard of progressive fiscal equity would be assured (Padoa-Schioppa, 1987, pp. 152–3). The system would lead to transfers from the rich to the poor but without the arbitrariness of the present system.

Conclusions

The search for adequate resources for the Union budget is a key element in the development of the Union's financial system. Because of the principle of budgetary balance, the pool of resources available to the Union determines the extent and scope of policy integration. There have been strict limits on the volume of resources channelled through the EU budget and each new decision on 'own resources' is the subject of extremely tough political bargaining.

During the 1970s, questions concerning the distributional consequences of the EU budget forced their way onto the agenda as problems of burden-sharing manifested themselves. Equity considerations were not to the fore when the original system of own resources was designed in the late 1960s. The importance of the 1970 decision was to embed the notion that 'own resources' were automatic in the budgetary *acquis*. The UK's disadvantaged position in relation to the budget meant that equity considerations could no longer be eschewed. In a tortuous fashion and with great reluctance, the Commission and the other member states began to take cognisance of the national incidence of the budget. Once calculations of who got what from the budget were published, however technically difficult the calculations were, the regressive nature of the budget was readily apparent. The national incidence of the budget bore little relationship to positions of relative wealth; poor countries like Ireland benefited but so too did relatively wealthy Denmark. Decisions on 'own resources' since Delors I give more weight to considerations of 'ability to pay'. Moreover, as the share of CAP in total expenditure decreases and the volume of aid through the structural funds increases, the redistributive character of the budget is more pronounced. However, the increased number of net contributors to the budget alters the dynamic of budgetary politics. The struggle for a budgetary deal to encompass the countries of East Central Europe is only beginning.

4

Making Budgets

The process of making budgets in the European Union involves the 'high politics' of European Summits, an annual budgetary cycle which includes tough battles between the two arms of the Budgetary Authority and thousands of decisions on individual budgetary lines. Those involved in moulding the annual budget form an important subsystem in the EU's decision-making system which is characterised by small groups of budgetary *cognoscenti* in all institutions. The technical nature of the budget and the complexity of the rules governing its formation tend to favour *specialists*, those involved in the budgetary cycle year in year in and year out, who have developed an 'insider' knowledge of the budgetary *acquis*. The *cognoscenti* work, however, within the political and financial boundaries established by the big budgetary bargains which evolve from negotiations in the General Affairs Council, ECOFIN, and the European Council.

The big decisions

Agreement on a multi-annual budgetary package called Delors I in 1988 heralded a new era of budgetary politics in the Union. Its successor, Delors II in 1993, further embedded a multiannual financial perspective within the Union. The budget evolved from a historical set of separate funds with distinct histories into a structured ensemble. The significance of these two agreements for Delors himself, the Commission and the wider Union is often underrated when placed beside the single market, monetary union and political union. However, both these agreements, though neglected after the Single European Act (SEA) and the Treaty on European Union (TEU), provided the essential financial and political underpinning for their success. And although they were finally agreed by the European Council with the full force of 'high politics', the Commission played a critical role in devising a new budgetary strategy and in persuading the member states of the need to move to a global multi-annual budgetary process. Both budgetary agreements are classical package deals involving complex linkages between different decision-making arenas, and varied policy preferences, and with mixed consequences for the member states.

The making of Delors I

The Commission established a critical policy and political link between the implementation of the 1992 programme and a stable budgetary framework for the EU's finances. Within weeks of agreement to the SEA, the Commission presented its seminal paper entitled *Making a Success of the Single Act* (see European Commission, 1987) proposing a new approach to the Union's finances. President Delors was convinced that the SEA needed financial underpinning in a number of important respects and he sought to take advantage of a 'window of opportunity' to stabilise and regularise budgetary politics in the Union. The Delors proposals were designed to respond to a number of interrelated issues:

- The budget's chronic resource problem, exacerbated by its size and the dominance of agricultural spending;
- The commitment in the SEA to 'economic and social cohesion';
- Endemic competition between the European Parliament and the Council on budgetary matters.

The Commission sought to transform the budget from a series of discrete financial instruments dominated by the European Agricultural Guidance and Guarantee Fund (EAGGF), into a coherent instrument that would enhance economic and political integration and the Union's autonomy. The kernel of the proposal envisaged a sizeable increase in budget resources, legal rules on budgetary discipline, particularly for agriculture, and a major commitment to economic and social cohesion over a five-year period (1988–93). The plan demanded much larger financial resources to be distributed according to new rules of the game. During the 1980s the Commission, entangled in the time-consuming and draining British budgetary conflict, had little opportunity to embed structural budgetary change in the *acquis communautaire*. This was its opportunity.

Agreement on the Delors I package took one year from the initial Commission launch in February 1987 to the special Brussels European Council in February 1988. During this period the package wound its way through highly technical discussions in working parties, various *ad hoc* groups, a high-level group reporting to the Committee of Permanent Representatives (COREPER), and COREPER itself, Council meetings of many hues, a failed Summit in Copenhagen to a final successful one in Brussels. The Commission submitted separate proposals on the four main aspects of the package:

- Budget discipline;
- Own resources;
- The UK budgetary rebate;
- Reform of the structural funds.

Negotiations on all four dossiers involved consideration of highly-technical issues to do with reform of the CAP, new regulations for the structural funds, and the comparability and uniformity of national GNP statistics, to mention but a few. Behind the technical discussions lay careful assessments of what the package might mean for national contributions to, and receipts from, the budget. Tortuous negotiations on what were on the face of it minor technical points underlined the seriousness with which all the member states approached the negotiations on Delors I. These proposals would transform many beneficiaries from the budget into net contributors for the first time. Moreover, the CAP, so dear to many states, was no longer impervious to outside influence.

The Danish presidency in the latter half of 1987 had the task of bringing the negotiations on Delors I to a conclusion at the Copenhagen European Council in December. However, an intensive schedule of preparatory Community and bilateral meetings in the lead-up to the Summit failed to generate sufficient agreement on major elements of the package. The difficulty in reaching agreement can be explained partly by the comprehensive nature of the dossiers under consideration, but was mostly due to the high stakes involved. The member states were being asked to agree to a major change in the rules which would leave many of them financially worse off.

When the package was unveiled in the earlier part of 1987, the UK was quick to register its opposition to the proposed budgetary increases. UK officials did not believe that the economic and social cohesion provisions of the SEA carried this expensive price tag. The proposals on agriculture were probably the most hotly disputed issues of all. France and Germany fought hard to ensure that agreement on cereal production and compensation for a proposed 'set aside' policy would meet the needs of their farmers. The Italians objected to the move away from a VAT system of 'own resources' to a GNP based system because of its implication for Italian contributions to the budget. The UK, France and Germany opposed the doubling of the structural fund resources right up to the final negotiations. The UK wanted increases limited to 35 per cent and France and Germany were willing to endorse a 50 per cent increase. The Commission and the poorer member states, on the other hand, held out for a doubling of the funds. The accession of the Iberian states greatly enhanced the 'cohesion' voice in the EU. As a consequence of the gap between the member states on major elements of the package, the European Council was adjourned to a special Council in Brussels 1988 under the German presidency.

Pressure was intense for agreement in February because the EC had entered the year without an agreed budget, there was a presidential election in France in June and the impetus created by the SEA might have faltered without this financial underpinning. In hindsight the conclusions of the Brussels Summit were a triumph for the German presidency and the Commission. The key to the success of the Brussels Summit was the role played by Chancellor Kohl as president of the Council. The Chancellor felt that the EC could not afford the luxury of continuing a divisive debate on budgetary matters given the high stakes involved. To avoid this, he was willing to delve deep into German coffers to pay for a larger and more redistributive budget. This took UK officials by surprise because they felt that the German Economics Ministry was in the austerity camp. Yet Chancellor Kohl accepted that the cohesion of the Union and the 1992 programme were worth a larger budget. The Commission and Jacques Delors played a critical role in the final agreement. The link between the SEA and Delors I was successfully sold to the member states. In addition, the Commission's determination to keep the proposals together as a package from which no element could be detached forced the member states to think in terms of a global agreement, rather than choosing those elements that best suited their interests.

The broad outline of the agreement corresponded to what the Commission wanted to achieve. Delors I was central to what insiders in the Delors cabinet called the 'Russian Doll' strategy of 'iterated episodes of strategic action to seize upon openings in the political opportunity structure, resource accumulation through success, and reinvestment of these resources in new actions to capitalise on new opportunities' (Ross, 1995, p. 39). The Commission had finally achieved a broadly-based agreement on the contours of EU finances. It got a stable budgetary framework for a period of five years which contained agricultural expenditure; the long search for enhanced cohesion was rewarded with a major financial commitment to the Union's poorer regions; and the Commission could look forward to a larger budget with which it could finance a range of developing policies. The Brussels agreement paved the way for the Council, Parliament and Commission to agree to an Inter-Institutional Agreement (IIA) aimed at controlling the endemic competition between the two arms of the budgetary authority.

The making of Delors II

The Commission quickly followed the signing of the TEU with its proposals on the next financial package, Delors II in February/ March 1992 in two papers entitled, *From the Single Act to Maastricht and Beyond: The Means to Match Our Ambitions,* and *The Community's Finances Between Now and 1997* (European Commission, 1992a and b).

The papers deliberately build on the Delors I agreement of a five-year medium-term strategy including a further commitment to structural fund spending, a new Cohesion Fund, containment of agricultural spending, a major increase in external spending and a range of internal policies to enhance European competitiveness. The proposals envisaged the growth of EU expenditure from 1.2 per cent GNP to 1.37 per cent by 1997. The Commission was once again asking many of the member states to commit more money to the Union budget as part of the process of building the Union.

Negotiations on Delors II proved no less tortuous and difficult than the original agreement. In many ways the environment was much less conducive to a successful outcome this time around. A *Financial Times* editorial in May 1992 underlined the difficulties in the following terms:

> When Mr. Jacques Delors spelled out plans in February for a one-third increase in European Community revenues during the next five years, the EC Commission President knew he was advancing into difficult terrain. The hostile response form the richer EC countries has shown that this campaign will be uphill all the way. (*Financial Times*, 12 May 1992)

This time the budget was not in crisis and there was even some scope left in the existing 'own resources' ceiling for budgetary growth. This allowed the UK government to argue with some merit that the package was too ambitious. The German government was struggling with the budgetary consequences of unification and the enormous needs of the new *Länder* which made them far less likely to endorse a much larger budget. The Delors I package had turned many more states into net contributors making them assess budgetary proposals with a wary eye. As 1992 progressed, the Western European economies slipped into recession, which reduced enthusiasm for more spending given the strained nature of national finances in many states. The Danish 'no' in June 1992, followed by the French '*petit oui*' in September, unleashed a crisis of confidence in integration and threatened the ratification of the TEU. Moreover, the Commission emerged during this time as a convenient scapegoat for the ills of the Community, which further undermined the credibility of its search for an even larger budget.

Negotiations on Delors II waxed and waned during the Portuguese presidency in the first half of 1992 and it fell to the

British presidency to complete the negotiations in the latter half of the year. By the Lisbon Summit in June, the Commission conceded the time-frame of its proposals by agreeing to a seven-year financial perspective rather than a five-year one. President Delors, however, decided to 'tough it out' on the other elements of the package. The budgetary negotiations then fell to the UK presidency. The budgetary dossier confronted the UK with a number of tricky issues because of their long-standing policy of containing public expenditure and the EU budget. In addition, the UK rebates from the budget, an integral part of Delors I, were questioned by a number of the other member states.

In a tactic designed to remove the core of Delors II negotiations from the Foreign Affairs Council, the presidency scheduled a number of Eco-Fin meetings on the matter because it felt that the latter were more likely to contain budgetary rises. The negotiations proceeded in the run up to the Edinburgh European Council in a series of official and ministerial meetings, including a special conclave of Finance and Foreign Affairs Ministers in November. The presidency put forward a compromise package to this meeting which represented a significant dilution of the original Commission proposals. Jacques Delors reacted to the UK proposals by sending a letter to all the delegations reinforcing his arguments about the *raison d'être* of the Commission proposals and the unacceptability of the presidency compromise. He ended his letter:

> I can but repeat my conviction that the ambitions of Maastricht cannot be achieved piecemeal. Closer cohesion, greater competitiveness, stronger Community policies and wider external responsibilities – all go together. What is at stake is the impetus of the European venture and its transition into economic and social terms and into foreign policy terms. (Commission internal briefing note)

The final negotiations on the package were left to the concluding Summit meeting of the UK presidency under John Major's chairmanship at Edinburgh.

The UK prime minister wanted a success at Edinburgh because the presidency was bedevilled by growing dissension in the Conservative Party about the TEU, the collapse of the ERM in September and the general crisis of confidence in integration.

Failure to reach agreement on Delors II would have greatly enhanced the sense of drift in the Union. Moreover, the opening of accession negotiations with the EFTA states depended on agreement to a new financial framework. Whereas the Community faced a financial crisis in February 1988 when Delors I was agreed, the crisis this time was political in nature.

The member states remained deeply divided on many issues in the run up to the European Council meeting. The cohesion states, led by Spain, were prepared to settle for nothing less than a doubling of cohesion finance. The Spanish Foreign Minister stated days before the meeting that 'better no agreement at Edinburgh than a bad one. There are plenty of other cities and lots of other dates' (*Financial Times*, 8 December 1992). The UK had the support of Germany, the Netherlands and to a lesser extent Italy for its presidency compromise. France, Denmark, Belgium and Luxembourg would support a compromise between the UK Treasury line and the demands of the poorer member states. The financial perspective was the last issue to be decided at Edinburgh because the Danish agreement was finalised on the first day. The Spanish Prime Minister, Felipe Gonzalez, appeared willing to veto the Danish agreement of the previous day unless he received satisfaction on the budgetary side.

Chancellor Kohl and President Mitterrand agreed over breakfast to a larger budget than the UK presidency had proposed. Chancellor Kohl's shift from opposition to meeting the demands of the poorer countries for more aid was decisive for the eventual agreement. The Delors II package did not represent the negotiating victory for the Commission that Delors I did, but then times had changed.

The consequences of Delors I and II

The most important consequence of the Delors I and II packages is that EU finances are now set in a medium-term financial perspective which can be altered only at the margins. Both agreements signalled a willingness on the part of the heads of government to provide a stable financial environment for the annual budgetary cycle and to contain the budgetary battles of the past. Budgetary discipline became an accepted part of the *acquis* with legally-based limits on expenditure. The budgetary packages led to the signing of interinstitutional agreements between the budgetary authority which established 'rules of the game' for the annual budgetary negotiations. The inclusion of expenditure ceilings by category of expenditure represents political decisions on policy priorities with a clear emphasis on containing agricultural expenditure, enhancing flows to the poorer parts of Europe, providing finance for flanking policies and responding to the changes in global politics. However, one of the biggest challenges facing the Union will be to extend the medium-term financial perspective beyond the millennium.

The annual budgetary cycle: formal and informal processes

The parameters of the budgetary cycle are established by Article 203 of the EEC Treaty which sets out a precise timetable and procedure for drafting the annual budget. The timetable set down in the Treaty has been modified by agreement of the budgetary authority to allow more time at each stage of the process. Decision-making power on budgetary matters is divided, albeit unevenly, between the Council and the European Parliament, the two arms of the budgetary authority. The Council opens the formal budgetary procedure by agreeing a draft budget which is then sent to the Parliament for a first reading. The budget returns to the Council for a second reading and then back to the Parliament. The Parliament closes the budgetary process by adopting or rejecting the budget.

Both arms of the budgetary authority have different powers over different parts of the budget depending on the categorisation of expenditure (see Box 4.1). The Council has the final say over what is termed 'compulsory expenditure' – expenditure necessarily arising form the treaties – and the Parliament has the final say over 'non-compulsory' expenditure subject to a 'maximum rate of increase' decided on each year on the basis of a statistical calculation. The importance of the 'maximum rate of increase' has been diluted considerably by the establishment of expenditure ceilings in the financial perspective. The distribution of budgetary power between the two arms of the budgetary

---

BOX 4.1
The financial perspective, 1993–99

Categories of expenditure

1. Common agricultural policy
2. Structural actions – Structural Funds, Cohesion Fund, EEA Financial mechanism
3. Internal policies:
   - training, youth, audio-visual, information and other social operations
   - energy, Euratom, environment
   - consumer protection, internal market, industry and TENs
   - research and technological development
4. External action
5. Administrative expenditure
6. Reserves
   - monetary reserve
   - guarantees
   - reserve for emergency aid
7. Compensation

---

authority is a source of conflict between the two institutions. The annual budgetary cycle involves five stages (see Box 4.2).

Stage one

The Commission has responsibility for preparing a *Preliminary Draft Budget* for submission to the budgetary authority. The preparatory work is carried out by the Budget Commissioner and Directorate General (DG 19) Budgets. The role of the Budget Commissioner is in no way comparable with a national Minister for Finance, who is generally second only to the prime minister. That said, the increased size of the budget since the end of the 1980s has enhanced the status of the Budget Commissioner within the Commission. Technical preparations fall to the various divisions of DG 19 which begin their work at the beginning of the year by collecting the necessary information for adjusting the financial perspective depending on projected GNP growth and inflation. Although largely technical, adjustments to the financial perspective establish the financial framework for the budgetary

---

BOX 4.2
The annual budgetary cycle
(following the Interinstitutional Agreement of 1993)

Budget to be adopted by 1 January each year

	Treaty Timetable	Timetable by Convention
Interinstitutional trialogue on the priorities for the 1995 Budget		April
Two ad hoc conciliation meetings on compulsory expenditure		July
Commission submits the PDB to Council	1 September	15 June

Conciliation meeting between the Council and the EP before Council first reading

Council first reading		31 July
Draft budget sent to EP	5 October	first half of September
EP first reading	19 November	25 October approx.

Conciliation meeting between Council and EP before Council second reading

| Council second reading | 4 December | 22 November approx. |
| EP second reading | within 15 days | second week of December |

EP President formally declares the budget adopted or EP rejects the budget

---

year. Less than expected GNP growth limits the pot of available money and forces choices on the spending directorates and the budgetary authority. Proposed adaptation of the financial perspective is decided on by the budgetary authority after a trialogue (a meeting between the three institutions responsible for framing the budget) involving the Council, the Parliament and the Commission which usually takes place in April.

In February, DG 19 sends a budgetary circular to all the Commission services explaining the budgetary framework, the underlying assumptions and the requirements that have to be met. DG 19 gives guidance on the amounts available and the margin the Commission wishes to leave unused to allow for the priorities of the Parliament and the Council. The Budget DG also indicates the major Commission priorities such as TransEuropean Networks (TENs) and external policy in recent years. In addition to budgetary requests for the following year, all DGs are expected to provide DG 19 with a medium-term (2–3 year) outlook of their financial needs.

After DG 19 has received the wish list from the various DGs, it conducts hearings with the *chef d'unité* for each section of the budget. Many budgetary bids are rejected at this stage of the process. The hearings are intended to allow the services to justify and elaborate on their budgetary requests. Negotiations between DG 19 and the services may be simply routine or may be conflictual, depending on the nature of the bid and how it fits with Commission guidelines. Most discussion revolves around the financing of category-3 expenditure (internal policy) given the limited room for manoeuvre on agricultural and structural spending, and on category 4 (external relations). Justification of budgetary requests is based on the medium-term planning for previous years, how existing budgetary appropriations have been spent, and value for money considerations. The latter consideration has become more important since the beginning of the 1990s since DGs are expected to justify new bids with well-prepared papers and a *fiche financière*. DG 19 is attempting to go beyond its traditional role of managing the preparation of the budget from an administrative and technical perspective to a position where it can help identify budgetary priorities. It wants the spending Directorates to examine more carefully the performance of each budgetary line. The lower than expected GNP figures for 1992/93 created a tighter budgetary environment than anticipated and hence forced choice between budgetary lines.

If DG 19 and the relevant service agree to the budget at the first hearing, the matter is closed. Disagreement will involve further hearings at the level of Director General, Commissioners and the Commission as a whole. Most budgetary lines are agreed at the lowest level with more contentious and political issues pushed up the hierarchy. DG 19 has adopted a practice of sending a number of selected budget lines to the full Commission for its consideration, to ensure that there is adequate discussion of new lines or significant increases to existing ones. The Commission generally decides on the text of the *Preliminary Draft Budget* (PDB) by May and then passes it onto the budgetary authority for its consideration. The PDB is a massive tome running to some 1500 pages outlining each budget line and the supporting arguments (European

Commission, 1995b). The Budget Commissioner and senior officials from DG 19 steer the PDB through the Council and the European Parliament, offering advice, potential compromises and assessments of what is technically feasible.

Stage two

While the Commission is in the process of preparing its PDB, the European Parliament makes its preparations for managing the annual budgetary cycle. The Parliament's Budget Committee, one of the most distinguished Committees in the EP, forms the central column of the Parliament's budgetary process. The division of responsibility within the Committee, already charted up to the year 1999, is decided by agreement among the political groups on chairmanship, on the main *rapporteurs* for the annual budget and on supporting responsibilities. Chairmanship of the Committee is one of the most influential political positions in the EP. Each year the Parliament appoints two *rapporteurs* for the budget, one for the operating and administrative budgets of the Commission and one for the administrative budgets of all other institutions. The *rapporteur* for the Commission budget is the central player in relation to the annual budget. Together with the Committee Chairman, the *rapporteur* is in a powerful position *vis-à-vis* the Parliament's sectoral committees and will be involved in all formal and informal contract with the Council and Commission. The *rapporteur* maintains constant contact with the *rapporteurs* of the specialised committees on the shape of their proposed amendments. The Budget Committee is a court of final appeal for the sectoral committees which come with their competing requests, priorities and pet projects. Each *rapporteur* attempts to put his or her stamp on the budget when the Parliament holds a debate and adopts a resolution on its budgetary priorities before the Commission publishes its PDB. The main emphasis at this stage is on the Parliament's own priorities.

Stage three

The Budget Council, composed of junior Ministers from the national Finance Ministries, is responsible for establishing the *Draft Budget* by 5 October, but usually will agree to it by the end of July before the summer recess. Because of the timing of the budgetary cycle, the establishment of a draft budget falls to the country holding the presidency in the second half of the year. The presidency in the first half of the year tries to get agreement on the budgets of the smaller institutions by the end of June to ease the workload on the incoming presidency. July is a very busy month for officials in the Council Secretariat responsible for the Budget and for the Council's Budget Committee.

Within the Council, the bulk of the work is done by the Budget Committee, a specialised committee consisting of the financial attachés in the Permanent Representations of the member states. The officials attending the Budget Committee have primary responsibility for overseeing the annual budgetary cycle from the perspective of the member states. The Budget Committee, like all permanent Council committees, has a character of its own because its members usually stay in Brussels for four to five years and all share a background in their national Finance Ministries. The process of socialisation in the Committee is aided by the intensity of work on the budget at particular times of the year, and the usual socialising occurs among a tightly-knit bunch of officials.

The Council's Budget Committee has four main tasks:

1. To reach the highest level of agreement possible on the draft budget.
2. To prepare COREPER's discussions concerning outstanding issues.
3. To formulate opinions on the financial aspects of proposed legislation.
4. To approve the estimates of expenditure of the Council Secretariat, the Economic and Social Committee and the Committee of the Regions.

The Budget Committee approaches the budget in a two-phased process. The first phase requires substantive discussions with questions to the Commission. The second phase involves voting only. Detailed line-by-line consideration of the PDB takes place in the Budget Committee which votes on the basis of qualified majority voting. In fact, the Draft Budget was always decided on by qualified majority voting even during the high point of the 1966 Luxembourg Compromise, which ruled out majority voting for legislative decision-making. The degree of independence exercised by the national member of the Budget Committee depends very much on national policy styles and national co-ordinating mechanisms. Some members of the Committee receive very detailed briefs on the national position on each budgetary item; others are left to gauge what is the best approach to follow. Some officials have clearly established priorities concerning spending, while others adopt a *laissez-faire* approach. Voting patterns in the Budget Committee are based on attitudes towards the budget, its distribution across policy areas and within policy areas. Old Brussels hands have a keen sense about the voting intentions of their partners and will trade their votes in informal bargaining.

COREPER and the Budget Council discuss only a limited number of budgetary lines at their meetings. This was not always the case. Council meetings in the early 1980s, when budgetary conflict was at its highest and the budget was a major agenda item, often went through the night. An official who attended the final Council meeting and conciliation meetings with the European Parliament on the 1980 budget describes the final stages in the following terms:

> The battle lines were drawn and the scene moved to an unusual third encounter between the two institutions, unusually held on Parliament's ground in Strasbourg and going on for an unusually long time. It was actually a string of meetings of the Council interspersed with meetings between the Council and the Parliament's Budget Committee. It is also etched on the memories of Council participants by the absence of any solid food – not even the legendary Council sandwiches – during the long night and early morning. (Nicoll, 1984, p. 9)

Relative budgetary peace since 1989 has meant that Council deliberations are usually very short. National positions are well-known on different budgetary lines with some member states adopting a position of austerity on all budgetary matters and others favouring those of interest to their national constituents. The major contributors – Germany, the UK and the Netherlands – are now looking more carefully at all budgetary lines. The tendency in the Budget Committee, COREPER and the Budget Council is to cut budgetary appropriations that the Parliament will in any case increase again. According to one observer, 'The approach of the Council is arithmetical rather than policy-oriented, except in the sense that it will look, of course, more favourably on items where they feel that the Commission proposals reflect previous decisions that they themselves have taken. The axe tends to fall most heavily on marginal areas that are not well established or that are not backed by Council legislation' (*The European Citizen*, July 1993, p. 11).

Before the Council adopts the Draft Budget, it will usually meet a delegation from the Parliament to discuss the latter's priorities. This meeting is largely ritualistic and involves a lunch between the Council and a Parliamentary delegation. The presidency speaks for the Council and is very formal. The other members of Council will tend not to contribute to the debate between the Council and the Parliament although the EP delegation may know that individual members of the Council favour the Parliament's stand on a number of issues. This set-piece conciliation meeting has been augmented by an additional meeting to discuss compulsory and non-compulsory expenditure following agreement on Delors II and by a trialogue on the priorities for the budget.

Stage four

Between September and December the budgetary process is at its most intense. When the Parliament receives the Draft Budget from the Council, it must co-ordinate the bids of the sectoral committees, and the Budget Committee must finalise its response to the budget. The *rapporteur* is in regular contact with the specialised committees, giving advice and support for particular amendments and indicating where the Budget Committee might have difficulty in supporting a proposed amendment. The Parliament may propose modifications to compulsory expenditure and amendments to non-compulsory expenditure.

The sectoral committees prepare their reports for the Budget Committee in September, usually advocating the reinsertion of lines taken out by the Council and cuts made by the Council. The critical stage is the three-day meeting held by the Budget Committee at the beginning of October when it responds to the amendments put forward by the specialised committees. The Committee decides on its response to the amendments from political groups and Committees at this meeting. The Budget

Committee's meeting on the 1995 Budget lasted for 21 hours and involved 400 amendments. There is considerable informal contact and horse trading between the chairman and *rapporteur* of the Budget Committee and the sectoral committees. Deals are struck within and between budgetary lines since this phase of the budgetary process is highly politicised. Representatives of the member states, Commission services and interest groups keep in close touch with the relevant Committee and the Budget Committee to ensure that their priorities are reflected in the final decision. Senior Commission staff will maintain contact not only with the specialised committee but also with the Budget Committee on disputed budgetary lines. The insertion of a budgetary line for the LIFE programme (environmental projects) in the 1992 budget illustrates the kinds of networks that are used. DG 11 (Environment) in the Commission failed to receive strong support for the proposed LIFE programme from the Delors cabinet and DG 19. Instead, senior officials in the DG used their contacts in the Parliament's Environment Committee to lobby for the programme. The *rapporteur* for the 1992 Budget, Alain Lamassure, was persuaded to adopt the LIFE programme as one of his projects for that year. Pascal Lamy, Delors's *chef de cabinet* accused the officials in DG 11 of using the tactics of the Vietcong!

Once the Budget Committee has decided on its response to specific amendments and modifications, discipline in the sectoral committees and among the political groups ensures that the Parliament's Plenary session votes the amendments approved by the Budget Committee with few exceptions. Hence the real work on the budget is done at the committee stage of the process (European Parliament, 1994).

Stage five

The Parliament's vote is then transmitted back to the Council for its second reading. Before the Council reacts, a second and critical conciliation meeting is held by the budgetary authority when both sides know the financial limits and the political environment within which they are operating. Unlike the earlier ritualistic conciliation meeting, this meeting attempts to reach agreement between the Parliament and Council on outstanding issues. The Council examines the EP's proposed modifications and amendments, some of which it may accept but the majority of which are rejected again. The results of the Council's reading are then sent back to the Parliament for its final reading. The process is relatively predictable; the EP restores the cuts made by the Council where it has authority. Last-minute negotiations between the Council and the EP are not uncommon right up to the time when the Parliament adopts the budget at its December hearing. The Parliament has the power to reject the budget, a power it was more willing to use in the days of unremitting conflict on budgetary matters with the Council. There has been no rejection since 1984. See Box 4.3 for an outline of the progress of the 1995 Budget through the institutions.

The evolution of interinstitutional relations on budgetary matters

The division of budgetary responsibility between the Parliament and the Council contains within it the seeds of conflict and division. In the early 1980s the annual budgetary cycle was punctuated with unending disputes between the institutions on what were relatively small amounts of money (Nicoll, 1984, p. 18). However, at stake were issues of principle and power between the Council, representing the member states, and the Parliament, attempting to forge a role for itself in the Union's institutional landscape. Budgetary power, granted in the 1975 Budget Treaty, gave the newly-elected parliament one of its few substantial powers. Following direct elections in 1979, the budget granted the Parliament leverage in EU decision-making, a leverage it was determined to wield. The Council of Ministers was no longer the sole budgetary authority. The unending battles between the two arms of the budgetary authority led to a series of conflict-ridden budgetary processes which ended only with the conclusion of Delors I in 1988 (Nicoll, 1984; European Commission, 1989).

In December 1979, the newly-elected parliament rejected the 1980 budget for the first time, which meant that the Commission had to operate on the basis of provisional-twelfths based on the preceding budgetary figures. The 1980 budgetary process was further complicated by a disputed supplementary budgetary process which involved alleged breaches of the budgetary rules. The Commission started infringement proceedings in the Court of Justice against

BOX 4.3
The 1995 budgetary procedure

Context
The 1995 budgetary procedure was the first to be conducted under the new procedures established by the Interinstitutional Agreement of 1993. It also took place against the backdrop of referenda in four applicants on accession which meant that the Preliminary Draft Budget prepared by the Commission was largely conditional on the outcome on enlargement. Accession inevitably would have an important impact on both the revenue and expenditure side of the budget. Discussion of the budget in the Council became embroiled with a problem concerning Italian contributions to 'own resources' because the Commission imposed heavy fines on Italy for non-implementation of the milk levy system. The Italians threatened non-implementation of the 1993 Delors II package which meant that there was a potential shortfall in receipts of 600 million ECU for 1995.

European Parliament priorities (EP debate, 23 March 1994)
- Agrees with the need for budgetary rigour
- Wants a revision of financial perspective re. enlargement
- Wants budgetisation of CFSP and ECSC
- Expressed concerns about agricultural expenditure
- Wanted a review of Phare and Tacis

Commission Preliminary Draft Budget
Volume of the Budget to grow by 4 per cent, just above the level of inflation
Tight agricultural spending
Increases in structural spending (+9%), research policy (+7.5%), TransEuropean Networks (+22%), training and youth policy (+12.6%)
Increases for East Central Europe, CIS and Mediterranean (+9%)
Substantial margins/reserves under headings 3, 4, 5 of the financial perspective.

Preliminary Draft Budget: 76 326 million ECU (commitments),
72 349 million ECU (payments)

Council First Reading (25 July under the German presidency)
The Council's Budget Committee and COREPER reached substantial agreement on CAP and structural policy, proposals to reduce the Commission's appropriations for internal policy by 450 million ECUs, but were deadlocked on the financing of the THERMIE 2 programme for energy technology.

BOX 4.3 (*continued*)

Ministers agreed to significant cuts in internal expenditure, with the exception of the Agriculture and cohesion policy, as proposed by the Budget Committee and COREPER. The cuts were aimed at the TENs, education, training, consumer measures, administrative expenditure and some external measures. Council's Draft Budget stayed within 1.2% of GNP ceiling as opposed to 1.21% envisaged at the Edinburgh Summit. Germany, France and the UK formed a 'blocking minority' to ensure that the THERMIE 2 programme had to be financed as part of the R&D programme.

Draft Budget: 75 745 million ECU (commitments), 71 955 million ECU (payments)

EP First Reading (27 October)
The Budget Committee took 21 hours to vote on 800 amendments to the draft budget which were then voted *en bloc* at Plenary. The EP restored the cuts made by the Council in its first reading. The EP froze certain amounts pending agreements to the 'own resources' decision, which was deadlocked in Council, and entered reserves for enlargement.

First Reading: 75 775 million ECU (commitments), 73 318 million ECU (payments)

Council Second Reading
Council opposed all modifications and all but six of the EP's 400 amendments; it opposed the Parliament's classification of certain expenditures and its treatment of pillar 2 financing.

The problem of enlargement
Following the results of the Norwegian referendum, the Commission published its proposals on the adjustment of the financial perspective with a view to enlargement of the Union. The Commission sent a letter of amendment to the budgetary authority outlining the adjustment to the financial perspective.

EP Second Reading
The EP takes account of the requirements of a larger Union but the enlargement related amounts were entered in a reserve to be allocated by a supplementary and amending budget in 1995. The EP restored the cuts made by the Council in its second reading.

President of the European Parliament approves the Budget for 1995

Total Budget: ECU 80 million ECU (commitments), 76 million ECU (payments) to take account of the additional amounts needed for the three additional member states.

three member states that refused to pay for the supplementary budget and was itself the subject of proceedings by Germany, which argued that the Commission's execution of the budget was illegal. The Court did not rule on these cases because agreement on a supplementary budget in 1981 covered the issues in dispute. The 1982 process was again the subject of intense discussion when the Parliament maintained its increases, even though they went beyond the 'maximum rate of increase'. When the Parliament's President declared the budget adopted in December 1981, the Council initiated proceedings against the Parliament in the Court of Justice. This was withdrawn in June 1982 when the two arms of the budgetary authority agreed to a joint declaration on the classification of compulsory and non-compulsory expenditure and on the roles of the respective parts of the budgetary authority.

This heralded a period of more intense conciliation between the Parliament and the Council on budgetary matters but did not lead to a normalisation of relations. The 1984 budget was marred by disputes about the classification of expenditure and on the amounts to be devoted to the Regional Fund, social expenditure and industrial policies. This was followed by the rejection of the 1985 budget by the Parliament and by an action in the Court of Justice over the 1986 budget. The Council brought the action on the grounds that the Parliament had exceeded the 'maximum rate of increase' on non-compulsory expenditure. The Court found for the Council against the Parliament, but insisted that the two arms of the budget authority had to reach agreement and could not act unilaterally. The 1986 budget was not adopted until July 1986, the second year during which the Commission had to operate on the basis of provisional-twelfths.

Conflict between the Parliament and the Council concerned institutional issues about their respective powers, issues of substance on policy priorities, classification of expenditure and the division of budgetary resources between compulsory and non-compulsory expenditure. Year-in and year-out highly-technical debates about relatively small amounts of money obscured issues of principle between the two institutions. Legal arguments and actions at the Court of Justice about the budgetary rules were deployed in what was in essence a political conflict, with the Parliament seeking to have the budgetary treaties interpreted in the widest possible manner and the Council adopting a restrictive position. The

Council was loath to cede power to the Parliament and sought to limit the sharing of power to the absolute minimum. Members of the Council, particularly France, were intent on protecting the privileged position of agricultural expenditure as compulsory expenditure. In addition, having failed to give the Parliament any say over revenue, the Council feared excessive expenditure demands or fiscal irresponsibility on the part of the Parliament. It is fair to say that the Parliament tended to concentrate on author-ising expenditure in the 1970s and 1980s rather than the more mundane issues of budgetary control and monitoring. In any event, the Parliament's proposed budgetary increases tended to be quite small – less than 1 per cent of the total budget. It was difficult to resolve problems between the Council and Parliament because intra-Council bargaining tended to push the Council to the limits of compromise – making it an uncomfortable partner in interinstitutional dialogue. The Council had great difficulty devel-oping a collective response to other EU institutions and in enter-ing genuine negotiations.

The Parliament wanted to use the only substantial power that it had to extract other concessions. The Parliament had five main priorities in relation to the budget.

1. It attempted to use its financial power to gain access to the Community's legislative process which was vested entirely in the Council. The Parliament's budgetary power was not matched by a corresponding power in the legislative domain. The Parliament argued that if appropriations were entered into the budget, the mere fact of a budgetary line cons-tituted a sufficient legal basis for their use. The Parliament proceeded to enter appropriations for new budgetary actions without a legal basis.

   The Council, on the other hand, argued strongly for the need for a legislative basis to accompany budgetary expenditure. The Commission found itself caught between the two battling institutions. Commissioner Tugendhat, Commissioner for Budgets, argued that 'without the appro-priate budgetary entry, there can be neither expenditure nor receipts. However, alone this basis is not always sufficient. There are cases where the legal basis constituted by the budget has to be underpinned by a separate legislative bases' (quoted in European Commission, 1989, p. 20). There were clashes almost each year on this issue between 1975 and 1982 until a joint declaration on 'various measures to improve the budgetary procedure' was signed. The declaration specified that a separate legal act was necessary for any 'significant action' involving budgetary appropriations.

2. The Parliament used its powers over 'non-compulsory' expenditure to promote its policy preferences. This involved an attempt, at least at the level of rhetoric, to contain agricultural expenditure and to expand the monies available for regional, social, transport, education and development assistance. For example, in 1978 the Parliament proposed an increase of commitment appropriations for the Regional Fund from 620 million EUA to 1000 billion EUA. When the Council could not overturn this decision by a qualified majority, the Parliament deemed its amendments accepted because they had not been rejected. However, the consequence of the Parliament's amendments was to increase the 'maximum rate of increase' of non-compulsory expenditure without the prior agreement of the Council. The dispute was resolved in March 1979 when the Council approved a supplementary budget which allocated 900 million EUA to the Regional Fund. A number of member states that had refused to regard the 1979 budget as legal, paid their contributions.

3. The Parliament sought to expand policies falling under the non-compulsory heading so that it had the final say over a larger part of the budget. Particularly contentious questions were the guidance element of the EAGGF, the common fisheries policy, UK rebates, and EMS interest subsidies.

4. The Parliament sought to ensure that intergovernmental agreements on the financing of particular policy instruments or intergovernmental mechanisms to deal with budgetary shortfalls should not erode the normal budgetary rules and its own role.

The Council, in an attempt to curtail Parliament's budgetary power, began to enter 'amounts deemed necessary' into legislative texts covering multi-annual programmes so that financial allocations would be predetermined. The Parliament rightly regarded this as a device to tie its hands in advance on budgetary matters. In

March 1995, an Interinstitutional Declaration established a *modus operandi* between the institutions on multi-annual programmes. The Parliament agreed that an overall budgetary target may be included in legislative acts under co-decision because the EP has important powers in this legislative process, but that for areas outside the co-decision procedure the inclusion of an overall budget allocation merely acts as a guide and is not binding on the budgetary authority (European Commission, 1995, p. 21). The legislative and the budgetary procedures are moving closer together.

A recurring theme in Parliamentary debate on the budget is the contrast between what MEPs perceive as the political approach of the Parliament and the technical approach of the Budget Council. The contrast is described in an EP publication in the following terms:

> The Council regards the budget as an accounting instrument, a simple reflection of the policies it has adopted and of inter-governmental negotiations, the conclusions of which may not be altered substantially; in short, it is a straight jacket. For Parliament, which has only limited legislative powers, despite the provisions of the Single Act, the budget is an assessment of the Community's needs, a chance to shape Community policies. (European Parliament, 1989)

The damaging effects of interinstitutional conflict during the annual budgetary cycle forced the two institutions to seek ways of establishing a *modus vivendi* on budgetary practice and principles. From 1970 onwards a series of devices was developed to structure budgetary discussion among the Council, the Parliament, and the Commission. This began with:

- Collaboration, dating from 1972, between the Council and Parliament during the budgetary cycle involving two meetings, one before the Council adopts the draft budget and one before the Parliament has its second reading of the budget;
- Conciliation, dating from 1975, on legislative acts with major financial implications.

These procedures were augmented in 1982 with the declaration noted above on the classification of expenditure and the powers of the budgetary authority. None of these devices could cope with the strain in relations between the Parliament and Council, given the tense budgetary environment for much of the 1980s. It was not until agreement on Delors I that the budgetary battles of the early 1980s were moderated by a new institutional device.

In June 1988, the Delors package led to the signing of an Interinstitutional Agreement (IIA) between the three institutions on 'Budgetary Discipline and Improvement of the Budgetary Procedure' (Nicoll, 1988; Zangel, 1989). Its opening Provision states that the main purpose of the agreement is to 'give effect to the conclusions of the Brussels European Council on budgetary discipline and accordingly to improve the functioning of the annual budgetary procedure' (European Communities, 1988a).All institutions agreed to respect the division of expenditure into six categories and to observe the ceilings placed on these separate categories of expenditure. Amounts not used under one heading could not be transferred to other headings. The institutions accepted that a strict ratio be applied to the relationship between commitments and payments so that the budget could not be burdened by the 'cost of the past' (Zangel, 1989, p. 683).

The IIA made provision for the revision of the financial perspective, the maximum rate of increase for non-compulsory expenditure and for budgetary discipline. The agreement benefited all participants in the budgetary process. The Commission could look forward to a reasonably stable budgetary environment within which to plan its expenditure programmes. The Council ensured that the decisions of the Brussels Council would be observed and that its relations with the Parliament would be less fraught. For the Parliament, the IIA meant that the Community had a multi-annual financial perspective which it favoured, and its long-standing policy priorities were endorsed concerning cohesion expenditure. The Parliament achieved increases in non-compulsory expenditure that would have been unimaginable in the 1980s. From then on, less energy was expended on budgetary battles. Although differences in interpretation of the agreement caused a number of interinstitutional debates, relative budgetary peace broke out between the Council and the Parliament. The Parliament passed the Budget into law on time for each of the years covered by Delors I despite the need for considerable changes to accommodate German unification and the collapse of communism in the former Soviet bloc (Shackleton, 1990).

The Budgetary institutions followed the successful outcome of Delors I and the IIA with an updated one in 1993. At Edinburgh in 1992, the member states agreed to a much more detailed financial structure which specified spending by category for each year of the financial perspective up to 1999. This left the Parliament less room for manoeuvre to negotiate on budgetary figures, but meant that it could extract concessions from the Council as the price of a new interinstitutional agreement. The Parliament was willing to offer the Council 'budget peace in exchange for political territory', according to Colom I. Navel, the *rapporteur* for the Budget Committee on this matter (European Parliament, 1993b). In return for accepting the amounts agreed at Edinburgh by the European Council, the Parliament won concessions on budgetary decision-making. The most significant features of the IIA, agreed in September 1993, are:

- The conciliation process is extended to include a trialogue meeting before the publication of the preliminary draft budget and *ad hoc* conciliation on compulsory expenditure.
- The agreement stipulates that all financial amounts in categories 2 and 3 are categorised as non-compulsory, over which the Parliament has the final say.
- The institutions agreed that any increase in compulsory expenditure would not be at the expense of non-compulsory expenditure.
- The establishment of an annual budget which leaves a margin beneath each ceiling to allow for unforeseen circumstances.
- The avoidance of budgetary lines involving small amounts of money. (Corbett, 1994; European Commission, 1995)

During the negotiations on the IIA, the Council agreed to review the budgetary procedure as part of the 1996 Intergovernmental Conference and to participate in a Parliament conference on 'own resources'. The budgetary process is part of the agenda on constitutional reform in the Union.

Although the medium-term financial package and the interinstitutional agreement marked a major improvement of the conflict-ridden budgetary procedure of the 1980s, a number of outstanding issues continue to bedevil Council/EP relations. First, the Parliament wishes to see the artificial distinction between compulsory and non-compulsory expenditure abolished completely. The Council has come to accept that more and more items of expenditure fall within the non-compulsory expenditure category; during the negotiations on the IIA, it conceded that financial protocols attached to international agreements should henceforth be non-compulsory. About 50 per cent of the budget is now in this category. That said, the main battle is about the status of the agricultural guarantee fund; the Council and especially some member states want to maintain its privileged position as compulsory expenditure. The Parliament received a set-back in November 1995 when the Court of Justice ruled that the 1995 budget as signed into law by the Parliament's president, Klaus Hansch, was invalid because agreement between the two arms of the budgetary authority was absent. The case was taken by the Council of Ministers because it argued that the parliament had not acted in good faith when it 'unilaterally and arbitrarily proceeded to reclassify compulsory and non-compulsory expenditure' (*European Voice*, 14–20 December 1995, p. 21). Moreover, conflict remains about the proper financing of Pillars 2 and 3 of the TEU. The Parliament is adamant that, if EU budgetary resources are used for joint actions, the normal budgetary procedures must apply.

Policy style in the budgetary domain

Making budgets is an important sub-system in the Union's decision-making process. It is characterised by well-established routines which rely on formal legal texts and the informal dynamics of intraorganisational and interinstitutional politics. Those with organisational responsibility for making the EU budget – DG 19, the Parliament's and Council's Budget Committees – exercise a horizontal/control role *vis-à-vis* the 'policy advocates' within their own institutions. The budgetary sub-system is dominated by a rather restricted number of people from DG 19, the competent Commissioner and one or two members of his cabinet, the Commission President and cabinet, national representatives on the Council's Budget Committee, the Council presidency, one or two senior Council officials, the

Budget Ministers, key members of the Parliament's Budget Committee, particularly the *rapporteur* and chairman of the Committee, and a small number of Parliament officials. The Commission is an ever-present player in the budgetary process, at hand with its political and technical advice for the two parts of the budgetary authority. The secretariats of both the Council and the Parliament play an important role in preparing technical dossiers and in maintaining day-to-day contact between the two institutions. They carry the institutional memories of previous debates and are adept at proposing solutions to very difficult problems.

Although it would be misleading to portray the Council/EP relationship as routine and conflict free, the current budgetary process lacks the tension and drama of the pre-Delors I days, captured by Nicoll in the following terms:

> The Budget Council of the European Union is like no other. It holds the second prize for the longest continuous meeting: its first reading in July 1983 began at 10 am. (nominal) on a Wednesday and ended at breakfast time on the Friday ... A French President once dismissed it as 'Brussels cinema' in comparison to his real work, but was later gripped by the thrill of the debate and worked mightily for its success. A President of the European Parliament's Committee on Budgets was once found unabashed in the interpreters' booths when the Council thought that it was in private conclave in the Parliament building in Strasbourg. (Nicoll, 1995, p. 180)

The development of conciliation since 1970 has meant that the Council has slowly and with considerable reservation come to terms with the presence of the Parliament in this policy field. Formal negotiations/trialogues between the institutions are conducted by a small number of key people from each institution who attempt to get beyond the ritual of well-established institutional positions. The annual budgetary cycle is now punctuated by trialogues, informal meetings, formal conciliation and convivial lunches that allow both arms of the budgetary authority to live with their shared agreements. The Council is inherently constrained in the conciliation process by its structure. The Presidency, acting on behalf of the Council, attempts to reach compromises with the EP without going beyond the mandate given to it by the Council. The difficulty of reaching agreement within the Council means that its mandate is usually very limited with little room for manoeuvre. The Parliament, for its part, continues to push the agenda on institutional and procedural issues in its search for an enhanced role in the EU's institutional landscape. In many ways, relative budgetary peace has meant that the 'stuff of politics' between the Council and the Parliament has moved to legislation as the Parliament seeks to establish itself as a partner in the legislative field. The experience gained in budgetary conciliation is deployed in other aspects of the policy process. Budgetary politics are no longer at the cutting edge of Council/Parliament relations.

Grantsmanship-or, while you are over there in Brussels, get us a grant!

Inevitably, the growing size of the EU budget and the expansion of its programmes attract the interest of potential beneficiaries in the member states. Although allocation of a large portion of the budget rests on negotiations between the member states and the Commission, a large number of programmes and Community initiatives are channelled directly to the beneficiaries. It is estimated that the Commission awards at least three separate contracts each day. Consequently it is the main focus of lobbying for EU funding. Voluntary groups, regional groups and interest organisations maintain contact with their MEPs, but the key relationship is with the relevant Commission service responsible for a programme. Finance for decentralised programmes, pilot projects, demonstration actions, information services and studies goes directly to those who win contracts from the Commission. Money from the R&D programme, Life, Phare and Tacis are all channelled directly to those winning contracts. The Commission also directly funds many voluntary groups based in Brussels, such as the European Women's Lobby, the European Forum for Migrants, and the Bureau for Lesser Used Languages.

There has been a proliferation of guides to funding from the EU prepared by Brussels-based consultants, Euro-groups, national interest groups and the Commission itself. Most guides contain information on the legal and policy content of particular programmes and the name and contact number of the relevant officials. Knowledge is a very important resource in negotiating the grants maze (Leeson, 1995). Reliable and accurate information about the development and priorities of a funding programme is essential for those seeking to get 'money from Brussels'. Such information can be gleaned from the Official Journal and newsletters issued by the relevant Commission services. Knowing how to sift through the plethora of information to distinguish what is important or not is difficult. Informal 'insider' knowledge can often make the difference between access to EU funding or not. Most EU programmes are oversubscribed, with the result that the best-prepared applications which accord with the priorities of the eligibility criteria have the greatest chance of success. Those with well-established personal contacts in the relevant Commission services tend to get copies of the draft guidelines on funding programmes before they are even published in the *Official Journal*, which gives them additional time to prepare a good application and to make the necessary contacts with partners. By the time a call for proposals is published, the resources may have already been unofficially allocated or the lead-in time for applications too short. A good working relationship with a desk officer allows a potential applicant to get an informal response from the relevant officials before the official deadline. Contact, of this kind, allows the applicant to mould the application to suit the evaluators. That said, potential applicants must be careful not to end up pestering hard-pressed Commission officials who will then be less-disposed towards their projects. Successful lobbying tends to be built on well-established relationships with Commission officials gained through professional contract and informal socialising at the usual round of receptions, the expatriate golf clubs and in a few well-known hostelries located near EU institutions.

Consultants based in Brussels or the national capitals play a growing role in assisting clients to gain access to Community funding, or in applying for contracts for their own purposes. They offer their clients 'insider knowledge' and a successful record in getting Commission funding. Some of them operate on the basis of a no-fund no-fee policy. In other words, they will charge only if the grant application is successful. Many Brussels-based consultants depend on the Commission for a large portion of their income. The rise and demise of independent consultancy firms tend to follow the Commission programme cycle to an extraordinary degree. When a programme is coming to an end, there is a fallow time for consultants as money dries up until the next phase of the programme is up and running.

The proliferation of regional offices in Brussels (95 in 1994) since the mid-1980s owes something to the expansion of the budget. Regional offices are interested in marrying potential projects in their region with funding opportunities from the Budget, especially structural funds, R&D, cultural and environmental funds. The structural funds are a central focus of much regional lobbying. Many regions falling outside Objective 1 status for the purposes of the structural funds find it necessary to have an office in Brussels to ensure that their region benefits from financial flows under other objectives. Poorer regions within wealthy member states may feel that direct representation in Brussels would serve their cause. The Northern Ireland Centre for Europe was established in 1992 largely for this reason. Some regions, notably Strathclyde and the Scottish Highlands and Islands, used their presence in Brussels to lobby successfully for Objective 1 status in the 1993 reform of the structural funds. The staff of regional offices develop 'insider status' and tend to have well-established contacts with Commission officials. One regional representative comments that 'the sources of soft information tend to be the ones from people you know on the inside. It's the tips, winks and nudges that are important' (quoted in Peter, 1995, p. 11). Regional offices are also a useful place for developing relations with other regions. Brussels has become a market-place for regional transactions (Peter, 1995, p. 11). Transnational applications for funding can be advanced in this manner, and most EU projects include a transnational dimension as a matter of course. Since 1992, Hesse, a German *Land*, has arranged a *jour fixe*, the first Monday of every month, for a meeting of the representatives of regional offices in Brussels at which they can forge transnational contacts.

The development and reform of the structural funds has led to the creation of transnational lobbying groups to ensure that the interests of particular regions – declining industrial regions or cities – are not neglected in the establishment of eligibility criteria and in the distribution of scarce resources. An apparent threat to the continuation of Objective 2 status (the 'Objectives' are discussed in the following Chapter, p. 134) under the structural funds led to the establishment in 1991 of an Objective 2 lobby which campaigned with the active endorsement of DG 16 for the continuation of Objective 2 status beyond 1993. Under the leadership of Strathclyde, a very active region on the European scene, the lobby engaged in an intense round of meetings with the relevant Commissioners, the Presidents of the Council, the member-state governments and the European Parliament. While the continuation of Objective 2 status cannot be attributed entirely to the activities of the lobby, their action in 1991–93 contributed to a heightened awareness of the continuing problems of Europe's declining industrial regions (McAleavey and Mitchell, 1994).

Conclusions

The central conclusion of this chapter is that the ability of the Union to agree to a multi-annual financial perspective dramatically altered the making of EU budgets. The Delors I package heralded the advent of relative budgetary peace after a decade of infighting about contributions and the role of the respective arms of the budgetary authority. Multi-annual budgetary packages are embedded in the Union's *acquis*. The adoption of a medium-term budgetary framework lent predictability to the annual budgetary cycle, and relations between the Parliament and the Council have improved beyond recognition in the budgetary domain. Gone are the night-long wrangles and threats of rejection; these have been replaced by deals brokered in conciliation committees, *ad hoc* trialogues and between the officials of the institutions. Budgetary matters have been largely, although not entirely, normalised. The Parliament still has its sights on compulsory expenditure and on establishing its remit in Pillars 2 and 3 via its budgetary power (the three Pillars of the European Union are discussed later in this volume: pp. 133–5, 142–4, etc.).

5
Building a Union: Internal EU Expenditure

The Union's financial instruments evolved from agreement among the member states about shared policy goals, with the Commission and the European Parliament playing the role of 'policy advocate' in relation to new facets of collective action. All the policies covered in this chapter exist in a complex relationship with other policies and with the balance of economic and political integration as a whole. There is a strong policy rationale behind each and every financial instrument and programme undertaken by the Union. Inevitably, however, there are tensions and ambiguities within and between policy domains about the reach of the Union's policy competence and the policy instruments that should be used.

All Union policies have their supporters and detractors – the 'party politics' differs from one policy to the next; for example, the interest structure in agriculture is different to cohesion policy which in turn differs from R&D and environmental policy. Social groups within and across the member states disagree about the level of resources that should be invested in different sectors. The introduction of the principle of subsidiarity in the Treaty on European Union (TEU) sharpens the debate about the division of responsibility between the EU and the national levels of governance. That said, this chapter shows that the Union's budgetary instruments grew significantly in the 1980s, albeit it in an incremental and pragmatic manner. With the notable exception of the CAP, policy competence is held concurrently by the member states and the Union. The purpose of EU funding programmes is to complement national policy and to generate 'added value' from transnational policies. Some of the policies analysed in this chapter are almost entirely driven by budgetary resources, whereas for many others, a budget line merely complements the Union's regulatory power, its principle instrument of public management. The purpose of this chapter is to analyse the medley of policy instruments designed to build the Union as an economic and political entity.

Pressure for new items of expenditure creates considerable strain between the legacy of past budgetary commitments, notably the CAP, and new policy objectives that compete for scarce financial resources. In the Council, Commission and Parliament, the various Directorates General (DGs), working parties and parliamentary committees vie for resources for their client groups and pet projects. Within each policy sector there is tension between the benefits of collective action and the desire to preserve national autonomy and policy choice. One of the main consequences of the expansion of financial instruments in the 1980s is that a vast web of institutions, groups and individuals are drawn into evolving EU-based policy communities which widens considerably those involved in the politics of 'grantsmanship'. EU finances are no longer simply a matter for budget ministers and central governments. Interest organisations, consultants, private firms, universities, local authorities, social groups, and even individual students in search of Erasmus grants, make it their business to be informed about EU financial instruments. Intimate knowledge of the Union budget is a highly marketable product in present-day Europe.

Policy integration

It is possible to identify some 90 different spending programmes that contribute to building the Union as an economic and political space. Recent analyses of public assignment in the Union conclude that there is an economic rationale on *efficiency* grounds for EU expenditure in four policy fields – environmental protection, European-wide infrastructure, research and development and, to a lesser extent, higher education because these spheres give rise to externalities and spillovers across jurisdictions (Reichenbach, 1994, p. 200; Costello, 1995). Ironically, agriculture, one of the main allocative policies in the Union, might be best managed at national level because of considerable differences in farm structure, income and policy goals across the Community. This underlines the fact that the level of policy integration is the outcome of political bargains cast at different stages of the integration process.

The assignment of responsibility for *redistribution* in a major issue in any polity because it goes to the heart of the political process. There is an acceptance that the Union must have a redistributive role, but the scope and scale of its endeavour here is heavily contested. Redistribution within states is of two kinds: it takes place at an interpersonal level, by means of national taxation and welfare system, and between regions. The transfer of responsibility for interpersonal equity to the EU level is unlikely from a political perspective and may be unnecessary from an economic perspective. The Union is, however, committed to strengthening its economic and social cohesion by transferring resources from the richer to the poorer regions in the Union.

Two themes emerge strongly in this chapter. First, the CAP and structural spending represent the predominant share (75 per cent) of EU financial expenditure (see Table 5.1 for an overview of the 1995 budget). The CAP, despite the reforms outlined below, continues to absorb over half the budget. Since Delors I, structural spending represents an ever-growing proportion of EU expenditure. Second, other policies, designed to complement market integration – R&D and TransEuropean Networks (TENs)

TABLE 5.1
The 1995 budget by category of expenditure, ECU million

Subsection	Amount	%
B1: EAGGF-guarantee	38 425.5	47.5
B2: Structural operations	26 638.1	32.9
B3: Training, youth, culture	730.8	0.9
B4: Energy, Euratom, environment	217.8	0.3
B5: Consumer, TENs, internal market	829.3	1.0
B6: R&D	2 968.7	3.7
B7: Developing countries	5 094.4	6.3
B8: Pillar 2	110.0	0.0
B0: Repayments, guarantees, reserves, administrative expenditure	1 870.0	2.3

Source: European Commission (1995a) *General Budget of the EU for the Financial Year 1995*, Sec(95), January 1995.

– and to build a People's Europe, have managed to establish a foothold in the Union's financial perspective, thereby leading to an expansion in the range of financial instruments managed by the Commission. The newer financial instruments that developed in the 1980s – R&D, environmental policy, cultural policy and media policy – highlight the Commission's role as a policy entrepreneur and policy advocate. In these sectors the Commission's strategy is to use the Union's financial resources, however restricted, to promote joint problem-solving strategies, innovative approaches to policy problems, and the diffusion of ideas across borders. Transnational networks of experts or policy specialists are a key feature of the Union's approach in the newer policy domains.

This chapter examines in turn the taming of the CAP, the enhancement of cohesion policy, the emergence of policies designed to promote Europe's competitiveness, the growth of financial instruments in the social field and the problem of financing co-operation on justice and home affairs which was included in the TEU as the third Pillar.

The taming of the CAP?

Europe's farmers, more than any other social group, understand the meaning and relevance of the European Union to them. The renowned distance between Brussels and Europe's citizens simply does not apply to the farming community. Specialist farm journals, radio and television programmes on farming are avidly listened to for the latest 'farm news', which in large measure means 'Brussels news'. The technical and tedious nature of much of the debate does not deter interest. Europe's farming communities in remote Donegal, the wheat-producing plains of France, olive-producing areas of the Algarve, wine-producing regions in the Mediterranean, or the dairy producing heartlands of Holland and Denmark are wedded to the multi-layered and complex Common Agriculture Policy. Farmers' economic prospects – the amount of money flowing into their households – depends in large measure on decisions taken in the annual price review of the CAP or the Commission's implementing committees. Agriculture is one of the few facets of public policy where responsibility has been transferred from national governments to the Community system.

The CAP has aroused more passion than any other subject of EU policy; support from its beneficiaries and odium from its detractors. Despite its complexity, the story of the CAP is relatively simple. The inclusion of agriculture in the Rome Treaty was the essential political bargain required to get French agreement to a Common Market. Moreover, the six original member states have a sizeable proportion of their labour forces living on the land in receipt of national support because of the vagaries of farm incomes and the political weight of the farming vote. The CAP was a policy designed to protect and support farm incomes by guaranteeing the level of prices they got for their produce. The price support mechanisms included buying surplus stocks into intervention, subsidising sales on the world market and imposing levies on the import of cheaper goods from outside the Community. CAP prices have traditionally been higher than the equivalent prices in the world market (see Box 5.1).

The first enlargement of the Community disturbed the cosy consensus on agriculture by changing the political balance on agricultural matters; the CAP was targeted by the UK from the

---

BOX 5.1
The European Guidance and Guarantee Fund (EAGGF)
The main financial instrument of the CAP

Guarantee Expenditure

The guarantee expenditure budget is drawn up each year for both plant and animal products based on the regulations in force in each agricultural market and on the basis of forecasts of market developments. The main policy instruments include export refunds, the cost of storage of surplus stocks, direct aids for producers, and set-aside. In 1995 the guarantee budget amounted to ECU 23 506.5 billion (62%) for plant products and ECU 11 069.0 billion (29.2%) for animal products.

The agricultural guideline for the Guarantee Fund was fixed at ECU 27.5 billion in 1988, with the annual increase thereafter limited to 74 per cent of the rate of increase of EU GDP (real rate, i.e. full account of inflation). Currency turmoil in 1992 and the effects of the MacSharry reform required an additional ECU 1 billion as a reserve for 1993/94, and half that amount for 1995 and 1996. The financial perspective was again threatened in 1995 because of the cost of the agri-monetary system which led to a significant reform in June 1995.

outset as a wasteful policy that was not in its interests, given the small size of the population living on the land. Ireland and Denmark on the other hand, as large exporters of agricultural produce, were enthusiastic members of the 'CAP supporters club'. Mediterranean enlargement in the 1980s added to the diversity of agricultural interests in the Community by tilting the balance from northern products to Mediterranean products. Traditionally the CAP favoured northern products such as cereals, milk, beef and veal. The 'olive oil line' introduced an important north/south divergence in the CAP. The growing number of Mediterranean members had a clear interest in redressing this imbalance by increasing support for fruit and vegetables, wine, tobacco and olive oil, which further added to the costs of the policy and the diversity of interests found in this 'policy community'. See Table 5.2 for an outline of the 1995 Agricultural budget.

TABLE 5.2
EAGGF guarantee budget, 1995, ECU million

	Amount	%
Plant products	23 506.5	62.0
Arable crops	14 779.0	39.0
Sugar	1 947.0	5.1
Olive oil	892.5	2.4
Dried fodder/vegetables	292.0	0.8
Fibre plants and silk worms	808.4	2.1
Fruit and vegetables	1 832.6	4.6
Vine-growing sector	1 515.0	4.0
Tobacco	1 119.0	3.0
Other	321.0	0.8
Animal products	11 069.0	29.2
Milk and milk products	4 050.0	10.7
Beef and veal	5 255.0	13.9
Sheepmeat and goatmeat	1 264.0	3.3
Pigmeat	159.0	0.4
Other	332.0	0.9
Ancillary expenditure	983.5	2.6
Income aid	44.5	0.1
Accompanying measures	1 372.0	3.6
Enlargement-related expenditure	950.0	2.5
Total	37 925.5	100.0

Source: European Commission (1995a) *General Budget of the European Union, 1995*, Sec(95), 10 January 1995.

As the 1970s progressed, problems with the CAP became increasingly visible, a factor that was exacerbated by the politicisation of the UK budgetary problem. The CAP system of *price support* for agricultural produce was expensive, insulated farmers from market forces, distorted world agricultural markets, led to higher food prices for Europe's consumers and had severe consequences for the Union's finances. Farmers inevitably responded to high EC prices by producing more and more of the relevant products. Newspaper reports of butter and beef mountains and wine and olive-oil lakes served to undermine the credibility of the Community both in Europe and internationally.

The CAP, as the Union's most comprehensive policy, has an immense influence on the Union's finances. In many ways the story of EU finances since the mid-1970s is the story of attempts to bring the juggernaut of incremental increases in agricultural expenditure under control, to tame runaway CAP spending. Agricultural price support, which absorbed 12.9 per cent of the budget in 1966 was devouring 68.4 per cent in 1985 (European Commission 1994, pp. 31–2). If structural expenditure on agriculture is added to these amounts, the proportion of the budget spent on agriculture rose to a staggering 80 per cent in 1985. Between 1974 and 1983, guarantee expenditure on agricultural products grew more than fivefold, from 3 billion ECUs in 1974 to almost 16 billion in 1983, a time when 'own resources' grew by less than two and a half times.

The amount of money spent on agricultural price support in any one year depended on a range of circumstances outside the control of the Commission and the member state governments, such as world prices, weather conditions, and the level of production. Thus the level of spending could neither be fixed nor forecast with any degree of certainty. The nature and predominance of CAP spending had wide-ranging consequences for the budget and policy integration more generally:

- It squeezed out other policies and made it difficult for the Community to extend its policy reach into new domains;
- The *open-ended* nature of the commitment to *price support* meant that figures entered in the budget for CAP expendi-

TABLE 5.3
Problems of budgetary management in the CAP, ECU million

EAGGF-guarantee	1983	1984	1985	1986
Preliminary draft	14 050	16 500	19 955	21 102
Actual expenditure	15 786	18 331	19 728	22 119
Over-run	+1 736	+1 831	−227	+1 017

Source: European Commission (1989) *Community Public Finance*, 31 May 1989,
p. 22.

ture were nominal and subject to frequent and dramatic
change, to the detriment of budgetary planning and budgetary discipline (see Table 5.3);

- CAP spending outstripped the growth of budgetary
  resources;
- the CAP conferred greater benefits on some states than
  others and on some sections of the farming community more
  than others, thereby raising issues of equity and burden-
  sharing; some 80 per cent of support went on 20 per cent of
  Europe's farmers (European Commission, 1991a, p. 2);
- The multiplicity of CAP rules and the intricacies of the
  management systems created a haven for large and small-
  scale fraud; extensive elements of the CAP simply cannot be
  adequately audited;
- The incentive to produce created a highly-intensive form of
  agriculture involving the wide-scale use of chemicals, the
  environmental consequences of which are only now being
  dealt with;
- The export of subsidised Community agricultural produce
  led to increasingly strained relations with Europe's trading
  partners, particularly the United States.

Although pressures on the CAP mounted during the 1980s,
reform of the CAP proved protracted and is not yet complete.

Global plans for comprehensive reform were diluted in
tortuous negotiations to emerge as piecemeal *ad hoc* measures.
Attempts at reform met fierce resistance from Agricultural
Ministers, who were under enormous pressure to protect farm

incomes. The farming lobby throughout Europe is famed for its capacity to pressurise Ministers of Agriculture whom they regard as their spokespersons and guardians of their interest. Agricultural Ministers in turn are comfortable in this role. In a number of member states with coalition governments, the Minister for Agriculture was frequently a member of a party that received a sizeable proportion of the farming vote. Officials in national Agricultural Ministries developed a strong clientele relationship with their farming community. Moreover, the transnational farming lobby in Brussels (COPA) is one of the oldest and most developed of the Brussels 'insider groups'. For historical reasons, the farming community benefited from policies that shifted the costs (some ECU 50 billion by OECD estimates) onto diffuse consumer and taxpayer interests.

Agricultural policy was largely crafted in a highly-insulated policy community which included the Commission's DG 6 (Agriculture), the Council's Agricultural Committee and Council of Ministers and a myriad management committees with responsibility for the various segments of agriculture. The people who paid for the CAP, Europe's consumers and taxpayers, had no countervailing power in this policy process and were represented only at the margins. The correspondence principle discussed in Chapter 2 is violated in decision-making on the CAP. The very complexity of the CAP made it the preserve of the 'insiders', those with technical and specialist knowledge. DG 6 in the Commission, one of the largest in terms of staff and dominated by French officials, for long regarded the CAP as its exclusive domain. It successfully undermined attempts by DG 19 (Budgets) to control the CAP budget. In the Council, an intensive annual cycle of meetings between Agricultural Ministers an their officials (on average 12–14 each year) fostered a club atmosphere. Agriculture Ministers refer to the informal atmosphere with ministers taking off their jackets 'to get down to work', in contrast to the Foreign Affairs Ministers who adopt a more diplomatic and formal approach. It was in the agricultural domain that the Union's style of package-deal bargaining was perfected, involving complex balancing of interests, costs and side-payments. Long marathon sessions, lubricated by whisky after midnight during the annual price review, added to the sense of community among Ministers for Agriculture. This did not detract from very tough bargaining between them as they fought for the interests of their particular producers.

Gradually the CAP's defences were breached and a process of reform set in train. The spiralling costs of the policy, international pressures, and the need to rebalance the relationship between production and demand all generated pressure for change. Successive UK governments were determined to curb agricultural spending and were able to exert sufficient pressure because of the budget's resource problems from the early 1980s onwards. The UK Minister of Agriculture disturbed the club atmosphere in the Agriculture Council by arguing that each set of Commission proposals did not go far enough in terms of reform. The wasteful nature of the policy and pressures for new Community policies lent weight to the UK position. Germany, as the largest contributor to the budget, joined the austerity camp. Germany's position was, however, equivocal because the Bavarian-based CSU party held the agricultural portfolio in any CDU-led coalition. Its commitment to income support for small Bavarian farmers led German Ministers to support policies in the Agricultural Council that were at variance with the official Bonn line on the EU budget. France, the promoter of the CAP from the outset, was the policy's main-defender supported by the smaller agricultural-exporting states. The opening of the Uruguay trade round in 1986 provided the US with the platform it needed to denounce the CAP; either the EU made concessions on agriculture or the GATT round would fail. This proved the most powerful catalyst for change, to date.

Reforming the CAP began with attempts to curb milk production from 1983 onwards with the introduction of levies on overproduction. A 1984 agreement among Finance Ministers that EAGGF guarantee expenditure should not increase faster than own resources was regarded by the Agricultural Ministers as a political commitment with no binding effect on them during the annual price review. It was not until the 1988 budgetary agreement that the first *legal* measures to curb CAP spending were taken. Delors I strengthened budgetary discipline by stipulating that:

1. The annual rate of growth of EAGGF guarantee expenditure should not exceed 74 per cent of the annual rate of

growth of Community GNP. The 1988 expenditure figure of EUC 27 500 million was taken as the base figure.

2. Mechanisms were put in place to reduce existing agricultural stocks by establishing limits on the amount of money available for intervention support.
3. Measures for containing overproduction were put in place for cereals as well as dairy.
4. An early-warning system was put in place to warn the Commission of impending problems. (European Commission, 1989, p. 27)

For the first time, agricultural expenditure would have to live within predetermined limits; the automatic nature of CAP expenditure was finally being controlled and agriculture's insulation from other political concerns in the Community was broken. The pattern of limiting budgetary resources for CAP expenditure continued in Delors II which set financial ceilings until 1999.

In 1990, Jacques Delors and his Agricultural Commissioner, Ray MacSharry, in the second Delos Commission (1989–92), grasped the nettle of CAP reform essentially because DG 6 itself became convinced that reform of the cereals and beef regimes was necessary or the system could face collapse. The so-called MacSharry proposals agreed by the Council in 1992, and the EU's commitment to its GATT partners as part of the Uruguay Round, provide the framework for the medium-term evolution of the CAP. The main elements of the MacSharry proposals, which were implemented in the 1992/93 production year, were:

- A partial shift from price support to direct income support;
- Price reductions for some commodities, notably cereals; and
- Income support dependent on quotas and set-aside policies to curb production.

The most important shift in the MacSharry reforms was the creation of new policy instruments to support farm incomes other than the traditional reliance on price support. In other words, for the first time production and farm incomes were decoupled.

Paradoxically, the reforms would cost more, not less, money but the transfers would become more visible and would go directly to farmers rather than to middle-men. Financing the reforms eats up a growing proportion of agricultural expenditure; in 1996, 16 billion of a total of 41 billion for the EAGGF represents the costs of the reforms.

The MacSharry measures were designed to enable the Community to deal with intense pressure from the USA during the GATT round. Despite violent opposition from France and to a lesser extent from Ireland, the Community agreed to lessen its aggregate level of support for the CAP and to reduce the volume of exports that it subsidies up to the year 2001. The Uruguay Round commitments involve predetermined ceilings on a schedule from 1995 to 2001. One assessment of the impact of GATT concludes that:

> Even though it does not mandate many price or policy changes in the immediate future, it effectively constrains future decisions. Specifically, it makes it difficult, if not impossible, to revert to the policy price levels that obtained before CAP reform. It makes it difficult to increase the level of compensation to farmers under CAP reform, or to relax setasides, without incurring the risk of challenge under the GATT. In effect it locks in the policy changes of the past few years, and makes any deviation from that path both politically and economically costly. (Tangermann *et al.*, 1994, p. 49)

The Commission sees little problem in meeting the GATT commitment although this is questioned by independent experts. Most commentators argue that the Union will have to engage in deeper reform of the dairy and beef market regimes and fundamental reform of sugar, wine, fruit and vegetable regimes (Grant, 1995, p. 10). The longer-term questions are whether or not the CAP can survive in however modified a form into the next century or will it be renationalised? The debate about the consequences of a continental enlargement for the Union's longest-standing common policy is just beginning.

The MacSharry reforms and the agreed figures in the financial perspective have not prevented the emergence of budgetary management problems. The issue in 1995 stemmed less from developments within agriculture itself than from the consequences of turmoil in the currency markets which had severe consequences for the agri-money system. In the absence of a single currency, the Union developed an increasingly complex and inefficient system of 'green money' for converting farm prices/subsidies into national currencies. The system is designed to protect the incomes of farmers in countries with revaluating currencies who would experience income-loss if adjustments were not made to the relationship between their currency and the 'green money' system.

Although a reformed agri-money system came into operation in January 1995, its viability was quickly threatened by currency fluctuations. The budgetary costs of adjusting the new agri-money system to take account of currency changes threatened the financial perspective. The Commission became increasingly concerned that it would overshoot the CAP budget in 1995 anyway without the added costs of revaluations. It estimated that a 3 per cent revaluation of five currencies would cost ECU 1 billion a year. Consequently the Commission tabled proposals for further reform of the system which met with fierce resistance from Germany in particular, ever ready to protect the interests of the Bavarian farmer. Protracted debate in the Council resulted in agreement (June 1995) to a new green currency system which may have wider implications for the future evolution of the CAP (see Box 5.2).

Solidarity and cohesion: a slow burn

The role of the budget in redistribution and the extent of such a role is one of the most vexed questions on the Union's agenda. The predominantly *laissez-faire* ethos of the Rome Treaty precluded a strong role for the Community at the outset. However, the accession of the UK and Ireland in 1973 followed by the Mediterranean enlargements of the 1980s altered the political and economic framework within which the issue of economic divergence and peripherality would be debated. The existence of high levels of economic divergence among the member states and regions cannot be disputed. Four member states – Spain, Greece, Portugal and Ireland – have a per capita GDP significantly below the EU average. The extent of regional disparities is still greater.

BOX 5.2
The dual green currency system

Main elements of the system agreed in June 1995

1. The common exchange rate mechanism for farm payments is replaced with a *two-tier* system which involves fixed exchange rates for strong currency countries and ECU linked rates for weaker currency countries. Rates for reform aid payments were frozen until January 1999 in strong currency countries. Direct aids have now been decoupled from revaluations since they are fixed in national currencies for the next three and a half years.
2. Mini-switchover system is scrapped. This system led automatically to raised support payments across the EU to compensate for exchange rate losses in just one member country.
3. Member states are allowed pay farmers flat rate aid to compensate for losses suffered over monetary movements between January 1994 and December 1995.

Denmark, Sweden and the UK voted against the proposals in the Agricultural Council but they were carried by a qualified majority in June 1995.

The Fifth Periodic Report on the Regions shows that the ten most prosperous regions out of a total of 180 had a GDP per head 3.5 times greater than the ten poorest regions, mostly found in Greece and Portugal (European Commission, 1995e). Income disparities in the Union are calculated to be almost double those found in the US, although there is evidence of some convergence since 1960.

During the 1960s the Commission began the slow process of developing a role for the Union in matters of regional policy and a stronger role in social policy. The Commission, in adopting the role of 'policy advocate' in this field, argued that the Union had to take the social and spatial consequences of market integration seriously. The literature on regional economics endorsed the view that the benefits of market integration would be felt unevenly. The Commission drew support for its views from analyses of fiscal federalism, particularly the 1977 MacDougall report on the role of public finance in integration. The establishment of the European Regional Development Fund (ERDF) in 1975, with puny financial resources, after protracted and difficult negotiations among Germany, France and the UK, gave the Commission the platform it needed to enhance the redistributive character of the Union's policy-reach in a number of ways.

First, it created a Directorate General for Regional Policy in the Commission, which would act as a powerful advocate of additional resources thereafter. Second, the European Social Fund began to take on a marked regional character with its funds increasingly going to the poorer regions. Third, the Commission began to use the terms 'structural funds' and 'structural policy' to refer to all Community financial instruments other than the price mechanism of the CAP. The Commission concentrated its energies on getting more resources for the structural funds and in enhancing its say over the disbursement of monies. It was very dependent on the member states because of the small amounts of transfers involved and the fact that it was essentially part-financing national measures. The period up to 1987 was characterised by incremental changes in the structural funds designed to strengthen the Commission's role in the policy process and to enhance the flow of resources to the poorer parts of Western Europe.

Disagreement about the appropriate role for Union in alleviating the consequences of regional disparities and economic divergence has never been fully resolved. Structural spending is justified by a number of different economic and political arguments:

1. There is a general, although not universal, acceptance that the Union should provide assistance to member states and regions to adjust to market integration.
2. There is agreement that the purpose of EU transfers is to enable the weaker regions to 'catch up' with the more prosperous ones.
3. Financial resources provide the Union with the capacity to make side-payments in bargaining on non-budgetary issues and hence lubricate the process of integration.
4. Budgetary transfers are part of political and not just economic cohesion in the Union and serve to distinguish the Union from traditional interstate relations.

There is no agreement among the member states that the Union should engage in permanent financial transfers akin to those found in federal systems. The communiqué from the Brussels European Council in 1978 emphasised that strengthening the economic potential of the less-prosperous countries was 'primarily the responsibility of the Member States concerned' (European Council, December 1978, point 2, p. 7). One year later, the European Council gave the Commission responsibility for examining 'in depth how the Community could make a greater contribution by means of all of its policies taken as a whole to achieving greater convergence of the economies of the Member States and to reduce disparities between them' (European Council, March 1979, point 4, p. 8).

The major breakthrough on structural policy came in 1985/86 with the Single European Act and its commitment to an acceleration of market integration by 1992. Economic analyses suggested that intensified market competition would further widen the gap in productive capacity and living standards between Europe's poor regions and the core. Hence, the SEA contained a new chapter on 'economic and social cohesion' which provided a treaty base to the Commission. Some of the SEA signatories, notably the UK, saw the cohesion chapter as largely symbolic and without further budgetary consequences. However, the balance of interest on the cohesion issue was shifting. The bargaining power of the cohesion countries was undoubtedly strengthened by the accession of the Iberian states, especially Spain. The SEA cohesion chapter should not be regarded as a mere sidepayment to Europe's poor regions for the 1992 project. Its inclusion also stemmed from a recognition among the richer continental member states that if the workings of market integration served to exacerbate economic disparity, countervailing measures were needed. The SEA embedded the values of cohesion and solidarity in the Union's system in a manner that will be difficult, although not impossible, to dislodge in the future. Tough battles continue on the scale of transfers, the geographic areas that should be eligible for funding and the efficiency of existing instruments.

Embedding the principle of cohesion

The policy changes in this field that accompanied the Delors I package represented a sizeable increase in the scale of

Community intervention and in the management of the funds. The Brussels package led to a doubling of financial transfers by 1993, a doubling of the flows to the cohesion regions (Objective 1) by 1992 and a major legislative reform of the structural funds. The financial commitment amounted to 60 billion ECU between 1989 and 1993. The new procedures governing the administration and implementation of the Funds were agreed by the Council in 1988. The Commission went into the reform negotiations with the aim of getting greater discretion over the use of the Funds and improving their operation. The new Fund regulations established the framework for the operation of the structural funds. The establishment of the following *five* priorities for action, in a clear attempt to concentrate resources on the neediest regions, was central to the reform:

- *Objective 1:* development of regions that are lagging in levels of economic development;
- *Objective 2:* converting areas of industrial decline;
- *Objective 3:* long-term unemployment;
- *Objective 4:* youth unemployment;
- *Objective 5:* speeding up the adjustment of agricultural structures;
- *Objective 5b:* rural development (European Communities, 1988).

Three of the objectives (1, 2 and 5b) are regional in nature whereas Objectives 3, 4 and 5a cover the entire Union. Objective 1 areas (per capita incomes of less than 75 per cent of the Community average) were to receive a doubling of their financial allocation by 1992. Areas designated as Objective 1 included Ireland, Greece, Portugal, a larger part of Spain, the Italian Mezzogiorno, the French overseas territories and Corsica. See Table 5.4 for a breakdown of structural fund spending on different objectives and Figure 5.1 for a breakdown by policy instrument.

The 1988 reform made important changes in the grant-awarding procedures, which altered relations between the national capitals and Brussels and disturbed central–local relations in many member states. The practice of awarding grants on the basis of

TABLE 5.4

**Distribution of monies for structural operations by objective, 1995
ECU millions – appropriation for commitment**

Structural funds	Amount	%
Objective 1	14 155	68
Objective 2	2 348	11
Objective 3	1 868	9
Objective 4	330	1
Objective 5a	1 036	5
Objective 5b	1 054	5

Source: European Commission (1995a) *General Budget of the EU*, Sec(95), 10 January 1995, p. 16.

FIGURE 5.1

Breakdown of structural monies by fund, 1995

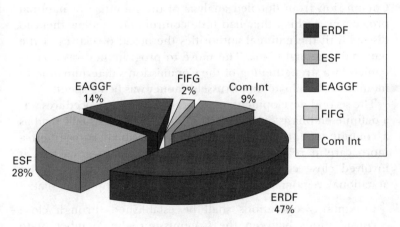

Note:

EAGGF	European Agricultural Guarantee and Guidance Fund
ESF	European Social Fund
ERDF	European Regional Development Fund
ComInt	Community Initiatives
FIFG	Financial Instrument for Fisheries Guidance

Source: European Commission (1995a) *General Budget of the EU*, Sec(95), 10 January 1995, p. 16.

individual projects was replaced by a system involving the submission of global programmes. This reflected similar developments in the US where the federal government, unable to control
categorical grants, moved to a system of block grants in the 1970s.
The Commission had been edging towards a programme approach during the 1980s with the Integrated Mediterranean
Programmes and the Integrated Programme for Belfast. The new
process included three steps. The member states or regions,
where appropriate, would submit a development plan to the
Commission which would in turn draft a Community Support
Framework setting out the level and nature of support over the
lifespan of the plan. This gave the Commission bargaining power
in the system for the first time, since it did not have simply to
rubber stamp the plans drawn up by the national governments
and regions. The Commission gained an important toehold in the
member states. The national authorities would then submit
operational programmes to draw down the grants from the
CSF. The programme approach was designed to release the
Commission from detailed analysis of the minutiae of national
projects over which they had little control and to allow them to
discuss with the national authorities the broad objectives of the
national/regional plans. The move to programmes was accompanied by a strengthening of the Commission's determination to
monitor and evaluate how Brussels' money was being spent.

The second development in the grant-awarding procedures was
a definite emphasis on 'partnership'. While this is usually read as
a commitment to partnership with sub-national authorities, a
more careful reading of the relevant article suggests that it
involved close collaboration between the relevant authorities
at national, regional and local levels. The article stipulated that:

> Community operations shall be established through close
> consultations between the Commission, the Member State
> concerned and the competent authorities designated by the
> latter at national, regional, local or other level. (European
> Communities, 1988)

Thus it was up to the member states to decide on the competent
sub-national authorities, and the Commission was acutely aware
of the continuing importance of its relations with the national
central governments. The Commission was and remains, however,

committed to regional mobilisation in the member states and to strengthening its links with public authorities below the level of central government. This strategy increases its reach into the national polities and may well increase its leverage in dealing with central governments. Regional mobilisation involving trans-national groups and public authorities within the member states has accelerated greatly in the Union since the mid-1980s as a con-sequence of the 1992 process and the reform of the Funds.

The 1988 legislation specified that structural fund spending in the member states should be *additional* to and not merely a re-placement for national expenditure on structural measures. The so-called principle of *additionality* had been a vexed one in rela-tions between the Commission and the member states in the 1980s. The lack of transparency in national budgets made it difficult to trace some forms of Community expenditure at national level. Moreover, the small size of the structural fund transfers in the 1980s lent an esoteric air to the ongoing debate on additionality. However, the significant increase in the size of the financial transfers in Delors I led the Commission to give renewed attention to additionality. In 1992, the Commission with-held over ECU 160 million in regional funding to regenerate British coal mining regions because of problems of additionality. This was followed by a protracted dispute between the Regional Commissioner, Bruce Millan, and the British government about the co-financing of local authorities that were in receipt of EU monies. The Commission was concerned that because of the lack of transparency in British procedures, monies destined for declin-ing industrial regions was leaking out to other local authorities in ineligible regions.

Structural spending is channelled through the three-phase process outlined above. In addition, the regulations made provi-sion for what are known as Community initiatives amounting to about 10 per cent of the total budget where the Commission could set aside special funds for measures of direct interest to the Community. Between 1990 and 1993 14 Community Initiative programmes were drawn up by the Commission, covering such diverse matters as environmental protection, cross-border devel-opment, energy networks, rural development, equal opportunities for women, and special training programmes. These programmes draw a large number of Commission DGs into the ambit of the structural funds. Community Initiatives are characterised by their support for cross-border or transnational co-operation, innovative approaches to policy problems, and a 'bottom-up' method of implementation (see Box 5.3).

Delors II: consolidation

The TEU and the Delors II package provided an opportunity for a reassessment of the funds and alterations to the basic framework regulations. The process was characterised by consolidation rather than policy or procedural innovation. The main principles of the 1988 reform were maintained, although adjustments were made in the light of the experience gained from the first reform. Commission DGs, national ministries, regional authorities, independent experts, the social partners and wider social groups participated in an intensive review of the operation of the Funds. The Commission's assessment was that fine tuning rather than radical change was necessary in the operation of the Funds. The

---

BOX 5.3
Community initiatives for structural spending
(9% of commitment appropriations – ECU 13.35 bn between
1994–99 at 1994 prices)

Community initiatives

INTERREG 2:	Cross-border and interregional co-operation
Leader 2:	Rural development
Regis 2:	Outermost regions
NOW, HORIZON, YOUTHSTART:	Employment and the development of human resources
ADAPT, RECHAR, RESIDER, RETEX, KONVER, SME's:	Management of industrial change
URBAN:	Crisis hit urban areas
PESCA:	Restructuring the fishing industry

Source: European Commission (1995b) *Preliminary Draft Budget of the European Communities 1996*, vol. 4, Com(95) 300.

BOX 5.4
Regions covered by Objective 1 status

Belgium:	Hainaut
Germany:	New Länder
Greece:	Entire country
Spain:	Andalucia, Asturias, Cantabria, Castilla, Ceuta y Melilla, Comunidad Valenciana, Extremadura, Galicia, Canary Islands, Murcia
France:	Overseas Departments, Corsica, Auvergne, Douai, Valenciennes
Ireland:	Entire country
Italy:	Abruzzi, Basilicata, Calabria, Campania, Molise, Apulia, Sardinia, Sicily
Netherlands:	Flevoland
Portugal:	Entire country
UK:	Highlands and Islands, Merseyside, Northern Ireland

Source: European Communities (1993a), Council Regulation (EEC) No. 2081/93, *Official Journal*, L 193/5, 31 July 1993.

1993 regulations significantly expand the number of geographic areas designated as Objective 1 (see Box 5.4), and the proportion of the Community's population living in Objective 1 areas grew from 21.7 per cent to 26.6 per cent under the new system. Only two members, Denmark and Luxembourg, have no priority regions. This development suggests that the principle of concentration established by the 1988 reform was seriously diluted and that structural fund monies are flowing to the wealthy as well as to the poorer parts of Europe.

A major attempt was made in the new regulations to increase the level of transparency in dividing up the structural fund pie and to reduce the level of political influence in the process. This implied that criteria such as national and regional prosperity, population in the regions and levels of unemployment would determine the flow of money to the various member states and regions. Other changes of significance were:

- Expansion in the scope of the Funds related to social policy, fisheries, and rural development;

- 'Partnership' to include economic and social interests in the member states;
- Simplification of the decision-making procedures from three stages to two;
- Environmental concerns given greater weight;
- Clarification of the principle of additionality. (European Commission, 1993d)

The programming period for the new system runs from 1994 to 1999, although three-year phases have been decided on for Objective 2 measures. The main focus of the 1993 reform was to strengthen partnership, clarify the position on additionality and improve transparency while simplifying the grant-awarding procedures. (European Commission, 1995d) Because of the significant increase in the volume of transfers, the net contributors to the budget are asking if the cohesion effort represents value for money. An Eastern enlargement will test just how embedded the principles of solidarity and cohesion are in the Union's *acquis*.

The cohesion fund

The TEU established a new financial instrument of a redistributive nature, the Cohesion Financial Instrument, commonly known as the Cohesion Fund. Article 130d of the TEU made provision for the establishment of a fund to provide a financial contribution to projects in the fields of environment and trans-European networks in transport infrastructure. The Edinburgh European Council agreed that over seven years a total of ECU 15 billion would be allocated to the Cohesion Fund, starting with ECU 1.5 billion in 1993. The allocation of the pool of money between different member states is as follows: Spain (52–58%), Greece (16–20%), Portugal (16–20%) and Ireland (7–10%). The origin of the Cohesion Fund can be traced to papers on cohesion submitted by the Spanish and Irish to the Intergovernmental Conference. The Spanish paper, in particular, called for the establishment of a new financial instrument to augment the existing structural funds in aspects of human and physical development not covered by the Funds (*Agence Europe*, 8 March 1991). The main plank of the Spanish proposals was the need for an automatic system of fiscal equalisation, especially in light of EMU. The inclusion of a provision for a Cohesion Fund went some way to respond to the Spanish concerns and their sense that their allocation from the existing structural funds left something to be desired. The allocation of over 50 per cent of the Cohesion Fund to Spain demonstrates that this fund was in many ways a response to special Spanish problems, just like the Integrated Mediterranean Programmes (IMPs) were a response to Greece's demands for renegotiation.

The objectives, tasks, scope and organisation of the Cohesion Fund was set out in Article 130d which suggests that the member states wanted to establish a limited and narrow framework for its operation. The geographical coverage of the Fund was limited to member states whose per capita income is less than 90 per cent of the Community average – Spain, Greece, Portugal and Ireland. This was seen as a mechanism to exclude the Italian Mezzogiorno. The rate of assistance from the Fund is very generous – between 80 and 85 per cent of the cost of a project can be financed from the Fund. There are four important differences between the structural funds and the Cohesion Fund:

1. No additionality is required for the Cohesion Fund;
2. An explicit link was made for the first time in a budgetary instrument between the use of funds and convergence programmes aimed at achieving the TEU convergence criteria;
3. No partnership required for Cohesion Fund measures;
4. The Cohesion Fund is based on projects not programmes.

The inclusion of a strong element of conditionality in a budgetary instrument established the link between the Cohesion Fund and the EMU. Although the TEU was not finally ratified until November 1993, the Cohesion Fund began to operate on a temporary basis in July 1993 when the first projects were financed.

The addition of a new policy instrument inevitably leads to management problems within the Commission and overlap between different cohesion instruments. A Court of Auditors Report on the Fund concluded that there were now too many 'windows' in various EU funds for the acceptance and approval of projects of the same kind. In fact, the Court found that some projects financed by the Fund were appraised and approved in several different departments of the Commission (European Court of Auditors, 1995). The member states seek to exploit different grant-awarding procedures to get maximum assistance for their preferred projects. The Court was critical of the Commission's management of some aspects of the Fund, especially in relation to the environmental impact of a number of projects.

Multilevelled policy-making and cross-national mobilisation

The 1988/93 reforms of the structural funds have had a number of important consequences for policy-making in this field. The new grant-awarding procedures greatly strengthened the position of the Commission in the system. It allows Commission officials to negotiate on a one-to-one basis with the relevant national authorities and to mould national and regional proposals in a manner that had eluded it heretofore. It now has the possibility of establishing a partnership relationship with the relevant national officials, particularly in the cohesion states and in areas receiving significant transfers. The presence of Commission officials on the monitoring committees has greatly enhanced their position in the policy process and gives them access to a variety of governmental and non-governmental bodies in the member states. The Commission is no longer a passive participant in the policy network, but a partner in a bargaining process about how EU finances should be spent.

Structural fund transfers, which amounted to a significant percentage of total investment for Greece (11 per cent), Ireland (7 per cent) and Portugal (8 per cent) respectively over the period 1989 to 1993, carry great political salience in the member states that benefit from Objective 1 status. For national governments, the structural funds represent a highly-visible means of 'bringing home the bacon' which can be used in national electoral and party competition. Prime ministers and their governmental colleagues use the planning process to associate themselves with Brussels bounty. The Edinburgh Agreement on the Delors II package was used by the then Irish prime minister, Albert Reynolds, to form a coalition government after he had done badly in a national election. Structural fund transfers were the carrot that brought the opposition Labour Party into coalition.

The increase in the level of funding and the enlarged scope of operation has facilitated mobilisation in the member states. Increasingly, sub-national authorities and social groups have responded to the existence of the Funds and want to participate in their operation and implementation. The Commission's Community Initiatives, such as LEADER and INTERREG, have helped empower local communities in their fight against economic decline and depopulation. The multilevelled policy process and the Commission's commitment to partnership has triggered institutional adaptation in some although not in all member states. As a consequence of the structural funds, the tentacles of the Community stretch down into the regions, cities and localities of the member states. Representatives of urban and rural groups, trade unions and industry representatives, environmentalists, community groups and those representing the poorer sections of society have mobilised especially in those regions that benefit from regional transfers. The disbursement of EU monies causes considerable conflict as different social groups and interests jostle to ensure that their priorities are reflected in the national and regional development plans. Although technocrats and sectoral interests continue to dominate in the planning process, diffuse social groups have impinged on the restricted and narrow policy networks.

During the life of the Delors I package, a campaign to *green* the structural funds developed from local protests by environmental groups fighting against what one activist called 'the invasion of EC-funded bulldozers' (Corrie, 1994, p. 19). As implementation of Community Support Frameworks proceeded, it became clear that there was considerable tension between development objectives, on the one hand, and environmental objectives on the other. The objective of the structural funds at the outset was to make peripheral Europe more like core Europe, regardless of the impact of development on unspoilt natural habitats (see Box 5.5 for an outline of some controversial projects). The construction of fish farms in the middle of important wetlands in the Prespa National Park in Greece began a campaign which was to develop from local protests into a transnational campaign in Brussels.

BOX 5.5
Controversial environmental projects funded by
Structural Fund monies

- *River Acheloos, Greece*: The Greek government applied for ECU 80 million for plans to dam and divert one-third of the flow from the Acheloos river to generate electricity and irrigate the Thesasly plains. The government did not assess the environmental impact in their original proposal and were forced to alter the plans
- *Coto Donana, Spain*: Environmentalists highlighted the possible impact of Spanish proposals for irrigation which would affect the Coto Donana national park. The Spanish Government was forced to alter their plans under pressure from environmental groups.
- *Burren Ireland*: Plans to build an interpretative centre, financed by EU monies, in an area with a unique and delicate habitat. Local, national and transnational environmental bodies were involved in a sustained campaign to alter the governments' plans. Modifications were made but the centre is being built.

Environmentalists complained that large-scale infrastructure projects, many tourist developments, irrigation programmes and afforestation schemes were planned and executed without sufficient attention to their potential damaging impact on the environment.

In 1989 a transnational campaign was launched by The Worldwide Fund for Nature and the Institute for European Environmental Policy (WWF/IEEP) which involved three full-time lobbyists in Brussels, together with national and local groups. The groups concentrated their energies on:

- lobbying politicians at a local, national and European level,
- issuing formal complaints to the Commission,
- getting media attention for the various campaigns,
- participation in planning appeals, site visits and local consultation,
- using the courts if necessary.

The pressure from environmental groups was augmented by pressure from within the Commission itself where the DG acts as the protector of the environment for the Commission. As a consequence of the campaign the reformed regulations in 1993 are far tighter on environmental control than the earlier regulations. The strengthening of environmental conditionality in the management of the funds has been resisted by the southern member states as undue interference in their affairs and a breach of subsidiarity. However, the new regulations mean that the Objective 1 regions will have to take the environmental consequences of their development plans more seriously because the Commission and DG16 can no longer be seen to disregard the environment.

The involvement of the EU level in the territorial politics of the member states disturbed central/regional/local relations in many states. 'Europe' was an added dimension in territorial politics. Highly-centralised states such as Ireland, Greece and Portugal came under considerable pressure to adapt their administrative structures to include a regional dimension. This in turn generated considerable tension in relations between levels of government within states. National governments needed to satisfy the Commission by including a 'regional' dimension in the planning process, but wanted to maintain as much autonomy for national policy as possible. There is evidence that the three small cohesion states adapted their administrative structures in a pragmatic and highly symbolic manner at the outset, but that the process of multi-levelled planning and implementation may in the longer term change policy networks in a more fundamental manner.

Strengthening competitiveness and market integration

Concern about Europe's ability to compete with the other economic giants and the newly-industrialising states was at the heart of the 1992 project. The sense that Europe had failed to adapt adequately to the changes in world capitalism following the collapse of the golden period of economic growth led Europe's governments, the Commission and industrialists to accelerate market integration by launching the drive to complete the internal market by 1992. Although 'regulation' was the main instrument of public policy used in this drive, the need for appropriate flanking policies soon became apparent. The Union developed three policies of an interventionist nature to complement and enhance market integration, a programme on research and

TABLE 5.5
Internal expenditure other than CAP and structural operations, 1995 appropriations for commitments, ECU million

Policy area	Amount	%
R&D	2968.7	65
Transport	24.0	
Fisheries	26.1	
Eduction, training, youth	361.5	8
Culture/audiovisual	137.7	3
Information	57.0	1
Energy	62.0	1
Euratom	18.8	
Environment	137.0	3
Consumer protection	20.8	
Internal market	152.5	4
Industry	117.7	3
Information market	13.0	
TENs	381.0	8
Pillar 3	5.0	
Reserve for internal policies	100.0	2
Total	45 828.0	98

Source: European Commission (1995a) *General Budget of the EU, 1995*, Sec(95), 10, p. 18.

development, aid to small and medium-sized firms, and more recently TransEuropean Networks. See Table 5.5 for an overview of internal spending other than the CAP and Structural Operations in 1995.

Research and development

If cohesion policy stems from a desire to ensure that Europe's peripheral regions responded to market integration, R&D policy reflects an acute fear that Europe suffers from a serious technological gap *vis-à-vis* the USA and Japan. The figures on market share in semiconductors, for example, show that Europe's share of the world market fell from 18 per cent in 1978 to 10 per cent in 1990 (Sandholtz, 1992, p. 8). The technological gap was attributed in large measure to the failure of European national champions to keep up with the pace of change in high technology.

Serious involvement by the Union in R&D dates from the early 1980s when the Belgian Commissioner, Viscount Davignon, gathered together a group of Europe's leading industrialists to analyse the needs of European industry and the role of the EU. In an iterative process the 'Roundtable Twelve' as the companies were known, outside experts, research laboratories and the Commission developed a strategy for a major programme in high technology that was presented to the Council of Ministers in May 1982. Community R&D policy was in effect the proxy for an EU industrial policy (Grahl and Teague, 1990). The major companies were involved in drafting the proposals which included very precise proposals on the sorts of programmes that should be financed. According to Sandholtz,

> the key to winning the approval of the national governments was the alliance struck by the Commission with industry. (Sandholtz, 1992, p. 16)

The proposed programme was called ESPRIT (European Strategic Programme for Research and Development in Information Technologies) which was the catalyst for the development of a large number of related programmes (15 by 1994) in other facets of technology. The Community's R&D programmes cover such diverse matters as information technology, biotechnology, environmental research, marine science, telematics and transport. As the Commission gained in experience, it developed an approach based on a 'Framework Programme' which provided a multi-annual budget for a series of programmes dealing with different sectors or forms of technology. The Community's first programme ran from 1984 to 1987, followed by a second programme from 1987 to 1991, a third programme which overlapped with the second from 1990 to 1994 and a fourth framework programme which is set to run between 1995 and 1998. The Community's R&D programmes have a number of features in common, notably:

- An emphasis on pre-competitive research;
- Shared costs between the Union, industry and the universities;
- Cross-national research teams;
- Access to the research results on a relatively wide basis.

As a consequence of the R&D programmes, a dense network of collaborative research programmes has developed between European industry and university laboratories across the member states. Although the level of EU financing is considerably less than the amount spent by national governments and industry, EU programmes have been instrumental in opening companies' eyes to the potential of the internal market as a launch pad to the world market (Scharp and Pavitt, 1993, p. 136).

There has been a substantial upgrading in the financial resources devoted to the Community's R&D programme since the early 1980s. Budgetary expansion was facilitated by the inclusion in the SEA of a Treaty mandate (Article 130.1) in technological policy which made provision for a multi-annual framework programme that would set out the objectives of policy and the financial means required. In addition to the SEA, the enthusiasm for the programme from European industry was critical. The R&D budget increased from ECU 311 million in 1981 to ECU 2.7 billion in 1995. Decisions on the financial commitments to the framework programmes have proved highly-contentious in the Council of Ministers, largely because the UK wants to limit the reach and scope of EU R&D policy. In 1986 when Commissioner Narjes wanted to treble the budget (to 10 billion ECU) over a five-year period 1987–92, he met fierce opposition from the UK in the Council. The British finally agreed to a figure of 5.3 billion ECUs, which represented an increase on the 3.7 billion in the first programme. The final allocation for the third framework programme (5.7 billion) again fell short of the Commission's initial bid (Laffan, 1992, p. 101). Agreement on financing for the fourth framework programme was equally fraught. In June 1993, the Commission proposed a budget of ECU 13.1 billion which was reduced to ECU 12 billion by the Brussels European Council (December 1993) with a possible 1 billion in reserve depending on the Union's budgetary situation. A figure of ECU 12.3 billion for the five-year programme was adopted by the Research Council; this amount rose to ECU 13.6 billion following the accession in January 1995 of three new member states. See Table 5.6 for the distribution of R&D money by programme and Figure 5.2 by category of expenditure.

There is a continuing tension in EU technology policy between the need to strengthen Europe's technological base to cope with global competition and the fear that the policy will lead to a

TABLE 5.6
R&D fourth framework (1994–95)*
Expenditure by programme, ECU million

Activity	Budget
IT	3.405
Industrial technologies	1.995
Environment	1.080
Life sciences	1.572
Energy	2.256
Transport	240
Socio-economic research	138
International co-operation	540
Dissemination of results	330
Training and mobility of researchers	744
Total	12.300

Note: * The total of ECU 12.3 billion was adjusted upwards to ECU 13.16 following the 1995 enlargement
Source: University College Dublin (1995) Research Bulletin no. 59, p. 11.

FIGURE 5.2

R&D – fourth framework programme, 1994–98
13.16 billion ECU-budget*
Category of expenditure

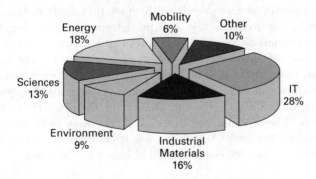

Note:
* Original agreement of 12.3 billion ECU amended to take account of enlargement
Source: *European Voice*, 14 December 1995, p. 29.

further concentration of technological capacity, to the detriment of Europe's lagging regions. An assessment of the framework programme concluded that 'the informal, corporatist development of industrial policy under Etienne Davignon could only work by privileging the very largest companies in the formation of policy, and has resulted in structures which continue to favour the strongest and most powerful economic agents' (Grahl and Teague, 1990, p. 177). Concern that large firms in the core regions have received a disproportionate share of R&D funding (the big-Twelve received 70 per cent of the first tranche of R&D grants) at the expense of the peripheral states and small and medium-sized firms, has led to attempts to rebalance the flow of funding. Programmes such as VALUE and CRAFT are designed to facilitate small firms in gaining access to the results of European research and allowing them to enter partnerships with larger firms. A number of Community Initiatives in the structural funds, notably STRIDE, are designed to promote technology transfer to Objective 1 and 2 regions. That said, the central objective of the Community's R&D programmes is to ensure that European companies are capable of withstanding the pace and intensity of global competition.

The Commissioner for R&D in the Santer Commission, Edith Cresson, a former French prime minister who took over responsibility in January 1995, would like to shift the balance of R&D from pre-competitive research to a quasi industrial policy. The Commissioner is hampered by the fact that R&D monies are locked into a five-year cycle with predetermined priorities and a predetermined division across different programmes. M. Cresson set up six task forces to work on key technologies for the future: the car, train, aircraft of the future, vaccines, combined transport and multimedia software. The next stage is to tap into the reserve funding of ECU 700 million to finance further research on these subjects. The creation of the task forces may well signal an impending shift in R&D policy towards competitive research for industry with finance concentrated in Europe's big firms.

TransEuropean Networks

TransEuropean Networks, or TENs as they are more frequently called, are central to the post-1992 agenda. Once the bulk of single market legislation was on the statute books, if not in all cases implemented and enforced, the Commission turned its attention to non-legal barriers that impede market integration. The downturn in economic activity in Europe in 1991 and the growing importance of unemployment led to renewed attention to Europe's structural economic problems. A series of European Councils from Edinburgh in 1992 to Essen in 1994 began to take seriously the need for concerted economic action. Buffeted by recession and rising structural unemployment, the Edinburgh European Council (December 1992) launched the 'Edinburgh Growth Initiative', aimed at accelerating the financing of infrastructure projects in an attempt to generate economic activity. The Council called for the establishment of a European Investment Fund intended to finance projects with a common European interest. The Copenhagen European Council (June 1993) requested the Commission President Jacques Delors to prepare a White Paper on *Growth, Competitiveness and Employment* for its consideration in December. A central theme in the Delors White Paper was the need to overcome continuing barriers to economic exchange by creating the necessary 'networks', described as the arteries of the single market. The report argued strongly for the development of:

1. Information networks for a range of electronic services;
2. Transport networks – high speed trains, roads, traffic management systems;
3. Energy networks. (European Commission, 1993c, pp. 22–31)

The Delors paper included an assessment of the enormous costs of upgrading infrastructural provision in energy, transport and electronic communications. Financing is cited amounting to ECU 67 billion for information networks, ECU 82 billion for transport and a further ECU 13 billion for energy by the end of the decade (European Commission, 1993c). Delors envisaged an annual investment of between ECU 20–30 billion in TransEuropean networks.

The substantial financing required for the TENs was a major consideration from the outset. The White Paper recognised that the state of the Community's and member-state finances left little margin to increase public expenditure beyond what was planned, and that new forms of public and private financing would be needed. The Commission saw itself playing a role as catalyst in seeking the appropriate financial backing for the priority network projects. The Commission made a play in the White Paper for a new financial instrument, 'Union bonds', which would be raised on the international capital markets to provide cheap loans, using the EU's favourable credit rating. Although there was general agreement among the heads of government about the desirability of European networks, there was lukewarm support for the development of a new financial instrument. Germany and the UK opposed the development of further non-budgetary instruments. Chancellor Kohl is reputed to have said that 'it is important not to create a "new pot" into which money would be poured just for show' (*Financial Times*, 5 December 1993). Moreover, the national political leaders felt that the Commission was attempting to bypass the European Investment Bank, which was already responsible for lending to infrastructure projects. The Brussels European Council endorsed the strengthening of European networks and set up a group of personal representatives chaired by Commissioner Christophersen to co-ordinate the implementation of priority projects and to analyse the financing of TENs in general. The European Investment Bank emerged as a major player in their financing (see Chapter 8).

The Commission has highlighted problems in the financing of the TENs and has requested additional finance for them from the Community budget, while acknowledging that the bulk of the finance will have to come from non-Community sources. Commission attempts to release additional monies for the TENs has met with considerable opposition from France, the UK and Germany. The Florence European Council in June 1996 failed to agree to President Santer's demand for additional monies although it recognised that a number of the networks, particularly high speed railways, need additional financing. The German Finance Minister, Theo Waigel, argued that the fiscal restraint facing the member states because of the Maastricht convergence criteria should be matched by the EU.

Creating a civil society

From the end of the 1960s, the social dimension of integration began to impinge more and more on the policy agenda. Chancellor Willy Brandt, at the Hague Summit in 1969, called for integration with a 'human face'. This reflected an aspiration to create a political community and to bring integration closer to the people. The Monnet method, which had been used to good effect in the 1960s, was excessively focused on Europe's élites and the imperatives of market integration. The desire to take more cognisance of the social impact of integration led to the first Social Action Programme which was launched in 1973. Michael Shanks, the Director General of the Commission's Social Affairs Directorate, argues that the SAP developed at a time when 'the Community was groping for a "human face", for a programme which would render it more meaningful to the ordinary men in the street, the field and the factory' (Shanks, 1977, p. 14).

Gradually, but in the teeth of considerable resistance, the policy-reach of the European Union was extended into policy domains that had a bearing on working and living conditions in the member states, with the EU budget playing a very important role in extending the tentacles of the Union into the national societies and not just economies. The Single European Act and the Treaty on European Union expanded the Union's policy-reach and gave a surer legislative foundation to policies that had already been developed. The Commission and the European Parliament have used their budgetary competence to augment policies that highlight the relevance of integration for Europe's peoples. The budget is used symbolically to enhance the legitimacy of the European Union for the population at large. Often small amounts of money are deployed to part-finance an experimental pilot programme or a transnational network in education, training, the environment and so on. As a consequence, a very wide range of national agencies, voluntary groups, educational establishments, companies and individuals are drawn into the Union's budgetary maze. Described as 'Europe's most colourful flowers' by a leading Non-Governmental Organisation (NGO) lobby, many obscure budgetary lines are used to create an embryonic civil society that is transnational in nature and to counteract the excessive representation of producer interests in the Union's governance structures.

A people's Europe

Although much of the Union's effort in the social field is based on its regulatory power, the Union budget has been an essential complement to its legislative capacity. The Union has a number of budgetary instruments, notably:

- The European Social Fund;
- Community Initiatives in the social field;
- Measures to combat poverty;
- Socrates, Leonardo and Youth for Europe – all designed to increase educational mobility;
- Public health and consumer protection;
- Environmental policy;
- Cultural policy;
- Special programmes to aid the peace programme in Northern Ireland.

The European Social Fund, which was originally established to aid the mobility of agricultural workers from southern Italy to the industrial heartlands of Germany, is the Union's main policy instrument to combat unemployment. The title Social Fund is a misnomer because the ESF is a labour market fund with the power to part-finance vocational training and employment-subsidy schemes in the member states. With the inexorable rise in unemployment in Europe from 1973 onwards, the ESF increasingly focused on the long-term unemployed and young unemployed people who had failed to make the transition from school to work. The ESF has also been used to bolster EU transfers to the lesser-developed regions of the Union in conjunction with the other structural funds. Three Community initiatives channel finance to particular categories of people who might not receive adequate attention in the national and regional development plans. These are NOW, which aims to promote employment opportunities for Women; HORIZON, which is directed towards the disabled and other disadvantaged groups; and YOUTHSTART, which is designed to help unqualified young people. Community initiatives provide finance for the most vulnerable and marginalised groups in society. Many ventures eligible for funding under the Community Initiatives scheme tend to have a transnational component and are designed as experimental demonstration projects that can be emulated later in other parts of the Union. In this way rather small amounts of money may encourage policy innovation in the member states.

In 1975 the Community, controversially, launched its First Combat Poverty Programme with 20 million ECU for five years. There was considerable resistance from a number of the wealthier member states whose policy-makers resisted the argument that all West European societies continued to have pockets of deprivation despite the welfare state. Since then, there have been two further programmes which have shifted the focus from research on poverty and small pilot projects to larger scale ventures. Attempts by the European Parliament to increase the resources devoted to combating poverty have met with the implacable opposition of the Council.

With the signing of the SEA, the Union began to turn its attention to educational policy and the mobility of young people. The Union's schemes have contributed to the internationalisation of university education in Europe and have reoriented students away from the United States towards European countries. A series of programmes – notably Erasmus, Lingua, Commett and Petra – were designed to promote the mobility of university students, young workers, training networks between industry and universities, and language training for young people. All these programmes were organised on the basis of networks of institutions in the member states. The impact of the programmes is considerable in that some 500 000 young people studied in other member states with the aid of Erasmus grants, and young workers had the opportunity to work in another country abroad. Although the numbers of students who actually availed of scarce Erasmus funding was limited, the influx of Erasmus students to university campuses gave them a cosmopolitan flavour and served to add a 'European dimension' to national educational policies in a very cost-effective manner from the Commission's point of view. The multiplicity of educational and training programmes has been regrouped into three overarching programmes – Socrates, Leonardo and Youth for Europe – which have all received greatly increased funding. Since 1990, the Commission has part-financed over 1000 teaching and research initiatives as part of the Jean Monnet scheme which ensures that courses on European integration are part of the undergraduate curriculum on most social science degrees.

During the 1980s the Union assumed responsibility for some aspects of public health and consumer protection. Both subjects were underpinned by the TEU which made provision for an explicit Union role in these domains. The Treaty calls on the member states to co-ordinate their policies on public health and makes provision for the Union to take 'incentive measures and supportive actions' (Article 129, TEU). This allows the Union to pursue its established programmes of action against cancer, drug and alcohol abuse and AIDS. Budgetary limitations and the principle of subsidiarity mean that the Union's role in public health will be limited to health information and some research, rather than the delivery of health care. Consumer protection policies which expand as a result of the internal market include EU-sponsored awareness programmes and consumer information funded from the budget.

The European Union, despite the original weakness of its legislative competence in the field, played a major role in the development of a 'European' dimension to environmental policy by gradually extending its regulatory reach to cover all major forms of pollution and by linking environmental issues to market integration. In 1981, the Directorate General for the Environment was established within the Commission which gave environmental issues a firm foothold in the Union's bureaucracy and a base from which to ensure that the environmental consequences of other EU policies would be taken seriously. The SEA enhanced the Union's Treaty basis for environmental policy and gave the Commission a sound legal base from which to operate. Commitments in the EU budget to environmental policy have grown from ECU 30 million in 1986 to ECU 76 million in 1995. This money is spent on environmental awareness campaigns, on gathering environmental information from the member states, on the newly-established Environmental Protection Agency in Copenhagen, and on a specific financial programme, LIFE, which finances demonstration projects (111 in 1993) and innovative ways of protecting the environment in the member states. The structural funds also finance environmental infrastructure and environmental job creation. Tensions persist in the Commission and in the member states between the rhetorical commitment to sustainable development and the TransEuropean Networks which will add some 12 000 km of motorways to the landscape.

Cultural policy is one of the most ambiguous policies that the Union pursues. Vague and rather bland references to Europe's cultural heritage and to the need to promote cultural integration have appeared in official thinking about the EU for many years. At the outset, EU policy consisted of a number of uncoordinated projects which did not amount to a policy. Rather small amounts of money have been used to promote cultural exchange, the translation of books into other Community languages, conservation projects and audio-visual co-operation. The TEU formally includes a treaty article on culture which says that the Community shall 'contribute to the flowering of the cultures of the member states, while respecting their national and regional diversity and at the same time bringing the common cultural heritage to the fore' (Article 128, TEU). EU policy in the cultural field has a strong symbolic intent and is clearly part of a deliberate attempt to generate the sense of the Union as a common cultural space. EU finance is used to fund:

- Pilot conservation projects;
- Cultural events like the 'European City of Culture';
- The MEDIA programme for the audio visual sector;
- The Kaleidoscope programme for cultural exchange.

The funds available for spending on these schemes, although extremely limited, are dispersed widely among a large number of projects. In 1993, over 200 projects were financed, costing less than 4 million ECU.

Justice and home affairs: financing the third pillar

The inclusion in the TEU of provision for Co-operation in Justice and Home Affairs, known as Pillar 3 of the TEU, represented the codification of activity that had been developing in the EC since 1975 when the Trevi Group was set up to help combat terrorism. Gradually other concerns – notably drug abuse, serious crime and immigration – were added to the list of subjects for co-operation that took place in an intergovernmental framework parallel to the formal treaties. The TEU provisions are largely intergovernmental, albeit with a role of the Commission in proposing measures and a more limited consultative role for the EP. The Treaty makes provision for three policy instruments (Article K3): common actions, common positions and conventions. Financing activities under the third Pillar is highly contentious because a distinction is made between administrative expenditure and operational expenditure (Article K8.2, TEU). Administrative expenditure is to be charged to the Union budget and the Council may decide:

- unanimously that operational expenditure, to which the implementation of those provisions gives rise, is to be charged to the budget of the European Communities; in that event, the budgetary procedure laid down in the treaty establishing the EC shall be applicable; or
- determine that such expenditure shall be charged to the member states, where appropriate, in accordance with a scale to be decided.

Problems have arisen because there is no definition of what 'operational expenditure' might entail. Moreover, financing Pillar 3 under the established budgetary rules provides the EP with an important channel of influence and would make such expenditure subject to established auditory procedures. One commentator underlined the problem of definition by suggesting that 'the range of possibilities is enormous and can spread from, at one extreme, the commissioning of studies and the financing of seminars to, at the other extreme, providing financial support for the strengthening of the Greek and Portuguese navies to enable them to patrol their part of the Community's external frontier efficiently' (Fortescue, 1994, p. 6). A number of member states, in their effort to conserve as far as possible the intergovernmental nature of Pillar 3, are refusing to charge what might be considered operational expenditure to the Community budget because of the political and institutional consequences of such a decision.

For example, expenses arising from the 'Piranha' surveillance operation are being borne by the member states themselves. The financing of Pillar 3 will remain contentious for some time to come.

Conclusions

The medley of policies and expenditure programmes outlined in this chapter have been moulded by the legacy of the past and the evolving dynamic of integration, especially new policy goals and enlargement. The finances of the Union have been essential to the integration process. The CAP was a necessary complement to market liberalisation in the 1960s, and structural policy was essential to the internal market. All major episodes of constitution building in the Union have been accompanied by a new budgetary deal. Such deals have acted as sidepayments to lubricate negotiations but also fulfill wider welfare functions. Liberalisation without compensatory mechanisms might not survive the inevitable tensions it brings.

The Common Agricultural Policy continues to weigh heavily on the EU budget, absorbing over 50 per cent of financial resources in 1995. The dominance of CAP expenditure in the EU budget is one of the most compelling features of EU finances. Its prominence owes much to the fact that the income of farmers was assured by manipulating prices through subsidies and storage. The insulation of Farm Ministers in the EU's decision-making system contributed to the explosion of CAP expenditure in the 1980s. The global nature of the Delors I package enabled linkages to be established between ceilings on CAP expenditure and wider budgetary concerns. By 1991, however, CAP expenditure was rising again and there were pressures on the Union from its trading partners in the GATT. A combination of internal and external pressures led to the MacSharry reforms which radically altered the CAP's policy instruments with the introduction of direct income support to farmers.

The second remarkable feature of EU finances since the mid-1980s has been the growth of spending on structural policy. The struggle to embed the principle of cohesion in the *acquis communautaire*, which occupied much of the 1980s, culminated in the

Delors I and II decisions which increased the proportion of the EU budget devoted to structural fund spending from 16 per cent in 1986 to 33 per cent in 1995. Although the scale of structural fund spending is limited in relation to Community GDP, the budgetary increases represent an important commitment by the Union to increase financial flows to the poorer parts of Europe. The fact that these increases were possible during a period of economic austerity and restrictive national budgets is in many ways remarkable. The richer member states view cohesion monies as limited in time and designed to enable peripheral Europe to 'catch up', whereas the poorer countries, notably Spain, argue for continuing interregional transfers.

The remaining 20 per cent of the budget has two main purposes: enhancing the competitiveness of the European economy (R&D and TENs) and building up a people's Europe (social policy, cultural policy, media and education). Spending on these policies goes directly to individuals and organisations within the member states and not through national budgets. Relatively small amounts of seed money are used to finance transnational projects and programmes which contribute to the Europeanisation of governmental agencies, para-statal institutions, and interest organisations. The main characteristic of this spending is an emphasis on a European model of internationalisation characterised by transnational networks and innovative problem-solving.

6
The External Reach of the Union

The European Union has gradually, albeit in a piecemeal manner, amassed a range of financial policy instruments to deploy outside its borders. Money has come to play a central role in the Union's search for a role in world politics since spending on what might be broadly termed foreign policy actions grew significantly since the mid-1980s. The Edinburgh Agreement of December 1992, which envisaged a doubling of external spending between 1993 and 1999, represents the most sizeable increase in the financial resources available to the EU for external action ever agreed. External expenditure (EU budget and European Development Fund) has grown from 3.3 billion ECU in 1990 to 7.3 billion ECU in 1995. Although external actions constitute only 5.4 per cent (1995 budget) of total budgetary expenditure, there has been a dramatic growth in the Union's external financial commitments and the range of policy instruments deployed across the globe. Direct budgetary expenditure is augmented by the dramatic rise in the international lending activities of the European Investment Bank. The Union's external policies provide a powerful lens though which to analyse the Union's international capacity. This chapter examines the nature of the EU as a player in world politics, the financial policy instruments it deploys and its relations with different parts of the world.

Inevitably, the growth of the Union's external financial reach over such a short period has been accompanied by considerable disagreement about the level of external funding and the purposes to which it should be put. Future splits may well concern the Union's internal policy remit and its external commitments, between the benefits accruing to existing member states and the growing international demands on the Union. Debate will also focus on issues of 'inclusion' and 'exclusion', of the terms of membership of what was once an exclusive West European club. Conflict already manifests itself in internal bargaining about the division of the Union's external financial cake among different parts of the globe.

The external ambit of the EU

Categorising the hybrid international role of the European Union tends to frustrate most analysts because the Union defies the traditional categories attributed to international actors (Hill, 1993; Smith, 1994). Although the range and capacity of EU action falls well short of the attributes associated with state power in world politics, the Union is a 'civilian power' of long standing that has gradually amassed political clout. Precisely because of its 'civilian' status, the Union relies heavily on *soft* policy instruments such as aid and trade rather than on coercive capacity. Soft policy instruments may well be more appropriate to the needs of the post-cold-war world and the security issues facing present-day Europe. The Union may be powerless to maintain peace in the Transcaucasia but with food aid can keep starvation at bay and contribute to the local economy.

Academic analyses tend to highlight the weakness of the EU in world politics rather than the growing reach of its external activities and the increasing sophistication of its policy instruments. Assertions that the Union is plagued by a gap between international expectations and its capacity to deliver reverberate in the academic debate (Hill, 1993). Images of a convoy moving at the speed of the slowest ship abound. Yet the rapid evolution of the external financial instruments deployed by the EU points to an impressive array of policy instruments and an expanding geographical reach (see Figure 6.1 – map of international flows). Some 157 states are formally accredited to the Commission in Brussels and the EU maintains 107 delegations in third countries. The EU is the world's largest trading bloc, accounting for some 24 per cent of world trade.

FIGURE 6.1

Map of financial flows from the Union around the world

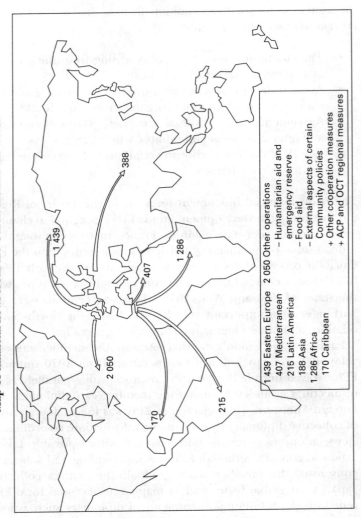

1 439 Eastern Europe   2 050 Other operations
407 Mediterranean   – Humanitarian aid and
215 Latin America   emergency reserve
188 Asia   – Food aid
1 286 Africa   – External aspects of certain
170 Caribbean   Community policies
                                    + Other cooperation measures
                                    + ACP and OCT regional measures

Source: European Commission (1994) *The Community Budget: The Facts in Figures,* Sec(94)1100, p. 93.

The role of the Union has been shaped by the gradual expansion of its treaty-based provisions, the development of a parallel process of European Political Co-operation (EPC) and pressures from the international system. The foundation treaties provided the legal basis for what are traditionally described as the Union's *external relations*, which include:

- The common commercial policy arising from the creation of a common market (Article 113);
- Association agreements with individual countries, groups of countries and international organisations (Article 238);
- Agreements with individual countries, groups of countries and international organisations (Article 228);
- Part IV of the Treaty covering relations with overseas territories and dependencies.

The main financial instrument foreseen in the Treaty of Rome was the European Development Fund (EDF) designed to channel aid to the member-state colonies. France successfully sought to offload some of the financial burden of its colonies onto the EC. Once the process of decolonisation accelerated in the early 1960s, the Union concluded the Arusha and Yaoundé Conventions with the states of East and West Africa. These agreements were the harbinger of a important role for the Union in North–South relations and in development co-operation generally.

Parallel to the Union's external relations, the member states developed European Political Co-operation from 1970 onwards. EPC evolved outside the Treaty framework with a parallel system of meetings at all levels among the member state diplomats and Foreign Ministers. The objective of EPC was to develop a system of collective diplomacy by exchanging information, co-ordinating views, adopting common positions and where possible taking action in concert. Although EPC was non-binding and subject to consensus, the member states gradually built up a collective capacity on global issues and in major international fora. EPC relied on the traditional instruments of diplomacy such as joint statements and *démarches*, but increasingly tapped into the economic instruments of the Rome Treaties in the 1980s.

Events in the 1980s heightened the ambitions of the Union as an international actor and increased the external pressures on the

EU. There were growing demands on the Union to marry its Treaty-based international powers with political co-operation to create a more complete and coherent presence for the EU in the international system. The SEA, although primarily concerned with the 1992 programme, codified the provisions on EPC for the first time and extended the scope of EPC to the field of security. The launch of the single market programme did much to increase the salience of the Union in the international political economy. Market creation in Western Europe challenged all of Europe's trading partners and their multinational companies. The US, Japan and the EFTA states were concerned that the 1992 project might turn into a 'Fortress Europe' project. This in turn led to a serious reappraisal by all EFTA states of their European policies and to a structural change in the relationship between the EU and EFTA. Subsequently, the majority of EFTA states applied for full membership of the EU.

The systemic transformation of the communist bloc following the 1989 revolutions in the former satellite states provided Western Europe with its most serious continental challenge to date. The geopolitical imperatives of the New Europe are far removed from the certainties of cold-war Europe. The retreat from empire fatally damaged the Soviet Union which began to disintegrate in 1991. The fragmentation of the relatively stable postwar order has left both parts of Europe searching from a new order that will deliver economic prosperity and peace. The euphoria which accompanied the end of the cold war was short-lived when it became readily apparent that international orders disintegrate rather more quickly than they can be built. The former communist states are striving, with mixed results, to transform themselves into market economies and liberal democratic political systems. This has involved changes in their constitutions, political institutions, judicial systems, property relationships, banking and commerce. The economic and social cost of transition has placed enormous strain on their populations which serves to undermine their nascent democracies. The states of the former Soviet Union face even more formidable difficulties given the unstable nature of Russia and interstate relations in this part of Europe. The disintegration of Yugoslavia reopened historical animosities in the Balkans and ended in bloody conflict between Serbia and the other successor states.

Western Europe, an island of stability in the New Europe, was called upon to lift its sights to the needs of the wider Europe. The states of East Central Europe look to the EU to support them in their transition. Accession to the EU and other western institutions as quickly as possible is the central foreign policy goal of these new states. The Hungarian government, in its statement at the entry into force of the European Agreements, argued that 'the attainment of membership of what has now become the European Union is a strategic aim of the Hungarian government and a priority in our foreign, security and economic policy alike' (Hungary 1994). The Czech president, Václav Havel, in his address to the European Parliament emphasised the importance of integration as a value to the countries of the East when he said 'we are intensely aware that the idea of European integration is an enormous historic opportunity for Europe as a whole, and for us' (Havel, 1994). The collapse of the cold-war order gives them the opportunity to re-establish their historical ties with the West and to 'return to' and 'rejoin' their natural partners. The New Europe poses acute dilemmas for the EU because it will have to face up to tough and difficult decisions about the process, timing and scope of continental enlargement and a potential membership of some 25–30 states.

The Maastricht Treaty formally created the European Union which, although it rests on a single institutional framework, consists of three Pillars. Pillar 1 includes provisions on the common market, EMU and a series of flanking policies. Pillar 2 deals with a 'Common Foreign and Security Policy', and Pillar 3 covers 'Justice and Home Affairs'. The segmentation of the Treaty reflects deep-seated conflict about the rules that should govern the different kinds of activities and the powers of the EU and national levels of governance. Although the compartmentalisation of the Treaty is not designed to achieve coherence and firmness of action, Article C in the Preamble specifically states that 'the Union shall in particular ensure the consistency of its external activities as a whole in the context of its external relations, security, economic and development policies (Article C, TEU). Consistency in the Union's actions remains a procedural ambition at best.

Pillar 2 builds on the scope and working methods of European Political Co-operation (EPC) as they evolved over two decades. The institutional provisions of Pillar 2 were laid down as follows:

- The Commission was given a right of initiative although not an exclusive right;
- Decision-making rests with the European Council and the Council of Ministers with different decision rules for 'common positions' and 'joint actions';
- The Council Presidency to represent the Union internationally;
- The jurisdiction of the Court of Justice does not extend to Pillar 2;
- The merging of the EPC Secretariat with the Council Secretariat;
- A consultative role for the EP;
- An enhanced role for COREPER (Title 5, TEU).

The objective of a Common Foreign and Security Policy (CFSP) is pursued by agreement on 'common positions' among the member states and 'joint actions'. The former corresponds to the practice in EPC, whereas 'joint actions' are new, though agreement depends on a very complicated decision-making process. The scope of the CFSP was extended to include 'all questions relating to the security of the Union, including the eventual framing of a common defence policy, which might in time lead to a common defence' (Article J.4). Although a common defence is well in the future, the Treaty abolished the artificial distinction between the economic and military aspects of security that had characterised EPC in the past. Security and defence policy remains unfinished business and will be revisited at the 1996/1997 IGC. If the EU is ever to develop a common defence, this will clearly involve difficult negotiations about equity and burden-sharing, issues that have dogged NATO in the past. The continuing debate about the financing of the CFSP is taken up below.

Pressures from the continental environment and the wider international system have led the EU into a more ambitious international presence and profile. The financial instruments described here evolved from the Union's original treaty basis, the external implications of its internal policies and more recent developments in Pillar 2. Unresolved dilemmas surround the relationship between Pillar 2 activities and traditional Community competencies, on the one hand, and the relationship between national

---

BOX 6.1
A medley of external financial instruments

The EU's international financial instruments can be broadly categorised as:

- *Development co-operation funds*: these include the financial commitments (development aid) that accompany the Union's agreements with a variety of Third World states;
- *Horizontal measures*: humanitarian aid, emergency food aid, environment and health, support for democratic institutions;
- *Financial and technical co-operation*: financial aid for the EU's neighbouring states to support their economic transformation;
- *Loans*: disbursed by the EIB to the Third World and to the former communist states;
- *Externalisation*: a number of the Union's internal policies notably, in R&D and education, include participation from third countries;
- *CFSP*: joint actions under Pillar 2 of the TEU.

---

policies and EU ones. See Box 6.1 for an outline of the EU's financial instruments in the external domain.

These financial instruments are managed by the relevant Commission services, committees of national civil servants, the Commission's delegations in third countries, the services of the European Investment Bank, international organisations, non-governmental agencies, private consultancy firms, and the administrations of the beneficiary countries. Managing external funding poses considerable challenges because of geographic distance, the weakness in many cases of governance in the receiving countries, and the complexities of the programmes themselves.

The Delors II package reflected the growing importance of external expenditure by including a separate heading for this category of spending in the Financial Perspective (1993–99). This was clearly an attempt to give added coherence to external spending and to provide the Union with predetermined sums for external action in the 1990s (Rey, 1993). A separate budgetary heading (B7/8) regroups the diverse and fragmented financial instruments under one rubric and will serve to insulate external spending from the dangers of being raided if other shortfalls occur in the budget. See Table 6.1 for an outline of external expenditure (B7) in the 1995 budget and Figure 6.2 for its distribution by region. The flexibility of the EU's external budget is enhanced by special reserves covering emergency aid and budgetary guarantees for EIB loans which allow for rapid use of the credits when and if necessary. A major lacuna in the Union's external budget is the continuing separation of the European Development Fund (EDF) from the main budget. This separation, largely motivated by France's desire to protect the privileged flow of aid to Africa, was confirmed by a declaration attached to the TEU, which stated that the EDF 'will continue to be financed by national contributions in accordance with the current provisions' (EU Treaty on European Union, TEU, Declaration on the EDF).

We turn now to an examination of the flow of EU funding to different parts of the world, starting with the budgetary issues raised in the negotiations between the EU and the EFTA states.

TABLE 6.1
External action (B7) 1995 budget

External action	Amount (ECU millions)	%
Geographic area		
Central/Eastern Europe/CIS	1582.6	32.4
Asia and Latin America	670.5	13.7
Mediterranean	487.4	10.0
Other non-members	52.0	1.1
Humanitarian aid		
Food aid	591.9	12.1
Humanitarian aid	256.0	5.2
General co-operation		
External aspects of EU policies	294.2	6.0
Other	646.8	13.2
Pillar 2	110.0	2.3
Reserve	190.0	4.0
Total	4881.4	100.0

Source: European Commission (1995a) *General Budget 1995*, p. 13.

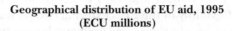

FIGURE 6.2

Geographical distribution of EU aid, 1995
(ECU millions)

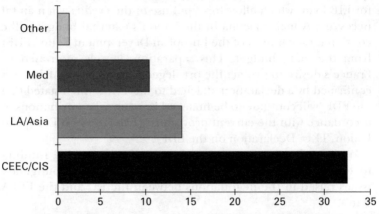

Source: European Commission (1995a) *General Budget of the EU 1995*, p. 13.

The EFTA states: questions of equity and burden-sharing

In 1989, the EU and the EFTA states embarked on a wide-ranging review of their relations with a view to concluding an agreement on a European Economic Area. In brief, the objective was to extend the internal market programme to the EFTA states and to give them some influence over the shaping of internal market legislation. Although the EEA Agreement was largely superseded by the subsequent enlargement negotiations and Swedish, Austrian and Finnish membership of the Union, budgetary issues surfaced during the EEA negotiations in an interesting manner. The cohesion states, particularly Spain, resisted offering the EFTA states an extension of the internal market as 'free riders' in their minds. The poorer EU states made a strong negotiating link between the agreement and an EFTA contribution to what for them was a corollary of the 1992 process – economic and social cohesion. Swedish and Austrian representatives appeared willing to contribute to a fair burden-sharing in the EEA and to maintaining its cohesion. This commitment emerged in the final agreement as an EEA Cohesion Fund which has now been subsumed into the EU budget following the EFTA enlargement.

Under the terms of the EEA Treaty, it was agreed that the EFTA states would contribute ECU 500 million over five years for projects in Ireland, Greece, Portugal and parts of Spain (Protocol 38, EEA Agreement). This has been reduced to take account of Finnish, Swedish and Austrian membership of the EU. Norway, Iceland and Liechtenstein remain in the EFTA pillar of the EEA. Norway has taken over responsibility for a much reduced Cohesion Fund. The EEA Agreement which is vital to Norway following the 'no' vote in the November 1994 referendum, is vulnerable to the charge that it wants the benefits of economic Europe without paying in terms of solidarity. This issue may resurface if the remaining EEA states want to deepen their relationship with the Union beyond its present level.

The EU's continental commitment

The need to respond to the circumstances of the New Europe is the most salient explanation for the increase in the EU's external expenditure since 1988. The 1993 Copenhagen European Council concluded that 'the Community will continue to devote a considerable part of budgetary resources foreseen for external action to the central and eastern European countries, in particular through the Phare programme' (Conclusions, Copenhagen European Council, June 1993). Pressure on the Union to devise a strategy for dealing with post-cold-war Europe forced it to enhance the co-ordination of its Treaty-based instruments and EPC. The EU quickly assumed the mantle of leading support for the process of transition to its East. The Union saw itself, and was perceived by others, as having a major role to play in establishing a European-wide framework following the end of the cold war. For the Union, this entails not just a reassessment of external action but also the internal workings of the Union itself and the existing policy *acquis*. The Union has a major stake in, and responsibility to aid, the process of transformation. In December 1989, the European Council emphasised its role in the following terms:

In this time of profound and swift change, the Community is –
and must also be in the future – a firm point of reference with
a strong power of attraction. It remains the cornerstone of a
new European architecture and in its desire for openness, the
stabilising influence in a future European balance. (European
Council, 1989)

The group of 24 countries (G24) asked the EU Commission to
co-ordinate the G24 programme of aid for Poland and Hungary,
the two states at the vanguard of the reform movement. The
significance of this should not be underestimated. For the first
time since the end of World War II, Europeans themselves, with
the support of the Bush administration, were adopting a leadership posture, not the superpowers. Moreover, the use of the
Commission to co-ordinate the G24 aid was a landmark of
international recognition of the Community. It established the
Commission's central role in an extensive programme of technical and financial aid known as Phare for the countries of East
Central Europe, a programme complemented by TACIS for the
CIS states in 1991. The member states and the Union contributed
50 per cent of all assistance committed by the G24 to the Central
and East European Countries (CEEC) between 1990 and the end
of 1992. The EFTA states contributed a further 11.8 per cent of
aid (see Table 6.2).

EU policy towards the former communist bloc is characterised
by the development of *institutionalised* co-operation between the
Twelve and the new European democracies. The nature and
extent of co-operation is determined by each country's reform

TABLE 6.2
**Assistance to the Central and Eastern Countries (CEEC) by donor,
1990–92**

Donor	ECU million	%
EU member states	14 412.07	38.1
EU	8 666.15	23.3
EFTA	4 253.71	11.1
Other	10 454.89	27.5
Total	37 786.82	100

Source: European Commission (1993f) 'G24 take stock of assistance to central
and eastern Europe', Press Release, IP(93)341.

process and its proximity to the EU's borders. The EU opted for a highly *differentiated* approach to the states for the former Soviet bloc. Put simply, the politics of 'inclusion' and 'exclusion' became highly variegated in the Union after 1989 (Smith, 1996). A clear distinction was drawn between the states of East Central Europe, on the one hand, and Russia and CIS states, on the other. Moreover, the Union adopted a differentiated approach to the states of East Central Europe themselves, depending on their proximity to the Union and the process of transition.

The question of EU membership hovered over policy deliberations from the outset with member states staking out various positions. Sustained pressure from the Visegrad states (Poland, Hungary, the Czech Republic and Slovakia) and a number of member states led to the Copenhagen declaration in June 1993 that 'the associated countries in central and eastern Europe that so desire shall become members of the European Union' (Final Communique, Copenhagen European Council, June 1993). Thereafter, the debate moved from the issue of whether or not membership would happen to 'how and when' the CEEC states would join the club. The Essen European Council (December 1994) set out a detailed pre-accession strategy based on what is called a 'structured relationship', which leaves some really tough decisions ahead on budgetary issues, institutional reform in the Union, and the adaptation of internal policies. Increasingly, Central and Eastern Europe straddles the boundary between what is external Union policy and the internal *acquis*.

The main German priority from the outset was to stabilise the countries on its borders, but also reflected the fact that reform had progressed more rapidly in the states nearest the EU. A distinct 'pyramid of privilege' evolved in the Union's relations with its non-member European neighbours. Four clusters of states characterised by the nature of the agreement that the EU was willing to offer them is readily apparent. First, the Union offered association agreements known as Europe Agreements, to Poland, Hungary, the Czech Republic and Slovakia (the Visegrad states) and on a slower timetable to Bulgaria, Romania and Slovenia. Second, the Union signed Trade and Co-operation Agreements with the three Baltic states – Latvia, Lithuania and Estonia – which were later offered Europe Agreements. These two groups of states were gradually incorporated into the Phare programme. Third, the EU signed or is negotiating co-operation agreements with the states of the CIS. The states of the former Yugoslavia represent a distinct category where the EU's effort is concentrated on peace-keeping and alleviating the consequences of war. An important, albeit unacknowledged, distinction was made between those states that were seen as future members of the Union and those that would remain outside as neighbours but not as partners. The Phare programme embraced potential members, whereas Tacis was for Russia and the states of the CIS.

Trade and financial aid are the two main policy instruments available to the EU in its dealings with the former communist states. So-called 'first generation' trade agreements were signed during 1991 with all of the Central and East European states following the EEC Council for Mutual Economic Assistance Declaration of June 1988. These were quickly super-seded by 'second generation' Europe Agreements and since the Copenhagen European Council, by preparations for eventual membership of the Union. When negotiating the Europe Agreements, the Union was unwilling to include specific financial commitments in the texts. The financial implications of the Agreements were worked out by the Union in its internal bud-getary process without the involvement of the associated states. In practice, the amount of EU financial aid going to Europe's continental neighbours has grown dramatically from ECU 500 million in 1990 to ECU 1.5 billion in 1995. The main assistance programmes are:

1. *Phare and Tacis*: reconstruction, environmental measures, technical assistance and skills transfer; see Tables 6.3, 6.4 and 6.5;
2. *Emergency Aid*: balance-of-payments difficulties and food aid;
3. *European Investment Bank*: loans;
4. *European Coal and Steel Community*: restructuring the coal and steel industries;
5. *European Bank for Reconstruction and Development*: loans;
6. *Tempus/ACE*: academic exchange.

A notable characteristic of the assistance programmes is their *conditional* nature. Five criteria have always governed access to the Phare programme: the establishment of the rule of law, respect for human rights, free elections, political pluralism and progress

TABLE 6.3
Breakdown of Phare commitments by partner country, 1990–94
(ECU million)

Country	Commitments	% Total
Albania	244.0	6
Bulgaria	393.5	10
Estonia	44.5	1
Hungary	409.8	12
Latvia	62.5	2
Lithuania	84.0	2
Poland	1011.6	25
Romania	541.7	14
Former Czechoslovakia	233.0	6
Czech Republic	120.0	3
Slovakia	80.0	2
Former Yugoslavia	141.1	3
Slovenia	44.0	1
Ex-GDR	35.0	1
Regional programmes	475.1	12
Total	4008.8	100

Note: A figure of ECU 247.6 million for other programmes brings the total
Phare programme to ECU million 4248.5.
Source: European Parliament (1995c) *Summary of Phare Financial Performance*,
Committee on Budgets, 12 April.

TABLE 6.4
Breakdown of Phare commitments by sector, 1990–94
(ECU million)

Sectors	Commitments	%
Administration	209.2	5
Agriculture	400.5	9
Democratisation	25.2	1
Education, training	599.3	14
Environment/nuclear	401.4	9
Financial sector	207.7	5
Food aid	367.8	9
Infrastructure	587.4	14
Consumer protection	4.0	–
Privatisation	723.9	17
Regional measures	34.8	1
Social development	130.2	3
Public health	99.5	2
Other	457.4	11
Total	4248.3	100

Source: European Parliament (1995c) *Summary of Phare Financial Performance*,
Committee on Budgets, 12 April.

TABLE 6.5
TACIS programme breakdown by country, 1991–94
(ECU million)

Country	Amount
Armenia	20.05
Azerbaijan	20.5
Belarus	40.07
Georgia	22.23
Kazakhstan	56.4
Kyrgyzstan	19.93
Moldova	20.2
Mongolia	8
Russia	630.89
Tajikstan	4
Turkmenistan	17.8
Ukraine	170.93
Uzbekistan	35.27
Baltic	15
Interstate	22
Humanitarian	521.01
Other	122.54

Source: European Parliament (1995d) *Summary of Tacis Financial Performance*, Committee on Budget, 12 April.

towards a market economy. Phare's policy guidelines display a strong bias towards market-led reform. The recipient states are free to make other choices but cannot count on EU finance to help them go in any direction other than free market mechanisms (Tommel, 1993). The conditionality introduced into Eastern European aid programmes reverberated in the Union's relations with Third World states, as we shall see later.

Phare and Tacis are mammoth programmes of financial and technical assistance involving national and regional programmes and humanitarian aid. Although they cannot substitute for private sector capital, because the monies are transferred in grant form, the programmes are very attractive to the recipients. The Phare model of transferring assistance was expanded to Tacis when it began in 1991. In 1993 the Phare management process adopted a total of 87 financing decisions including 66 national sectoral programmes and 10 regional co-operation programmes. These programme decisions are followed by a process of tendering for specific parts of the programme to private and public agencies (European Commission, 1993g, Phare Report). The remit of the Phare programme includes aid towards economic restructuring, training of personnel, environmental measures, agricultural restructuring, aid to small and medium-sized companies, assistance for the financial and banking sectors, reform of public administration, and programmes to develop democracy and civil society. National programmes depend very much on the rate of internal change in the recipient state. For example, Poland, Hungary and the Czech Republic implement far more sophisticated programmes than either Albania or Romania. See Table 6.3 for a breakdown of Phare assistance by partner country between 1990 and 1994.

The main emphasis in the Phare programme is on:

- 'Demand-led' *national programmes* submitted by each recipient state based on its own reform policies and shaped very much by the stage of reform (see Box 6.2 for an overview of the Polish programmes);
- *Regional programmes* to enhance regional links of all kinds between the CEEC states;

BOX 6.2
Overview of Poland's indicative programme signed in 1994

The 1994 indicative programme commits ECU 208.8 million to nine specific areas:

- Financial sector development;
- Investment in transport infrastructure;
- Cross-border co-operation;
- Higher-education (TEMPUS);
- Supporting democratic institutions/civil society;
- Worker protection;
- Forestry protection;
- Industrial restructuring and privatisation;
- Fiesta 11 – a multi-sectoral facility.

Source: European Commission (1994c) Phare Annual Report, p. 25.

- *Multidisciplinary measures* designed to allow for global grants, which can then be allocated for smaller projects without an individual Commission decision;
- *Humanitarian aid* to countries such as Albania and the former Yugoslavia.

(European Commission (1993g and Phare Report)

The design, implementation and management of the technical assistance programmes for the CEEC and the CIS pose enormous challenges to the Union and the Commission because of the intrinsic difficulties associated with the transition process, the wide divergences between the CEECs on the scope, timing and strategy for transition, and the unstable nature of politics in some states. Moreover, the number and diversity of public and private institutions involved in programme implementation create problems of delivery, evaluation and accountability. In a process much akin to policy domains, the Commission has gradually refined its approach to policy design, implementation and management through a process of institutional learning. This was influenced by the findings of commissioned research on existing programmes, a process of dialogue with the recipient states and the experience of the EU's internal structural policies.

The rapid expansion in the number of states benefiting from Phare, from two in 1990 to 11 in 1993, put enormous pressure on the Commission which was not adequately staffed for the demands of the programme. It tended to rely on non-statutory staff to manage the programme. In 1991, 72 people out of a total of 108 staff in the Phare unit were not Commission officials. A deliberate policy to gradually replace non-statutory staff was evident by 1993, when the permanent staff increased to 66 (+27) and the non-statutory staffed declined to 59 (−25), but they continue to constitute a high proportion of the total staff.

The first phase of Phare lasted from 1990 to the end of 1992 when a major review was undertaken. The focus in the first phase reflected the first stage of reform, with an emphasis on traditional technical assistance such as studies, training and the transfer of expertise. The second phase of Phare is designed to contribute to the fundamental long-term transformation of the national economies. The reform of the programme was influenced by a number of decisions taken by the European Council at

Copenhagen, the experience of the first phase of implementation and the implementation of the Europe Agreements. The changes included both substantive policy issues and the management of the grant-awarding process. The Phare guidelines for 1993–97 defined a number of new principles for the operation of Phare, notably:

1. The adaptation of a multi-annual approach to programming aid, based on close relations between the Commission and the recipient state.
2. A flexible response to the needs of the different countries, reflecting the stage of transformation and progress with reform. Actual receipts from Phare will carry greater conditionality. If a state is disbursing Phare assistance very slowly, or if the reform process is put into reverse, Phare finance is adjusted to take account of this.
3. A concentration on a limited number of strategic matters to achieve the critical mass necessary to achieve the desired impact. Since Copenhagen, the emphasis in Phare has shifted from expensive technical assistance to investment aid, particularly on infrastructural projects. The Essen Summit lifted the 15 per cent ceiling in Phare for financing investment projects to 25 per cent.
4. Financial assistance to help the CEECs adapt their institutions and laws to future EU membership.

The emphasis on programming reflected the Commission's approach to the management of internal cohesion grants. It stems from a desire to get beyond short-term, *ad hoc* interventions in the recipient states and to get them to develop a more strategic approach to the transformation process. The priorities of the Phare programme are increasingly geared towards the process of preparing these states for eventual EU membership. This is reflected in the proportion of Phare monies going to administrative reform and infrastructural development. See Table 6.5 for a breakdown of Phare assistance by sector between 1990 and 1994.

In developing its policies towards Eastern Europe, the EU has tended to rely on its traditional policies of aid and trade. However, the degree of conditionality attached to aid is new, as is the commitment to market solutions. Consultants acting as policy experts have played a crucial role in relations with the associated states. Private consultants act as intermediaries between the Commission and the representatives of the recipient states. According to Tommel, consultants provide 'policy advice in all fields, prepare or influence concrete decisions and serve as tutors in the policy process' (Tommel, 1993). One of the consequences of using consultants is a 'bias in actual expenditure away from the intended CEEC beneficiaries towards West European and international intermediaries' (Sedelmeier and Wallace, 1996, p. 362). The role of the Commission in the Phare process is also critical. Although Phare is implemented in a decentralised manner, the Commission has ample opportunity to influence substantive policy and procedural issues. The Commission is at the hub of a vast programme of technical assistance that includes all the activities of the G24.

The main focus in the EU's relations with the former communist bloc has moved from diplomatic statecraft in 1989/90 to an institutionalisation of relations between East and West that envisages a gradual enmeshing of the East into Western norms and practices. The beacon of membership is held up to those states that persevere with market reform and strive for political stability. The challenge for the Union is to transform what is still external action into a strategy for internalising the problems of East Central Europe with a view to the accession of these states to the Union. There is considerable tension between the commitment to a continental enlargement and the internal implications of such a move for the existing balance of policies and institutions of the Union. If Eastern Europe provides the Union with its most challenging internal/external problem, the growing importance of continental relations has disturbed Western Europe's relations with other neighbouring regions, notably the Mediterranean.

The EU and the Mediterranean

Unlike Eastern Europe, where the Union's relations were heavily restricted by COMECON's non-recognition of the EC until 1988, the EU has long-standing relations with the countries of the Mediterranean. See Table 6.6 for an overview of agreements and

TABLE 6.6
Agreements and protocols with Mediterranean states, ECU million

State	Signed	Protocol 1		Protocol 2		Protocol 3		Protocol 4	
		Grant	Loan	Grant	Loan	Grant	Loan	Grant	Loan
Algeria	1976	44	70	44	107	56	183	70	280
Tunisia	1976	54	41	61	78	93	131	116	168
Moroco	1976	74	56	109	90	173	151	218	220
Egypt	1977	77	93	126	150	200	249	258	310
Jordan	1977	22	18	26	37	37	63	46	80
Lebanon	1977	10	20	16	34	20	53	24	45
Syria	1977	26	34	33	64	36	110	43	115
Israel	1975	–	30	–	40	–	63	–	82
Turkey	1963	175	–	195	25	220	90		
Cyprus	1972	10	20	16	28	18	44		
Malta	1970	10	16	13.5	16	15	23		

Source: European Commission (1994d) Internal Memo/94/74 'The European Union's Relations with the Mediterranean', 6 December 1994, p. 4.

financial protocols between the EU and the Mediterranean states. The intensification of relations with its continental neighbours has forced the issue of the Mediterranean states onto the Union's external agenda. The southern member states – notably Italy, Spain and France – fearful that Germany's concentration on its eastern borders would be to the detriment of the Union's southern borders, pressed with increasing urgency for a reconsideration of the Union's Mediterranean policy in 1994. The Union is attempting to devise a Mediterranean strategy to run in tandem with its eastern policies. The desire to portray a 'dual track' or parallel policy is evident in Commissioner Marin's (Commissioner with responsibility for relations with the Mediterranean) statement after the November 1994 Foreign Ministers Council that:

> The parallelism between the two main priorities of the European Union's foreign policy, the East and the Mediterranean, has clearly been confirmed by the Council.
> The European Union has already made a great effort towards establishing a partnership with Eastern Europe and it will continue to do so. This is the utmost priority. Now we need to further consolidate our partnership with the Mediterranean. (European Commission, 1994j)

The Union is engaged in an attempt to marry an ambitious strategy to its east with an equally ambitious strategy to its south. This drive is motivated by two powerful political imperatives. First, the countries on the southern shores of the Mediterranean have rapidly growing populations, with high levels of poverty and unemployment. It is estimated that the population of the southern Mediterranean countries will grow from 209 million inhabitants in 1992 to 304 million by 2010, with a corresponding growth of 29 million in the EU states (European Commission, 1994d). The southern EU states are clearly fearful of further migratory pressures from North Africa as a burgeoning population seeks employment in the EU. The rise of xenophobic populist parties in the member states points to the sensitivity of immigration in the domestic politics of the EU. Second, political instability in North Africa, most notably in Algeria, raises fears of the destabilising effects of Islamic fundamentalism and its potential for destabilisation in the EU itself. The southern member states are determined that the EU will take due cognisance of its external environment to its south and not just to its east.

The EU's policies towards the Mediterranean are influenced by the legacy of past agreements with this part of the globe. Since the early 1970s the EU has signed co-operation agreements with all states on the southern shores of the Mediterranean with the exception of Libya, and association agreements with Turkey, Cyprus and Malta. Association agreements imply a commitment to membership of the Union, although the history of EU/Turkish relations implies that the commitment is less than fullsome on the EU's side. In 1976 the Union signed agreements with the Arab Maghreb (Morocco, Tunisia and Algeria) followed by agreements with the Arab Mashreq (Egypt, Jordan, Lebanon and Syria) in 1977. Israel signed a free-trade and association agreement in 1975. These agreements represented the core of the Union's global policy on the Mediterranean. The Union is now attempting to translate this legacy of accords into what the Essen European Council called a Euro-Mediterranean Partnership. The Council reaffirmed that the 'Mediterranean represents a priority area of strategic importance for the European Union' (European Council, 1994).

EU accords with the Mediterranean consisted of the two key elements of market access and financial assistance. The original agreements included provision of aid in the form of financial protocols of five years duration attached to each agreement. There is an inbuilt tension in the Union on the appropriate balance between trade concessions and financial transfers. The northern member states have always argued that economic development, and hence political stability, in these countries depended on more open access to the EU markets whereas the Mediterranean member states favoured budgetary transfers rather than competition from cheaper producers. The new Mediterranean policy provides for further but limited concessions for agricultural exports and a major increase in budgetary resources directed towards the Mediterranean. The Commission has strongly argued that it will require a substantial increase in technical and financial assistance for this region. Decisions on financial aid between 1992–95 include:

- A renewal of the Financial Protocols amounting to around ECU 2 billion in grants from the EU budget and loans from the EIB;
- A special financial envelope (ECU 300 million) destined for structural adjustment policies in these countries;
- Special funds to cater for regional co-operation and environmental projects;
- An extension of the model of a number of internal EU policies such as co-operation between universities (Med-Campus) and between municipal authorities (Med-Urbes).

Budgetary commitments foresee that total funds, including grants from the EU budget and EIB loans will amount to roughly ECU 4.5 billion, nearly three times the financial support to the southern Mediterranean between 1987 and 1991 (European Commission, 1994d). The countries of East Central Europe will continue to receive larger amounts of EU aid (see Table 6.7).

The Commission strategy is clearly to emulate its experience with Phare in the Mediterranean region and gradually to institutionalise relations between the Union and the southern Mediterranean states. The Union's capacity to influence internal developments in these states is however much weaker than its corresponding influence in Eastern Europe because it cannot hold out the beacon of membership and the unstable nature of intra-

TABLE 6.7
Financial flows to the CEEC and Mediterranean 1995–99
(ECU million)

Year	CEEC	Mediterranean
1995	1154	550
1996	1235	900
1997	1273	1000
1998	1397	1092
1999	1634	1143
Total	6693	4685

Source: European Council (*Conclusions*), 26/27 June 1995, p. 39.

and interstate relations in the Arab world. The Arab states may be less than open to the conditionality implied in Union policy which clearly states the intention to co-operate most closely with those states that undertake far-reaching modernisation, and that co-operate with the Union in the management of the inter-dependencies that tie both sides of the Mediterranean. The up-grading of relations with the Mediterranean was highlighted in November 1995 at the Euro-Mediterranean conference involving 27 states, which agreed to a wide-ranging declaration on future relations at the centre of which is a free trade area by 2010. In return for a substantial increase in Union aid, the poorer Mediterranean states will open their economies to increased trade and investment from the Union's member states. With the EU's growing commitment to its immediate environment, a question can be raised about the EU's traditional policies towards the Third World.

Development co-operation: a quest for coherence

The European Union is an important player in its own right in development co-operation, and is referred to as the 'thirteenth donor' in the OECD's Development Assistance Committee (DAC). The Union is now attempting to transform a range of piecemeal policies, programmes and funds that have grown up since the 1950s into a development co-operation policy as envisaged by Article 130u of the Treaty on European Union. For the first time, development co-operation has been recognised in legal terms as falling within the competence of the EU, and the co-ordination of EU policy and national policies is at least a procedural ambition in the Treaty. The Union inherits a range of policies that can be characterised by a 'pyramid of privilege', at the apex of which sits the Lomé states, then the Mediterranean states and finally non-associated developing countries which benefit from a number of global policies. The EU's internal politics on development co-operation suffer from a number of competing claims as different member states seek to map out the future of EU policy. The Iberian enlargement brought pressure for a move from a predominantly regional aid policy to a more balanced worldwide policy (Hewitt, 1993). France continues to champion the privileged position of the African, Caribbean and Pacific (ACP) states, while Germany is preoccupied with the development needs of its immediate neighbours, and Spain does not want Latin America left out.

The EU and Lomé: traditional concerns versus competing demands

The Lomé Conventions and their antecedent Agreements constitute the core of the Union's traditional external commitments. Co-operation with one-time colonies formed a major part of the Union's external reach in the 1960s and was augmented by UK accession in 1973. The first enlargement and the growing debate on North–South relations provided the incentive for a wide-ranging reassessment of the Union's relations with the former colonies of the member states. This culminated with the signing of the Lomé Convention in 1975 between the EC and 44 African, Caribbean and Pacific (ACP) countries known collectively as the ACP states. The fourth Lomé Convention was signed in Togo in December 1989 for a period of ten years with 69 ACP states (see Box 6.3 for a summary of the main features of the Convention). The Conventions are negotiated on a bloc-to-bloc basis between the EU and the 69 ACP states. Consequently, internal negotiations within each group are as important as EU/ACP negotiations.

BOX 6.3
Summary of the main features of the Lomé Convention

Lome IV is divided into *five* parts

Part 1	Sets out the general objective of ACP–EU co-operation:
	legally binding system
	equality between partners
	each state to determine its own political, social, cultural and economic policies
Part 2	Funds can be deployed for 20 different policies specified in Article 229
Part 3	Instruments of co-operation
	trade co-operation
	commodities
	financial and technical co-operation
	special arrangements for land-locked, least-developed states
Part 4	Institutions
	ACP–EEC Council of Ministers
	ACP–EEC Committee of Ambassadors
	ACP–Joint Assembly
Part 5	Final provisions
Protocols	

Source: European Communities (1990a) Text of IV Lomé Convention.

Lomé was touted as the beginning of a new era of relations between the developed and developing world, based on a multilateral *partnership* between the EU and the ACP states. Article 2 of Lomé IV states that EU/ACP co-operation is based on the principles of:

- Equality between partners, respect for their sovereignty, mutual interest and interdependence.
- The right of each state to determine its own political, social cultural and economic policy options;
- Security of relations based on the *acquis* of the system of co-operation.

The principle of partnership if buttressed by an institutional-isation of relations, including an EU/ACP Ministerial Council, a joint Committee of Ambassadors and an ACP/EU Assembly. Despite the evident commitment to partnership in the Convention from the outset, the decline in the ACP's bargaining power since the height of commodity power in the mid-1970s leaves the ACP states in a weak bargaining position *vis-á-vis* the EU. Growing concern about the effectiveness of aid and human rights has undermined the partnership element of the Conventions. In addition, the disastrous decade of the 1980s when sub-Saharan Africa almost fell out of the world economy raised major questions about traditional development aid and the purposes to which European Development Fund (EDF) monies should be put. The assumption that the 'more aid the better', is increasingly questioned given the growing evidence of poor aid performance, particularly in Africa (Riddell, 1990).

Lomé follows the pattern of EU external policy instruments with a dual policy of trade and aid. Despite the Lomé states' desire for 'trade not aid', the ACP share of EU imports coming from the Lomé states declined from 7 per cent in 1973 to just 3 per cent in 1992, despite privileged trading relations. Consequently, 'more by default than design, the principle benefit of the Lomé Convention has come to lie in its provisions for technical and financial co-operation' (European Research Office, 1993, p. 1). Hence the pot of money negotiated with each Convention tends to be one of the most hotly debated issues, agreed only in the dying moments of each round of negotiations. Internal EU negotiations about the level of funding is far more important than EU/ACP discussions about the size of the EDF. The EU tends to present an offer in very much a 'take it or leave it' basis to the ACP states which can reject it but will receive at best a little more from the member states.

The financial negotiations on Lomé IV illustrate the nature of internal EU bargaining and how divergence on the financial envelope is worked out. The EU had still not agreed to a financial offer by 30 October 1989, after one year of negotiations, when an EU/ACP Ministerial meeting was held. The negotiations then continued with a restricted number of states in a specially convened presidency group under the auspices of the French presidency of the Council. A two-day Council meeting (26/27 November, 1989) finally agreed to a financial package which was then transmitted to the ACP states but rejected as insufficient.

The negotiations in the Council of Ministers were described as 'un travail difficile et harassant' by the French Foreign Minister, Roland Dumas. The French Presidency, given its traditional interest in Lomé, was determined to get the best deal it could for the ACP states. It had a difficult struggle to convince Germany and the UK to be more generous than they were prepared to be. Both states tend to favour trade rather than aid as a development strategy. Spanish negotiators were also reticent because of their traditional orientation towards Latin America. The Twelve agreed to a financial envelope of ECU 11.9 billion at the end of November which was rejected by the ACP states as falling well short of their request for ECU 15.5 billion. A determined effort by the French presidency over the following week led to an increase of 100 million ECU which brought the financial package over the ECU 12 billion barrier. Finances for the period 1990–95 amounted to ECU 12 billion in contrast to ECU 8.5 billion for Lome III, representing a 46 per cent increase in nominal terms and 25 percent in real terms (Cova, 1990; Nicora, 1990).

The financing of the EDF was reopened in 1995 when the financial provisions of Lomé IV had to be renegotiated. Once again, it fell to the French presidency (January–June 1995) to negotiate the financial details of the eighth EDF. Opposition to maintaining the level of spending in the EDF came largely from Germany and the UK. The Cannes European Council agreed to a total of ECU 13.3 billion, which fell short of the Commission's request and the ambitions of the Frech presidency (European Council, 1995, p. 40). In an effort to reach agreement, France became the largest donor to the eighth EDF contributing ECU 3120 million in contrast to ECU 3000 million from Germany. The figure agreed at Cannes simply maintains in real terms what the twelve member states provided between 1990 and 1995, with no increase for the 1995 enlargement (see Table 6.8).

The EU's finances for the ACP states are channelled through the European Development Fund (EDF) and loans from the EIB. The operation of financial and technical co-operation has been characterised by an expansion in the number of financial instruments and continuing refinements to the traditional ones. Changes are influenced by the evolution of thinking on development assistance and specific problems confronting the ACP states.

TABLE 6.8
**Financial resources contributed by the member states to the 8th
European Development Fund (EDF)
(ECU million)**

Member state	Amount	Scale	Scale for 7th EDF
Belgium	503	3.77	3.96
Denmark	275	2.06	2.08
Germany	3 000	22.54	26.06
Greece	160	1.20	1.24
Spain	750	5.63	6.66
France	3 120	23.44	23.58
Ireland	801	0.60	0.55
Italy	1 610	12.09	12.58
Luxembourg	37	0.27	0.19
Netherlands	670	5.03	5.64
Portugal	125	0.93	0.88
UK	1 630	12.24	16.58
Austria	340	2.55	–
Finland	190	1.42	–
Sweden	350	2.63	–
Other	350	2.63	–
Total	13 307		–

Source: European Council *Conclusions*, Cannes 26/27 June 1995.

Three mechanisms for financial assistance are found in the EDF/EIB Lomé provisions, namely:

- Programmable financial resources, allocated geographically at the beginning of each five-year financial cycle;
- Non-programmable resources, which are allocated for specific purposes including emergency aid, aid to support the integration of displaced persons, STABEX, SYSMIN, regional trade promotion and structural adjustment support;
- Loan financing through the European Investment Bank, part of the EDF and partly raised by the EIB on the international capital markets.

These three mechanisms for channelling aid to 69 ACP states necessitates a vast and complex delivery process involving DG 8

(Development Co-operation) in the Commission, Commission delegations in the ACP states, the recipient governments and bureaucracies, non-governmental aid agencies and other funding agencies, notably the World Bank.

What are known as programmable resources are decided on every five years in discussion between the individual ACP state and the Commission, which results in a National Indicative Programme (NIP). The Commission tells the ACP state the level of funding it can expect over five years and then draws up a draft programme setting out how it proposes to spend the money by sector and project. Once a NIP has been agreed, the ACP state is guaranteed a certain global figure which cannot be withdrawn even if it is under-utilised. National Indicative Programmes are sometimes accompanied by regional programmes to promote co-operation between the ACP states. The principle of the programming process is to ensure that the recipient state receives finance for its internal development strategies and needs. In reality the lack of capacity within the ministries of the ACP states may mean that the EC or particular interests within the EC attempt to fill the policy vacuum in a recipient state in the desire to get resources committed and spent. EU producers have a major interest in tendering for lucrative Lomé contracts.

The most significant and innovative non-programmable resources are financial instruments designed to cushion the ACP states from a loss of income arising from fluctuations in commodity prices. These are particularly important to those ACP states that are heavily dependent on one or two key commodities.

STABEX (Lomé 1)

This was designed as a financial system to compensate states for a loss of income when prices fall for agricultural commodities on the world market. STABEX payments are made when a number of conditions are met and can finance restructuring programmes. STABEX was established in the first Lomé Convention at a time when commodity prices were rising, but it has had to cope with a significant deterioration in market prices during the 1980s. In 1990, admissible applications for STABEX aid amounted to ECU 495 million when the level of resources available amounted to

ECU 141 million. Although the amount of funding for STABEX was increased in 1990, it still only managed to meet 51 per cent of eligible demands (Simmonds, 1991, p. 329). The operation of the STABEX fund was a constant source of conflict between the ACP/EU Association Council during the operation of Lomé III. The fourth Convention reflected this concern by increasing the financial resources available for STABEX by 62 per cent between 1990 and 1995.

SYSMIN

This mechanism was established as part of Lomé II to help states dependent on the export of minerals to deal with the loss of export earnings. Its purpose is to rehabilitate and modernise the mining sectors in the ACP states and to promote diversification into other sources of export earnings. The scheme works some-what like STABEX on the basis of conditions of admissibility and dependency thresholds.

Structural adjustment support

This is the major innovation in Lomé IV although it came long after other donors began to pay attention to economic adjust-ment in the ACP states. It complements the traditional develop-ment projects and programmes financed by the EDF. A fund of ECU 1150 million has been set aside to finance support prog-rammes for structural adjustment aimed at generating economic growth, enhanced productivity, and balance-of-payments relief (European Communities, 1990a, Lomé IV, Articles 243–4). The focus on structural adjustment reflected the worsening economic crisis in many developing countries during the 1980s.

Concern about the operation of Lome's financial instruments has grown over the life of the Conventions. The two main issues, which were made apparent in a debate involving the European Parliament, the ACP states, non-governmental aid agencies and the Commission, are:

- The management and delivery systems for aid; and
- The need to link aid with human rights and democracy.

The administration of Lomé aid has been increasingly criticised in recent years. One scholar concludes that 'The EC has tended to be good at devising aid instruments (Stabex, indicative programming, a Convention which is a 'partnership of equals') but often weak at executing development policy' (Hewitt, 1993, p. 310). The programming and project process moves very slowly, with the result that there is a build-up of unused resources from the first three conventions. It can take up to 20–30 months between the submission of a project and the financing decision, and even longer before monies are actually disbursed (Robins, 1994, p. 66). Financial and technical bottlenecks occur in both the Commission and the ACP states. In an attempt to improve the delivery systems, the Commission is seeking to amass even greater control over the implementation of aid to overcome problems at the level of the individual states. A new project management cycle was implemented in 1993 and is now used for all EDF operations. The emphasis is on monitoring the impact of projects on the local population and more rigorous evaluation of policy outputs. ACP representatives complain that the Commission's administrative changes imply a retreat from the established system of partnership and co-management.

Partnership if also threatened by a renewed focus on conditionality. The readiness of the EU to attach considerable conditionality to financial transfers to its immediate neighbours has spilled over into ACP/EU relations. The emphasis in Phare and Tacis on human rights and good governance has heightened the centrality of the issue in North–South relations. Increasingly, the attitude of the donor states is reflected by Lynda Chalker, the UK's overseas development minister, when she said 'no taxpayer in any donor country should be asked to contribute to the Swiss bank accounts of corrupt third world politicians' (quoted in Robins, 1994). Although human rights is already recognised as a basic factor in development (Lomé, Article 5), the member states and the Commission increasingly insist on the need to focus on democracy and the rule of law as well, and would like to extend the human rights provision to make reference to good governance. In 1994 the EU suspended negotiations on financial transfers with ten ACP states because of the deteriorating political situation in those countries. In November 1995 the Commission suspended ECU 225 million of aid to Nigeria under the Lomé Convention following the execution of nine human-rights activists including the writer Ken Saro-Wiwa by the Nigerian military regime. The view that the EU cannot impose strict conditions on the former communist states without also imposing similar criteria on Third World states is gaining currency in EU circles. For their part, the ACP states are concerned that the EU is moving from the principles of partnership to unilateral decisions on the suspension of aid. Moreover, the privileged place of the ACP states is increasingly questioned by those interests in the EU with historical links in non-associated parts of the globe.

Financial and technical aid to Latin America and Asia

EU aid to the developed world outside the ACP circle has traditionally received little attention or political priority. The development of a budget line for aid to the non-associated developing countries made its appearance in 1976 when 20 million units of account were made available for non-ACP development assistance. The impetus for this stemmed from the UK's accession in 1973 and the need to do something for the Commonwealth states of Asia that were deemed non-associable. Disagreement in the Council on the extent and nature of this aid led the European Parliament to enter the figure of ECU 20 million in the 1976 budget as part of its margin of manoeuvre. The extent of this aid has grown since then as the Union strives to reduce the regional focus of its development co-operation policies. Aid under this budgetary line is channelled towards the poorer states in Asia and Latin America and is focused on rural development, and the fight against drugs. Most of the aid is channelled to India, the largest beneficiary, Bangladesh, Thailand, Pakistan, Bolivia and a number of Central American states. Until 1992 funding was made available on a yearly basis from the EU budget, but it is now based on' five-yearly plans. The 1992 Regulation commits a total of ECU 3 billion in aid between 1991 and 1995 which represents a sizeable increase on previous amounts. The increase in aid for Latin America is particularly marked and reflects the growing importance attached by the Union to relations with this part of the globe. Following the Iberian enlargement, the proportion of non-associated aid going to Latin America rose form 20 per cent to 25 per cent.

Deeply divided societies

The Union's aid to the peace process in Northern Ireland is echoed in similar aid to Palestine, South Africa and, following the Dayton Accords, to Bosnia. The Union has been involved in aid to the Palestinian people, particularly refugees, since 1970; this aid was accelerated in 1987 when a special budgetary line was created promoting development aid for the Occupied Territories. Financial transfers were seen as one means of giving substance to EU policies on the Middle East conflict. The peace settlement provided the impetus for further EU aid for the process of recon-struction, with some 500 million ECU pledged for use between 1994 an 1998; half of this aid (ECU 250 million) is in grant form, with a further ECU 250 million in EIB loans. EU assistance is centred on institutional development (Palestinian Police Force, elections), employment-generating projects, and major infra-structural projects.

The dismantling of apartheid in South Africa provided the impetus for a major reassessment of relations between the EU and Africa's wealthiest state. Opposition to apartheid was one of the most enduring policy concerns of European Political Co-operation, although agreement on the use of sanctions against South Africa was highly contested and was agreed only after long and tortuous negotiations in the Council. Policy towards South Africa included a budgetary element from 1985 onward when the 'Special Programme for the Victims of Apartheid' was launched with a budget of ECU 10 million. Between 1986 and 1993 a total of 671 individual projects were funded, from a budget of ECU 336 million. The Union used non-governmental organisations to channel aid to training projects, legal support against the security authorities, and social projects. The Special Programme budget of ECU 110 million (1994) is the largest programmable budget the Commission has with one single country. The transition to democracy in South Africa with the inauguration of the Mandela Government in May 1994 opened the way for the normalisation of EU/South Africa relations and the signing of a draft co-operation agreement which provides the framework for co-operation in the future. The Union has agreed to continue Special Programme aid until 1999 albeit in the altered circumstances of a democratically elected government. The South African elections in April pro-

vided the occasion for one of the first *joint actions* decided under
the new Pillar 2 provisions of the TEU (Holland, 1994). The EU
sent a team of 312 election observers to South Africa for the duration of the campaign, the financing of which is discussed below.

Horizontal measures: food aid and humanitarian aid

Food aid is a well-established and traditional form of aid deployed
by the EU in the Third World and more recently in the former
Communist bloc. It was traditionally portrayed as a convenient
means of dumping surplus agricultural produce, particularly
expensive milk powder and butter oil, under the guise of aid.
Persistent criticism by the European Parliament, the Court of
Auditors and many non-governmental aid agencies resulted in a
major review of the principles and purposes of food aid policy in
1986/87. The establishment of the European Community
Humanitarian Office (ECHO) in 1992, as a para-agency attached
to the Commission, significantly altered the management of EU
disaster relief of which food aid is an important component. The
delivery of EU humanitarian assistance involves important linkages with the UN World Food Programme and EuronAid, an
umbrella group of non-governmental agencies (NGOs) involved
in distributing aid locally in the recipient countries. Most aid is
distributed by third parties on behalf of the Union. Consequently,
the role of the Commission is to manage and monitor the
activities of a myriad of NGOs and UN agencies. In 1993 alone
700 contracts for the supply of emergency aid were agreed by the
ECHO.

In 1993, 56 states received EU emergency food supplies, evidence of its expanding reach. In 1994 aid was channelled to alleviate tribal strife in Brundi and Rwanda, and the effects of war in
the Sudan, Angola, Liberia and Somalia. Sometimes humanitarian aid is a substitute for political decisions and an inability to
prevent or contain war. Confronted with a series of conflicts in
the former Yugoslavia that it was powerless to influence, the
EU uses humanitarian aid as an instrument of foreign policy.
Financial expenditure in this region soared from ECU 13 million
in 1991 to ECU 410 million in 1993 (European Community
Humanitarian Office, Annual Report 1993).

FIGURE 6.3

EC humanitarian aid, 1990–93, ECU million

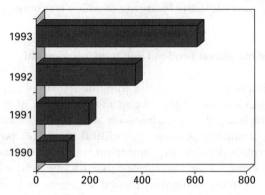

Source: European Community Humanitarian Office, *Annual Report, 1993*, p. 40.

Financial resources allocated to food aid and emergency aid has increased significantly since 1990, making the EU one of the world's leading donors (see Figure 6.3). Following the reform, the Commission has attempted to integrate food aid policy into its development co-operation policy and to enhance its management processes. A review of the new procedures by the Court of Auditors in 1992 was generally favourable and concluded that the reforms had improved efficiency and effectiveness. The EU is slowly attempting to shift the focus from emergency food aid to longer-term food security to prevent recurring famines. In addition to standard food aid programmes, the Union uses its budgetary resources to enhance storage facilities in the poorer countries and to provide the basis for food production, food processing and marketing.

Financing the Common Foreign and Security Policy (CFSP)

The existence of three Pillars in the European Union, with different decision rules and institutional responsibilities, inevitably gives rise to inter-institutional conflicts. The financing of Pillar 2 is set out in Article J.11 of the TEU, which establishes a distinction between administrative expenditure and operational expenditure. Administrative expenditure is charged to the Community budget whereas operational expenditure may be charged to the Community budget or to the member state budgets depending on a unanimous decision of the Council. In practice, those states favouring the retention of the pillar system, and wary of attempts to circumvent the system, prefer the latter method in principle. However, the need for speedy access to money for joint actions makes the EU budget an attractive proposition even for those states wedded to the pillar system.

Financing through the budget offered practical and financial advantages to the member states; each presidency could activate the resources for joint action without having to drag money out of national Finance Ministries. The Commission's report to the Reflection Group, established in June 1995 to prepare for the 1996 Intergovernmental Conference, acknowledged that 75 per cent of the cost of joint actions had been allocated to the Community budget which shows that, despite reservations, the member states agree that the Community budget provides the speediest and most efficient way to finance joint actions (European Commission, 1995). Otherwise joint action might be plagued by non-payment from the member states, a common feature of UN action.

Since the coming into operation of the TEU in November 1993, unresolved controversy and contention has characterised the debate on financing Pillar 2 measures. The sources of conflict include the following issues:

1. The distinction between administrative and operational expenditure is not clear-cut.
2. If operational expenditure is charged to the Community budget, it falls within the ambit of the normal budgetary process which gives the EP a say over CFSP financing, highlighting the imbalance between the European Parliament's political powers on CFSP matters and its budgetary powers. CFSP finance is regarded as non-compulsory, giving the Parliament the last word on expenditure decided by the Council. Yet those who negotiated the TEU had no intention of giving the EP influence over the detailed implementation of the CFSP.

3. The Council, in an attempt to curtail the power of the EP, would prefer a system whereby as much CFSP finance as possible forms part of the Council budget and is therefore subject to the 'gentlemen's agreement' whereby the Council and Parliament refrain from interfering in each other's internal administrative expenditure.

The Council, in its desire to limit the role of the Parliament, at the outset sought to charge the costs of the Union's administration of Mostar (ECU 115 million) to the Council's own administrative budget in 1994 by diverting money from internal Council administration to joint actions. The Parliament retaliated by reducing the Council's budget by the equivalent amount in 1995. The Mostar joint action is now charged to a special CFSP line in the budget, but the Parliament has frozen these commitments and will transfer them only on an *ad hoc* basis until agreed procedures about Pillar 2 financing are arrived at. Problems with financing the CFSP mean that each decision on joint action is accompanied by a procedural debate on how it should be funded rather than on the substance of the action itself. Decisions about who should pay CFSP staff in the Council Secretariat, about who should pay EU administrators in Mostar, or election observers in South Africa and Palestine have taken up an inordinate amount of time in the Council and have soured relations with the Commission and the Parliament. If the member states have a preference for financing the CFSP out of the Community budget they will have to give the Parliament a greater say in Pillar 2, and will have to give the Commission executive responsibility for the financial dimension of joint actions, neither of which is particularly palatable to the United Kingdom or France. Even if a *modus vivendi* is arrived at on Pillar 2 financing, difficult issues lie ahead if the Union's foreign policy ambitions grow and if CFSP procedures allow for 'positive abstention' or 'opting out' of joint actions. Will 'opting out' allow a state to 'opt out' of financing measures as well, or will financial solidarity prevail here?

Conclusions

The Union budget is a central part of its presence in international politics and is thus no longer merely a instrument for building the Union internally. The external reach of the Union and its deployment of financial resources as an instrument of foreign policy increased dramatically in the 1990s. The inclusion of a separate heading – external action – in the financial perspective (1993–99) highlights the significance of the change. The European Development Fund, which was the Union's main external financial instrument, is no longer centre-stage. The reasons for the change are threefold. First, the Union has a major interest in prosperity and stability throughout the European continent. It has thus had to accord major priority to institutionalising links with the former communist states. Financial assistance through Phare and Tacis constitutes a major component of the Union's external budget. Following the Copenhagen European Council (June 1993), what were 'external' Union objectives have been transformed into 'internal' Union objectives with the prospect of a continental enlargement. Just as enlargements in the past altered the dynamic of budgetary politics in the Union, a widening to the east is set to challenge not just the Union's external policies but the internal budgetary *acquis*. Second, the shift in the centre of gravity towards the east led the Mediterranean member states to draw attention to Europe's southern borders and shores. As a consequence, the Union embarked on an upgrading of its relations with the poorer Mediterranean states, necessitating a substantial increase in financial transfers. Third, the Union is attempting to rebalance its traditional development co-operation policies (Lomé) with a more broadly-based global policy.

Finance plays a more central role in the Union's international profile than it does for the individual member states. Together with trade it provides the Union with a range of foreign policy instruments. In fact given the inevitable difficulties which accompany all trade concessions, financial aid is frequently used as a side payment to disgruntled third parties. The Commission has been innovative in many of its external policies – STABEX, SYSMIN, Phare and Tacis. However, it faces considerable management problems when dealing with the extensive growth of programmes of financial and technical assistance. Staff shortages in the Commission have led to an over-reliance on outside experts and consultants to manage many of the external programmes. This leads to problems of controlling the quality of programmes and ensuring that the Union gets 'value for money' in relation to its external expenditure.

7

Managing the Finances of the Union

The Union's budget of some ECU 80 billion, like the finances of all multi-leveled governance structures, raises particular management challenges. Formally, the Commission is responsible for implementing the budget but, in practice, implementation involves very complex procedures with responsibility widely-scattered between EU-level institutions, central governments, para-governmental agencies, local and regional authorities, private companies and individuals. The analysis of EU finances so far draws attention to the multiplicity of programmes and thousands of individual budgetary lines which give rise to over 400 000 individual authorisations of expenditure and payments each year. The day-to-day implementation of the budget involves the Commission in the management of elaborate application procedures in all its spending directorates, the formal authorisation of expenditure, the clearance of payments and evaluation of how EU monies have been spent. The Commission is at the centre of a vast web of heterogeneous interorganisational and intergovernmental networks stretching from Brussels to the remote corners of the member states and beyond.

This chapter traces the growing salience of management issues in the budgetary politics of the Union. It stems from an awareness at EU level and in the member states of the need to pay more attention to better management. The Commission, Court of Auditors, the Parliament and the Council have all responded to the management issue although there are continuing difficulties of embedding 'value for money' as a norm in the Union. The search for a larger budget has been accompanied by a rising concern with how EU money is spent. Financial management is assuming greater importance in the Union because of the growing size of the budget, the concerns of the net contributors and the politicisation of fraud. Newspaper headlines highlighting fraud, with disappearing wheat, tinned tuna which was not tuna, bags of bones instead of meat in intervention, have undermined public confidence in the management of EU finances.

The management challenge

The Commission is a 'policy innovator' *par excellence* constantly searching for new ideas to enhance the reach of Union policies and to intensify integration. As a 'policy entrepreneur' and 'policy advocate', the Commission is a unique multicultural organisation in the realm of public policy-making. However, the Commission has traditionally been less interested and less capable when it comes to actually implementing programmes and in managing the dispersed delivery systems it has to cope with. In the past, far more political and organisational energy went into expanding the policy remit of the Union than into establishing the administrative and management capacity to actually deliver the programmes. The claim that 'Mr. Delors showed more interest in the big idea than the balance sheet, and never got to grips with managing his own organisation' is difficult to refute (*Financial Times*, 4 April 1995, p. 20). A report by the European Policy Forum, a London think-tank with a minimalist approach to the European project, argues that 'The Commission's lure to spend has always overwhelmed its sense of responsibility for financial discipline. The temptation for the Commission is to put its energies into devising new ways of spending money rather than in the less glamorous function of checking whether existing programmes are meeting their goals and terminating those that do not' (Vibert, 1994, p. 10).

Chapters 5 and 6 bear testimony to the impressive expansion in the policy responsibilities of the Union and in its financial programmes during the 1980s, highlighted by the reach of EU monies in the member states and throughout the globe. However, the expansion in competence has not necessarily been matched by a strengthening of capacity. Metcalfe, one of the few scholars to analyse this issue, concludes that the Commission suffers from a 'management deficit' no less damaging than the more talked about 'democratic deficit'. He argues that:

> Though the EC is distinctive in being more than just an inter-governmental organisation, it is also true that the hard-fought battles over the pace of integration has left quantitative and qualitative questions of administrative capacity unresolved. The form of integration – federal or not – has been the focus of vigorous controversy. The substance of integration – whether there are adequate and appropriate capacities to implement policies effectively – has not received anything like the same attention. (Metcalfe, 1992, p. 118)

Yet the management of EU programmes is critical in the long-term evolution of the Union. The member states must be persuaded that joint programmes are well-managed or they will be unwilling to invest scarce resources in the EU budget. Weak management or evidence of fraud damages the credibility of the Union and its worth in the eyes of the ordinary citizen. The Commission's political authority is undermined if EU funding is seen to be badly-managed or if the Commission adopts a spendthrift approach to financial management.

Although the Commission is solely responsible for the implementation of the EU budget under Article 205 (EEC), it relies on systems of *shared management* largely beyond its control. EU finances are channelled in essentially four different ways. First, the Commission administers some programmes directly, such as the Fourth Framework Programme for Research and Development (R&D) and the European Development Fund (EDF). Second, many of the funds and a high proportion of the budget (80 per cent) are managed by the member states for the Commission. Third, during the 1980s the Commission increasingly used outside consultants, who bid for contracts to manage programmes on its behalf particularly in the education, audio-visual and training fields. This system of external management relied on so-called Technical Assistance Bureaux, known in Brussels parlance as BATs. The latter emerged as an additional and important element in the Union's administrative landscape (see Box 7.1 for a list of the responsibilities of a typical Bureau). BATs were established for the Petra programme (youth exchange), Erasmus (student exchange), Now (training for women), and

---

BOX 7.1
The role of a technical bureau

The Bureau assists the Commission

- To implement the logistics of a programme
- Prepare the calls for proposals
- Assist with the selection process
- Provide administrative and financial management services for various contracts awarded under a programme
- Assist with the spread of information
- Assist in planning, follow-up and evaluation
- Provide internal management and organisational services

Source: European Communities (1994b) Commission tender for technical support for the Leonardo programme, OJ C 245/10, 10 September 1994.

Lingua (language training). Four, the evolution of the Union in the 1980s was accompanied by the creation of many additional specialised agencies, such as the European Monetary Institute, the European Medical Evaluation Agency, and the European Environment Agency which have a major role to play in their respective spheres.

All four spending channels raise different issues of control, management and evaluation for the Union. The Commission services have a limited capacity to implement financial programmes directly because of paltry administrative resources and distance from the beneficiaries. Its grasp of the socio-economic realities of the member states is limited. Hence most programmes are characterised by decentralised management which is supported by the new emphasis on subsidiarity. The Commission works with and through other organisations by establishing administrative networks. Reliance on national authorities is inevitable but problematic since the member states have very different administrative cultures and practices. The capacity of the domestic public services actually to manage the complex task of multi-leveled governance is highly variegated. Moreover, national administrations were not created to administer EU programmes but for other purposes. Involvement in the EU's governance structures frequently disturbs national policy networks, which means that there is a 'management of change' problem for the EU and the member states (Sutherland, 1992).

The management of EU finances relies on the development of administrative and policy partnerships between Brussels and the domestic public services. Yet member states and their representatives may not be that open to the presence of the Commission and the Court of Auditors on their national territory. According to the British Chancellor of the Exchequer, Kenneth Clarke, Ministers are,

> more interested in getting a fair proportion of whatever expenditure it is than they are in all this minutiae which they regard as more important to accountants! The idea that when some particular country has triumphed in obtaining a large allocation of funds for some particular interest group or some particular part of the country, that this might then be followed up with some querying of how the money is then spent in that particular country, is quite strange. (House of Lords, evidence, 6th Report 1994)

National authorities may be unwilling or unable to invest their management resources in EU programmes; weaknesses of national management capacity impair the attainment of European objectives; and the Commission has a limited ability to coerce national authorities into doing its bidding. It relies mainly on persuasion and on creating norms of compliance although the legal framework has been strengthened in recent years. The fostering of partnerships with national bodies requires considerable patience and continuing discussions with national players, the results of which are uncertain.

The development of BATs, as a management tool in the 1980s, was the direct result of the growing number of new programmes administered by the Commission. Faced with staff shortages and administrative overload the Commission came increasingly to rely on external consultants for technical assistance for project management, financial management and computing. BATs allowed the Commission to bypass the lengthy recruitment processes required for in-house staff. In addition, Commission staff tended not to have expertise in the newly-developing concerns such a education, audio-visual and specialist training.

The development of BATs raises a number of important issues for the management of EU finances. First, the BATs appeared very quickly and were not backed by a clearly-articulated rationale; they were a response to programme overload. The remit of various BATs differed one from the other depending on the DG responsible. Second, the relationship between a BAT and the Commission differed considerably. In some cases the Commission maintained tighter control over the BAT than others. Decentralised management by private consultants inevitably raises issues of control over the grant-awarding process, the potential for conflict of interest and the management of policy. As a consequence of the experience with the BATs, the Commission, although not abandoning this management technique, is placing increased emphasis on policy control. The Commission is assisted by two BATs for the new education programmes – Socrates and Leonardo – but with a much narrower remit than the technical bureaux in the past. The tender document clearly stated that the Commission retained sole responsibility for the implementation of Council decisions (European Communities (1994b) September).

Control and accountability: the Schmidhuber testimonial

A former Budget Commissioner, Peter Schmidhuber, who left Brussels in January 1995 at the end of the third Delors presidency, bequeathed a memo on financial management to his successor. The Schmidhuber memo offered a damaging analysis of the Commission's financial management. The memo was widely circulated towards the end of 1994 and was finally tabled at the last meeting of the Delors Commission on 11 January 1995 against the wishes of the Commission president. The Schmidhuber memo concluded that the management of EU finances suffers from a number of important defects, notably:

- Commission departments pay far less attention to the organisation and methods of financial management than to the content of policies;
- Budget planning, although improved with the financial perspective, could be strengthened;
- The implementation of the budget suffers from inadequate preparation, with the result that the bulk of appropriations

are settled just before the end of the financial year in rushed circumstances;

- Commission services depend too much on the Financial Controller to detect breaches of the Financial Regulations;
- There is inadequate evaluation of funding programmes.

(European Commission, 1995g)

The memo provided the incoming Santer Commission with the ammunition it needed to address financial management weaknesses. This task fell to the Finnish Commissioner, Erkki Liikanen, responsible for a reform project within the Commission designed to fundamentally change the management culture.

The formal system of control

The problems of administering a host of financial programmes in a multi-leveled system are matched by equally pressing problems of ensuring that the management systems allow for adequate control and accountability. There are three important criteria with respect to the control phase of the budgetary process:

- ensuring that monies have been legally spent;
- that financial management is sound; and
- that there is adequate evaluation of the added value from EU funding.

A number of different institutions share the task of financial management in the Union Each institution has a financial Controller and a specialised directorate exercising an *internal audit* function. *External audit* is vested in the Court of Auditors, which was established by the 1975 Brussels Treaty. In addition, the Commission created an Anti Fraud Unit (UCLAF) in 1988 (see Box 7.2). Political control is exercised by the Council and the European Parliament in an annual discharge procedure when the latter formally gives or refuses discharge to the Commission for the budget. The rules governing financial management are based on the provisions of the Treaties and a Financial Regulation, subject to revision by *unanimity* in the Council, which is applicable to the general budget and covers all institutions (European Communities, 1990). The financial Regulation is the basic

---

BOX 7.2
The system of financial management in the Union

Internal Audit
Financial Controller in all Institutions

External Audit
Court of Auditors (1977)

Political Control/Supervision
Budgetary Control Committee European Parliament
Parliament's Discharge to the Commission
Temporary Committees of Inquiry which may examine financial
matters
Council review of Court of Auditor's reports

UCLAF
Commission's Anti-Fraud Unit (1988)

---

operating text for all financial officers, the Court of Auditors, and
the spending services.

Financial management in the Commission

The control of the budget falls to DG 20 (Financial Control) and
specialised budget units in the spending directorates. The
SINCOM computer system provides budget managers with management information about the availability of appropriations both
for commitments and payments. Budget units in the various
Commission services differ greatly in their size and function
depending on the scale of the financial resources to be managed
and the traditions of the particular DGs. These units have 545
staff to manage an annual budget of some ECU 80 billion; staffing
has tended not to increase in line with the expansion of the
budget. The functions of the units are to produce annual budget
estimates, to monitor the implementation of appropriations
during the budgetary cycle and to maintain contact with the
major financial DGs 19 and 20. The budget units have few A
grade (official level) staff and are not seen as attractive place-
ments for career advancement; this causes difficulties in filling

vacancies. The status of the budget units is indicative of the fact that financial management has traditionally not been a valued part of the culture of the Commission.

DG 20, Financial Control, is the responsibility of the Financial Controller, an officer with designated tasks in the Financial Regulation. The main characteristic of the financial system is the need for prior approval of all commitments of money and payments of amounts owed. Without prior approval or a 'visa' as it is known, EU monies cannot be committed or paid out. The granting or withholding of a visa follows well-established procedures in spending services and in DG 20. The following criteria govern the granting of a visa:

1. That expenditure has been charged to the correct item;
2. That appropriations are available;
3. That expenditure is in order;
4. That the principles of sound financial management have been applied (European Communities, 1990, Article 38).

If the Financial Controller refuses a visa, his or her decision can be overturned, and sometimes is, by the Commission as a whole. Paradoxically, the impact of prior approval on the culture of financial management in the Commission is that spending directorates tend to neglect their responsibility for ongoing financial management. Once the 'visa' hurdle has been overcome, the spending directorates do not give priority to managing their budgetary lines. Because financial control is fragmented between DG 19 (Budgets), DG20 (Financial Control) and the spending directorates, responsibility is diluted. The Schmidhuber memo concluded that the 'authorising Commission departments rely heavily on the Financial Controller to detect any breaches of the Financial Regulation and to make the necessary corrections' (European Commission, 1995g).

In an effort to keep up with the explosion in the number of financial transactions, DG 20, with just 210 staff, is in the process of modernising and rationalising its style of control. Instead of looking at the dossiers on all transactions, this Directorate is concentrating on systems audit and the sampling of individual transactions. By analysing the systems that generate the transactions, Financial Control reduces the number of dossiers it must examine. A number of serious frauds which were masterminded from within the Commission services, notably in the tobacco division of DG 6 and the tourism unit, have forced DG 90 ⸱˗ ˪xamine the internal systems of controls more ⸱ˡ˻˻˪⸱y. Since 1990, DG 20 has carried out detailᵉ˙ ᶠ˻˻˻˻ıaı audits of the big-spending services on the basis of a rolling plan and conducted 'on the spot checks' in the member states. Seminars for in-house staff as well as national officials are a growing part of the work of DG 20 given that 80 per cent of the budget is channelled through national agencies.

In 1990, DG 20 established a small unit that would be responsible for 'cost effectiveness and cost-benefit studies' in response to Article 2 of the revised Financial Regulation which stipulated that budget appropriations must be used 'in accordance with the principles of sound financial management and in particular those of economy and cost effectiveness' (European Communities, 1990, Article 2). The unit, which is becoming more central in DG 20, is part of a continuing effort to alter the culture of financial management in the Commission, to get Commission staff thinking not just about the disbursement of moneys but its use as well. This it does through working with the spending departments, producing reports on evaluation techniques, and holding seminars. The unit works closely with DG 19 during budgetary hearings and is attempting to move the financial controllers from compliance-management to performance-management. This is a difficult task given the traditional emphasis on regularity rather than 'value for money' considerations.

Notwithstanding the growing concern with sound financial management, the former Budget Commissioner, Schmidhuber baldly concluded that 'The principle of sound financial management stated in Article 2 of the Financial Regulation and stressed repeatedly by the Court of Auditors is not acknowledged as a general maxim' in the Commission (European Commission, 1995g). The new Santer Commission, in contrast to the Delors Commissions of the past, has taken up the challenge left by the Schmidhuber memo. Sound financial management and combating fraud were recurring themes during the Parliamentary hearings on the new Commission. President Santer's interest in financial management stems partly from his long-standing connections with members of the Court of Auditors when he was Prime Minister of Luxembourg and partly from a desire to mark out a distinctive role for the new Commission.

The reform project

The new Commission President moved quickly to tackle the problem of financial management when he arrived in Brussels in January 1995. In his first proposals to the new Commission, President Santer got the approval of the College of Commissioners to three provisions concerning financial management. First, it was agreed that documents with implications for expenditure should not be distributed to the College without the approval of the Budget Commissioner unless specifically authorised by the President. This provision enhances the authority of the Budget Commissioner. Second, the staffing implications of all proposals have to be included in the financial statement to ensure that the Commission had the capacity and not just the willingness to carry out new programmes. Third, the College requested the Budget Commissioner to submit a report on how financial management might be reinforced in the Commission (European Commission, 1995h).

Commissioner Liikanen followed up with a report drafted in collaboration with the Swedish Commissioner, Anita Gradin, who has responsibility for combating fraud. The reform report was submitted to the Commission in March 1995 and further elaborated on in reports issued in June and November. These reports provide a broad overview of the strategy that is being adopted for the reform project entitled *2000 – Sound and Efficient Management*, which has as its stated aim a 'substantial and lasting reform of financial management culture' in the Commission (European Commission, 1995i). The March report was essentially a stocktaking exercise with strong echoes of the original Schmidhuber memo. The essential message is that the Commission's management of EU finances had not kept pace with the substantial increase in the size of the budget. The Commission's internal organisation, financial procedures and the pattern of management had remained largely unchanged despite its burgeoning financial responsibilities. The reports reverberate with phrases like 'reform-mindness', 'reform of financial management culture', and 'the Commission as a manager of public money' (European Commission, 1995i)

The Commission agreed to tackle the reform project on a phased basis to enable it to generate evidence of change quickly; this would then act as an impetus for a lasting improvement of the underlying management culture.

- *Phase 1* deals with the consolidation of the existing system within the Commission to show that it is willing and able to carry out the reform process.
- *Phase 2* aims at a substantial reform of the financial manage-ment culture within the Commission, including internal reorganisation and possible changes in the Financial Regulation. This phase aims at deeper reform within the Commission and may entail changes in the Financial Regulation which require unanimity in the Council.
- *Phase 3* is concerned with the operation of the system as a whole – execution, audit and control – including the management of EU funds by national authorities. The main emphasis is on closer partnerships with the member states where they are responsible for Community funds.

(European Commission, 1995j)

The elaboration of phase 1 is well-advanced in the Commission and involves the relevant Commissioners and a high-level re-stricted working party (Director General level). The working group consists of representatives of the horizontal services (DG 19, 20 and 9) involved in managing EU finances and representa-tives of three operational services.

The Commission adopted all of the main recommendations of the Phase 1 report on 21 June 1995. The aim of the reform project is to:

- Simplify financial management procedures;
- Enhance the evaluation and cost-effectiveness of Community programmes;
- Undertake practical action to follow up observations of the Court of Auditors and the observations of the Council and Parliament.

Decisions on the first phase in June 1995 were followed by detailed orientations in July and further measures agreed in November highlighting the intensity of activity in this field since the Santer Commission took office in January 1995.

As a first step, the Commission has decided that all DGs must have a specialist budget and financial unit reporting directly to the highest level in the DG to ensure that there is a uniform financial management culture within the Commission. The Director General or a deputy must take budgetary matters more seriously than in the past because they will have direct responsibility for the proposed budget units. According to Commissioner Liikanen, 'the personnel in the financial units of all DGs have to form a network of professionals who are able to set up the same standards for financial management in all parts of the Commission' (European Commission, 1995k). The EP is supporting the Commission by agreeing to the establishment of eight new A2 posts for financial management in the Commission. The responsibilities of these units/divisions must include an enhanced control function and more extensive contact with other Commission DGs and the external auditing bodies. The purpose of this proposal is to decentralise responsibility within the Commission to ensure that each DG actually assumes responsibility for its funds and does not rely too heavily on DG 20 for financial management. Organisational change is accompanied by a renewed emphasis on the training of staff with financial responsibilities, an updating of management information systems and a rationalisation of the financial procedures within the Commission. The last is concerned with speeding up the notoriously slow payment procedures and ensuring that all budgetary procedures are adhered to. See Box 7.3 for the detailed provisions of the reform project.

The Commission has decided to hold a budgetary policy debate each January to established financial priorities before the services engage in preparing their annual wish-list. The purpose of this debate is to enable the College of Commissioners to establish political priorities for the annual budget. The Commission has also required that the full cost of any proposed programme be submitted to it before it decides on new programmes. It is particularly insistent that the personnel requirements be adequately planned (European Commission, 1995l).

BOX 7.3
The Commission's reform project

Financial management

Phase 1 reform project

Budget units
1. All DGs must have one reporting directly to DG or deputy DG.
2. No outside staff except national experts.
3. Priority use of lists to fill vacant posts.
4. Organisation of specialist competitions to get trained staff.
5. Enhanced training for staff.

Responsibility of staff
1. Rotation of staff in sensitive positions involving contracts.
2. Upgrading the financial function for career development.

Procedures
1. Increased frequency of ACPC meetings on contracts.
2. Production of lists of contracts awarded.
3. Standardised tender notices.
4. Annual budget estimates, staff allocation and revision of internal budgetary rules to begin earlier each year.

Response to EP and Court of Auditors
1. Debate by College of Commissioners.
2. Increased involvement of senior officials.
3. More factual replies from departments.

Management instruments
1. Simpler management instruments.
2. Single manual of financial rules and procedures.
3. Modernisation of SINCOM.
4. Checklist of procedures for authorising officers.

Source: EU Commission (1995j) *Report on Improvement of Financial Management: Phase 1*, 1 Sec(95) 1013/5, 21 June 1995.

Evaluation and value for money

Enhancing budgetary control and accountability responds to only one dimension of the Union's management problems. Far more difficult is to ensure that EU finances are not wasted on the wrong things. EU spending priorities emerge from the functional requirements of integration and political bargaining about how scarce resources should be spent. In each spending programme, notions of 'value for money' come face to face with the demands of different member states and groups within them, all jostling for a slice of the Brussels pie. Ensuring that public expenditure conforms to the norm of 'value for money' is common to all budgets, be they national or European. It is difficult to establish priorities for public expenditure when faced with competing demands, and difficult to ensure that once priorities are established that money is spent wisely and well. The work of the analyst and evaluator comes face to face with the realities of politics.

The Commission reform project intends to go beyond sound financial management to issues of value for money and the value added by EU funding. The emphasis in the report on evaluation and the spread of an *evaluation culture* throughout the Commission is striking. The report insists that there must be an *ex ante* evaluation of all multi-annual programmes, followed by systems to monitor programme implementation and *ex post* evaluation of the results of programmes. In the process of preparing the Preliminary Draft Budget, DG 19 has been mandated to enhance the link between budget allocation and evaluation. An inventory of programming, evaluation and monitoring systems used by the Commission has been undertaken and a group of external experts are helping to establish a vade mecum for the evaluation of Community expenditure. The Commission intends to establish an interdepartmental network of evaluators and to train policy staff in evaluation techniques.

The need for a system of evaluating and monitoring EU spending programmes has been conventional wisdom in the Commission for many years. The legal framework of all spending programmes specifies the need for studies, evaluation and technical assistance to improve the effectiveness of programmes. The experimental nature of many EU policies implies a need to revise strategies and objectives on a phased basis. Second, the Commission in its search for greater autonomy and control over EU programmes, must be open to reform and must prove that it has not wasted money. Third, evaluation perpetuates an image of efficiency, rationality and accountability. It has an important ritualistic role in any organisation and is particularly important for an organisation that engages in extensive policy innovation.

Evaluation can contribute to policy-oriented learning in many important respects.

The report adopts a very rationalistic approach to evaluation, although evaluation is inherently political because it is designed to 'yield conclusions about the worth of programmes and in so doing, is intended to affect the allocation of resources' (Weiss, 1970, p. 56). The multicultural and multinational character of the Union complicates evaluation. Definitive answers about the worth of public programmes are elusive to say the least. Academic consultants employed to devise a methodology for assessing Social Fund expenditure highlighted a number of diverse problems including multiple objectives, the tailoring of national programmes to meet EU eligibility criteria, problems with the quality of statistical information and the difficulty of ensuring that evaluation is seriously taken into account at the planning stage of new programmes (Planas and Casal, 1994, p. 32). The Commission has some considerable way to go before evaluation is an integral part of budgetary allocation.

Relations with the Court of Auditors

The final section of the reform report deals with the vexed question of relations with the Court of Auditors and the Commission's response to the observations of the Court. Relations between the Court and the Commission reached their nadir in 1993 when the Commission President, Jacques Delors wrote to the President of the Court, Mr André Middelhoek, upbraiding him for his comments on the Structural Funds. President Santer, building on his contacts in Luxembourg, is determined to improve relations between the Court and the Commission. The reform report confirms new internal Commission guidelines on relations with the Court which include greater participation by senior officials in improving the quality of responses to the Court, the organisation of an in-depth discussion on each annual report and the involvement of members of the Commission itself in meetings with the Court. President Santer has clearly and quickly indicated that he accords a high priority to improving relations with the external audit authority. The Budget Commissioner, Mr Liikanen, has devoted considerable time to maintaining close links with the

Court of Auditors. That said, relations between those carrying out expenditure programmes and external auditors are inevitably tense and sometimes hostile.

Attention in the Commission is moving to the more sensitive but crucial part of the Reform Project, namely phase 3, which involves relations between the Commission and the member states. The Commission has adopted a strategy of working with the Court of Auditors in an attempt to get the member states to pay more attention to the management dimension of the budgetary process. The focus is on structured discussions with the national authorities and a new partnership between the Commission and the member states. This echoes Commission strategy concerning the implementation of Community law and the management of the internal market. The Commission has established a high-level group of personal representatives of Ministers of Finance and Budget under the chairmanship of a member of the Commission, to identify priority actions which need to be taken to ensure effective budget execution. The Commission can expect to find considerable support from the net contributors, concerned about the use of EU finances.

External audit: the European Court of Auditors

The European Court of Auditors, one of the lesser-known EU institutions, is located on the Kirchberg Plateau in Luxembourg, with the Court of Justice and the European Investment Bank. The Court was described as the 'financial conscience' of the Union by the President of the Court of Justice, Mr H. Kutscher, at the time of its inauguration in October 1977. The decision to establish an independent audit authority in the 1975 Brussels Treaty was part of the change in budgetary procedures which gave the European Parliament the exclusive power to grant the Commission a *discharge* for its management of the annual budget on the basis of a recommendation from the Council. The Court was appointed as an organ of the Community and not as a fully-fledged institution.

Before 1975 the audit function was carried out by what was called the European Audit Board, a committee of representatives of national audit boards which met infrequently to give an opinion on the financial control practices of EU institutions. The

Audit Board had limited access to Commission files and no control over the national agencies that spent EU monies. The external audit function suffered from inherent weaknesses that rendered its work purely symbolic. Given the growing size of the budget and the development of 'own resources', there was a growing realisation of the need to ensure that EU monies were collected in a transparent and correct manner. Moreover, the discharge authority had to base its assessment on evidence collected by an independent external audit authority. A German MEP, Mr Aigner, published a report, *The Case for a European Audit Office*, in 1973 which was very influential in placing the question of external audit on the agenda (European Parliament, 1973).

Although agreement was reached on the desirability of a European audit authority, there was considerable confusion about its organisation, role and function in the Union system. Weighty debate ensued about its composition; whether it should consist of a single auditor, a small committee of three or a collegiate body. In the end the tradition of national representation in EU institutions more generally, led to the establishment of a Court with one member per state although there is no legal requirement that members have the nationality of one of the member states. That said, each enlargement has brought additional members to the Court so that at present it has 15 members.

Members of the Court are appointed by the Council acting unanimously after consulting the European Parliament. The Parliament gives its opinion on individual nominations, in contrast with the situation that pertains to the appointment of the Commission. The EP has given negative opinions on nominations in the past. The Treaty specifies that nominees to the Court must be independent and may have belonged to the external audit offices of their member states or be 'specially qualified' for the office. The latter provision allows the member states to nominate non-professional auditors to the Court such as politicians, lawyers or civil servants. The varied backgrounds of the members is sometimes a source of tension within the Court between those who come from an audit background, those who are excessively legalistic, or former politicians who may find it difficult to make the transition to the highly-technical field of auditing. On balance, the presence of some former politicians is an advantage since the Court finds itself in a highly-politicised institutional environment.

Six of the current 15 Members have political backgrounds in the European Parliament, national parliaments, public accounts committees or ministerial experience at national or EU level.

The status of the Court

The Treaty on European Union made a number of important changes to the legal framework for budgetary and financial matters. New measures include inserting the principle of budgetary discipline into the Treaty and the first mention of the Financial Controller (Article 201a); the stipulation that the Commission follow the principles of sound financial management (Article 205); and references to protecting the financial interests of the Community (Article 209a). As part of the drive for better financial management, the Treaty removed the Court of Auditors from the category of 'other bodies' and raised it to the status of a full institution of the Community (Article 4). This elevation enhances the authority of the Court and gives it equality of status *vis-a-vis* the institutions it audits. The granting of institutional status to the Court has not been met with unrestrained enthusiasm by the other institutions. Some members of Parliament's Budgetary Control Committee feel that there should be an organic link between the Court as audit authority and the European Parliament as discharge authority. This would allow the Parliament to have a greater say over the work programme of the Court and would allow it to call on the services of the Court at will.

The internal organisation of the Court

The Court is both a collegiate body of 15 members who take decisions by majority voting and a bureaucracy of professional auditors. The College elects a president for a term of three years which may be renewable. The president is no more than *primus inter pares* with no special prerogatives, and he relies for his authority on the backing of the College. The President in public speaks on behalf of the College and presents the annual report to the European Parliament and the Council. The president's role is to mould the College into a cohesive group with an agreed work programme, something that has not always been easy to achieve.

Joe Carey, a former British member of the Court who retired in 1992, publicly stated that the institution was often like a 'rudderless ship' (*Financial Times*, 19 November 1994). In an effort to strengthen collegiality, the members of the Court work as part of audit groups within which individual members are responsible for distinct aspects of EU financial activity. The groundwork for the annual report and the Court's other activities is carried out by the audit groups. Notwithstanding the existence of these groups, individual members have considerable autonomy in their respective responsibilities (see Box 7.4). What is regarded as the top-heavy structure of the Court is criticised by some members of the Budgetary Control Committee in the Parliament and by the internal auditing staff of the Court. The Court has a staff of 500, only half of whom are involved directly with the audit function. Since the Court is a multinational body, considerable staffing resources are vested in language and support staff, and each member of the Court has a cabinet consisting of two personal assistants. There are 90 staff engaged in the translation services.

BOX 7.4
Internal organisation of the Court of Auditors

The President of the Court
General Secretariat

Audit Group 1: EAGGF – crops, EAGGF – management and budgetary control procedures, EAGGF – markets (livestock, sugar, fisheries).

Audit Group 2: Regional policy, tourism, transport, cohesion fund, social sector, guidance section EAGGF, ECSC, borrowing and lending, East Central Europe.

Audit Group 3: European Development Funds, administrative expenditure of the institutions, 'own resources', co-operation with third countries, excluding Eastern Europe.

ADAR Group: Co-ordination of annual report, auditing standards, work programme, audit manual.

Statement of Assurance Group: Implementation of statement of assurance, relations with the member states and national audit offices.

Source: *1994 Directory of EC Information Sources* (Brussels: Euroconfidential) 1995, pp. 37–8.

The work of the Court

One of the most difficult tasks faced by the Court of Auditors when it began work in July 1977 was to decide its approach to the audit function. This was highly problematic because its members came from very different national audit traditions and some of them had no previous auditing experience (Keemer, 1985). The Court had to slowly, and with considerable difficulty, formulate its own approach (Kok, 1989, pp. 353–5). External audit is concerned with two different facets of financial transactions:

- A concern with the *legality* and *regularity* of financial transactions; and
- A concern with questions of *value for money*.

National audit traditions differ greatly in the emphasis they place on the procedural aspects of the financial system, on the one hand, and the more difficult questions about 'value for money' on the other. North European audit practices are concerned with both aspects of financial management, whereas the Mediterranean countries place greater emphasis on regularity and legality. Once correct procedures have been followed and the paperwork is in order, the auditors are satisfied. They do not consider that their role involves judgements about the use of public monies.

The legal mandate of the Court embraces a broad definition of external audit by stating that the Court of Auditors:

> ... shall examine whether all revenue has been received and all expenditure incurred in a lawful and regular manner and whether the financial management has been sound.
>
> (TEU, Article 188c)

The Court itself, in its internal working procedures, opted for an approach that embraced compliance, a central feature of all auditing processes, and financial management defined as involving 'value for money' considerations. However, it did not define what it meant by 'value for money'. The second important decision that the Court took at an early stage was to concentrate on a *systems* approach to auditing, which aimed to ensure that the systems governing financial transactions were sound. The purpose of the audit is to examine 'whether and to what extent the system itself includes efficient controls to safeguard and ensure that the objectives of the legislative authority have been realised in an economic, efficient and effective way, and to examine where the system fails and what caused this failure (Kok, 1989, p. 355). The auditing approach adopted by the Court sat uneasily with its collegiate and top-heavy nature. One scholar concluded that the Court was a 'body with a Southern European structure and a Northern European remit' (Ó Halpin, 1988).

The work of the Court is based on an annual programme within a multi-annual cycle of four years that includes the production of an Annual Report each year, Special Reports on particular policies or forms of expenditure, and Opinions that are issued on the financial regulations and other matters. Between 1989 and 1995, the Court produced 96 reports including five annual reports. The contents of the reports are based on an evaluation of the financial systems, detailed control tests, and tests of the underlying transactions based on a sampling procedure. In addition, the Court carries out comprehensive audits of sections of budgetary management, including a financial audit and a sound financial management audit. Until the TEU, the Court did not, however, have to give an account of the accuracy of the accounts. In line with its elevation to the status of a full institution, the Court is now required to provide the Parliament and the Council with a 'Statement of Assurance' as to the 'reliability of the accounts and the legality and regularity of the underlying transactions' (Article 188c). This implies an expansion in the work of the Court and a change in its working methods, discussed further below.

Although reports are the most visible part of the Court's work, its opinions may be requested by other EU institutions. In 1983 the Stuttgart European Council asked the Court to draft a review on the sound financial management of Community activities. The report covered all the main expenditure programmes – EAGGF, Structural Funds and Development Assistance – highlighting the main weaknesses in the financial systems and recommending improvements. The themes raised in the report reflected the Court's concerns that had been frequently expressed in a succession of annual reports about the Community's financial systems. The Court's findings were not even discussed by the Council and no follow-up taken (Kok, 1989, p. 358).

When the Council was discussing the Delors II package in 1992, it again requested an Opinion from the Court on EU spending. While the Court acknowledged that there had been improvements made in budgetary discipline and the reform of the structural funds, it persisted with its identification of administrative and financial shortcomings. The most important conclusions of the report were:

- That the Community budget remained vulnerable to unforeseen fluctuations in agricultural expenditure;
- That Commission initiatives aimed at eliminating the worst excesses of overproduction had been blunted by the member states;
- That Community-led co-ordination of the structural funds was inadequate;
- That the partnership system had many failings;
- That even minimal additionality was not assured. (European Court of Auditors, 1992)

These conclusions were used by those opposing a doubling of the structural funds during the Delors II negotiations, to Jacques Delors' great ire. Notwithstanding Delors' response to the 1992 report, the views of the Court of Auditors were strongly echoed in the Schmidhuber memo.

The annual report

The production of an annual report within a very tight timescale, for presentation to the European Parliament and the Council in the year following the budgetary year being audited, forms a central part of the work of the Court. The annual report, a weighty tome running to over 450 pages, consists of three parts:

Part 1: Detailed chapters on different internal and external spending programmes;

Part 2: Observations on different kinds of administrative expenditure (travelling allowances and expenditure on buildings);

Part 3: The Commission's replies to the Court.

The report is drafted in an iterative fashion by the auditors, the cabinets and members of the Court, and the full Court based on draft reports, that wind their way through the different stages of the process. A special division in the Court (Audit Development and Reports) ADAR, is responsible for co-ordinating the work of the annual audit and ensuring that a timetable is adhered to.

The Court has adopted a procedure of having a *contre rapporteur* for each section of the annual report to ensure that no one member of the Court considers a particular functional area to be his or her exclusive mandate. Once the full Court has produced a draft, the observations are discussed with the Commission in a procedure (commonly known as the 'contradictory procedure') to allow the Commission to reply to the Court and to ensure that there is agreement on the facts. The 'contradictory procedure' normally involves meetings between the responsible auditors and members of the cabinet with the relevant Commission staff, but Court Members and Commissioners also participate as necessary. Once this process has reached a conclusion, the final report is drafted, including the Commission's comments, and is presented to the European Parliament and the Council in November of each year. The president of the Court presents the annual report to the Parliament in November and this represents the culmination of the annual cycle. The annual report receives extensive media coverage throughout the member states.

The purpose of the audit process and the annual report is to draw particular attention to failures and weaknesses in the management of EU resources and to propose improvements. The House of Lords Select Committee on the European Communities, in a very important report on the work of the Court, concluded that:

> Even with its limited existing resources, the Court of Auditors has drawn attention on numerous occasions to weaknesses in administration, failure to exercise adequate control and other grave irregularities. (House of Lords Report, 1989, para. 179)

Each annual report is a catalogue of questions about weaknesses in the financial management systems. The Court felt compelled to conclude in its 1993 report that many of the problems it identified in the Stuttgart Report in 1983 have not yet been overcome.

The statement of assurance

The decision to include a *statement of assurance* of the Court of Auditors in the TEU alongside the annual report may well radically alter the work of the Court over time. The statement of assurance obliges the Court to give the Parliament and the Council an assurance that the transactions underlying the budget are legal and regular. The Court must satisfy itself that the accounts are reliable. If the Court finds that the accounts are not reliable it can refuse to give the assurance or may give only a partial assurance. In contrast to the situation before the TEU, when the Court simply reported on the planned programmes of audit that went into the annual report, the Court must take a position on the accounts. If it cannot give an assurance it will have to clearly state why this is not the case. It has taken a long time and considerable effort by the Court to decide what the statement of assurance means and how it should go about carrying out its mandate in this respect. The 1994 budget was the first attempt to carry out the work related to this task.

The need to deliver a statement of assurance has meant a fundamental rethinking of the working methods of the Court. First, it has had to adapt its sampling techniques to ensure that it reviews a representative sample. Second, the volume of tests that must be carried out to gauge the accuracy of the accounts for the budget as a whole is much greater than anything the Court has undertaken in the past. Third, the auditors will have to follow the audit trail of its selected tests right down to the final beneficiaries of Community funding; this implies that the Court has to carry out much more extensive auditing in the member states than heretofore. It is often very difficult for the Court to gain access to the necessary financial data on individual transactions because of the complexities of the multi-leveled delivery system. In the longer term, the Court would like to work more closely with national audit offices and to be able to rely on their auditing work as part of the statement of assurance process. This is a highly-sensitive matter and it will take time to move from the current agreed process of liaison with national audit institutions to an auditing partnership between the Court of Auditors and the national level.

The *statement of assurance* is still largely experimental. The Budgetary Control Committee of the Parliament recommended that it be given 40 new staff to assist it with the inevitable increase in its workload. Within the Court, the statement of assurance is the responsibility of a member of the Court, but it must in the end be the collective responsibility of the entire College. The audit divisions have had to reorientate their work, and there is some tension between this work and 'value for money' audits, the other major part of the Court's mandate. While the official position is that the statement of assurance does not reduce the resources directed at 'value for money' considerations, individual auditors claim that the increased workload will result in less auditing of sound financial management.

The Court issued its report on the first statement of assurance in November 1995 at the same time as it published the annual report. The Court concluded that its investigations of Community revenue did not reveal any significant errors, but it was unable to give a positive assurance about the payments side of the budget because there were too many errors in the transactions underlying payments. Based on the results of the sampling process, the Court concluded that errors in the amount paid out of the budget amounted to between ECU 1500–3700 million or between 2.9 per cent and 5 per cent of total payments. In addition to these errors, the Court could not give an assurance on a further 14 per cent of payments (European Court of Auditors, 1995a, *Statement of Assurance*, November 1995, p. 81). Not surprisingly, the Court found the most serious errors in the EAGGF and structural fund expenditure. Moreover, the report concluded that the problems 'originate most often in bodies in the member states responsible for the administration of Community expenditure programmes' (ibid., p. 82). The Commission accepted the conclusions of the Court because the report acknowledged the Commission's attempts to improve financial management and further emphasised the role of the member states in the management of EU finances. The Commission draws a distinction between formal errors which occur in the Commission and what it calls substantial errors which occur at the level of the member states.

Relations between the Commission and the Court of Auditors

As a consequence of the statement of assurance work, the Court's relationship with the Commission is even more critical than in the past because of the need to gain speedy access to significantly more extensive Commission documentation. The Court's relations with other EU institutions (the auditees) inevitably involves a certain tension since the external audit function is designed to highlight weakness and absence of performance rather than to praise achievement. Given that the Commission is responsible for implementing the largest volume of EU finances, this is an important and difficult relationship for both partners. Relations were poor for many years. An early controversy broke out over the format of the annual report and the insertion of the replies of the institutions. The Court maintained for itself a right to 'the last word' concerning the observations of the audited institutions. The public controversy damaged relations for many years and was exacerbated by the attitude of the Budget Commissioner, Christopher Tugendhat, who was in office until 1984. Mr Tugendhat made no secret of his disregard for the Court and its work. In his evidence to the House of Lords Select Committee in 1989, Commissioner Tugendhat maintained that the Court had made two big mistakes in considering that the Parliament,

> was going to be a much more important institution than it turned out to be and that its principle interlocutor was the European parliament and in particular the Committee on Budgetary Control ... the second was that ... it strove after publicity and attention. (House of Lords, 1989, Tugendhat evidence, p. 37)

The claim that the Court concentrated on 'Sunday newspaper' issues and played politics reverberated in Commission attitudes towards the Court in the early 1980s and can still be heard in the corridors of the Commission.

Gradually the Court and the Commission established a *modus vivendi*, and the sense of open warfare was toned down as the Commission came to terms with the presence of the Court and recognised that it served a useful purpose in the Community (House of Lords, 1989, Pratley evidence, p. 59). As the Court gained more experience and more resources, the quality of its audit improved. The Commission is still concerned that the Court opts for eye-catching issues to publicise its work and has never fully come to terms with the 'value for money' approach which brings the Court into policy issues – the domain of the policy-making branch of the Union.

In the latter years of the Delors presidency, relations between the Court and the Commission appeared to deteriorate again when in 1989 the Commission refused to give information on cases where the Commission overruled its Financial Controller. President Delors was also antagonised by the views expressed by the Court on the structural funds during the negotiations on the Delors II package. The publication of the 1993 annual report in November 1994 caused further disharmony. This annual report was accompanied by an information note highlighting its most salient findings and drawing attention to the most important weaknesses in relation to spending in East Central Europe, the wine regime, and the failure of the European Parliament to enforce competitive tenders for its Brussels building programme. The report was taken up by the press and received extensive coverage across the member states, particularly in the UK where it coincided with the Parliamentary debate on the increase in 'own resources'. Bill Cash MP, a leading Conservative Euro-sceptic, seized on the report to argue that the 'British tax payers were contributing to a bottomless fraudulent pit' (*Financial Times*, 16 November 1994, p. 1). The Commission, because of the public-ity given to the Report, was quick to reply by pointing out that the Court's résumé of the 482 page report was neither comprehensive nor balanced. It was concerned that the report had been used to highlight fraud when in fact fraud was mentioned only once in the entire report. The Commission sought to point out that it was dependent on the Council to establish clear objectives for policy, and that the member states themselves had to tackle issues rela-ting to financial management and the protection of the Union's financial interests (European Commission, 1994e).

The Santer Commission has made improved relations with the Court of Auditors a central plank of its work programme. President Santer maintains regular contact with the president of the Court of Auditors, whereas Jacques Delors rarely met the current president of the Court. Individual Commissioners and the Directors General now take part in the Commission/Court of Auditors adversarial procedure. This upgrading of relations with the Court of Auditors is part of the Commission strategy discussed above.

The discharge procedure

The Court's relations with the Council and the European Parliament take place within the context of the so-called *discharge procedure*, whereby the Parliament has the power to grant or refuse the Commission a discharge for its implementation of the budget, based on a recommendation of the Council. The Commission is legally obliged to take into account the Parliament's discharge resolutions. The resolution is binding on the Commission which must make its best efforts to deal with the shortcomings identified in the discharge resolution. The procedure takes place in the second year following the completion of the budgetary year in question, usually at the April plenary. The procedure is managed internally in the Parliament by the Budgetary Control Committee established in 1979, which shares many members with the traditionally more powerful and prestigious Budget Committee. It could well be that the changing atmosphere in the Union on financial management may strengthen the role of the Committee on Budgetary Control to become more of an equal with the Budget Committee. The Committee on Budgetary Control examines the court's annual report and its special reports are part of its preparations for the discharge procedure. The Committee drafts a discharge report for each budget year based on the findings of the Court of Auditors. The *rapporteur* for the report and the chairman of the Committee have considerable influence over the approach to the discharge and the issues that are likely to be tackled. Individual members of the Committee are given the responsibility to monitor different spending programmes.

Contact between the Court of Auditors and the Budgetary Control Committee have always been substantial, because the latter relies to a large extent on the output of the Court. The Court assists the Parliament in the discharge process. Unlike the conflict-ridden relations with the Commission in the early years, the Court settled, from the outset, into a stable and co-operative relationship with the Parliament. Paradoxically, as relations with the Commission become more amicable, tension between the Court and the Budgetary Control Committee grew.

An EP report concluded that 'relations between the Court of Auditors and Parliament have sometimes shown signs of strain' (European Parliament, 1993). Some in the Parliament are resentful that the Court has been elevated to the status of a full institution which puts it on a par with the Parliament and does not allow the Parliament to require that the Court give priority to the Parliament's requests for assistance. However, whenever the Budget Control Committee or the Parliament's Plenary pass a resolution urging the Court to undertake a special report, for example on EAGGF expenditure in Portugal, these requests are responded to by the Court. The Court and the Parliament have agreed to work together in devising their respective work programmes and the Court has agreed to ensure that the Parliament receives Court reports before the press does. Notwithstanding procedural innovations, a certain inter-institutional rivalry is apparent.

Failure to grant a discharge to the Commission should on the face of it be an extremely powerful weapon in the hands of the Parliament. In 1977, the then Budget Commissioner, Christopher Tugendhat, concluded that failure to grant a discharge would necessitate the resignation of the Commission. In fact, when the Parliament refused the discharge in 1984 in respect of the 1982 budget, Mr Tugendhat did not resign nor did the Thorn Commission because it was within weeks of leaving office anyway. Had the Commission resigned, it would have given greater substance to the Parliament's formal budgetary control powers. As it is, it remains unclear what would happen if the Parliament again refused a discharge.

The Parliament postponed its decision on the discharge for the 1992 Budget in 1994 because of continuing conflict about the application of the milk quota scheme in Spain, Greece and Italy between 1989 and 1992. The three member states failed to apply the milk quota scheme and failed to collect the superlevy for a prolonged period. Successive Court of Auditor reports documented the blatant disregard for Community law. Concerning Spain and Italy, the Court of Auditors concluded that:

> Italy had not assigned individual quotas to farmers or dairies nor had it established figures for milk production per farmer or per dairy. Therefore, it was not in a position to collect the

superlevy. In regard to Spain, although it has assigned quotas
to producers, the collection of the levy was not enforced.
(European Court of Auditors, 1993, p. 48)

When this came to light during the annual clearance of the
EAGGF accounts, the Commission imposed substantial financial
corrections on the member states (ECU 536 million) which contested the decision and sought to have their milk quotas increased
and applied on a retroactive basis. In an attempt to solve the
problem politically, given intense pressure from the three member
states, the Commission devised a milk buy-back scheme for Italy
and Spain without any legal basis. The Commission's Financial
Controller refused a visa for the draft decision because he considered that the retroactive provisions were illegal. His decision was
overruled by the College of Commissioners, a decision that the
European Parliament denounced in the following terms:

> ... Deplores the Commission decision to overrule its Financial
> Controller's refusal of approval of a decision amending the de-
> cision concerning the clearance of EAGGF-Guarantee accounts
> for the 1989 budget, in respect of milk quotas to one Member
> State.
> Questions the independence of the Commission within the
> meaning of the Treaties from outside political pressures in up-
> holding the interests of the Community taxpayer in general.
> (European Parliament, 1994a)

The Parliament finally granted the discharge of the 1992 accounts in 1995, at the same time as the discharge for the 1993
accounts when the Commission and the Council removed the
most damaging aspects of decisions taken to deal with the milk
quota conflict. The Parliament did so with great reluctance
when stating that the 'Commission had continued to act in a
manner more compatible with the interests of certain Member
States and the political convenience of the Council than with
those of the Community budget and therefore of the
Community taxpayer at large' (European Parliament, 1995a).
This case underlies very clearly why deliberate abuse of EU
finances is becoming as pressing an issue as the flaunting of the
rules by national governments.

Fighting fraud

The question of fraud against the EU budget has always been part of the agenda on EU finances, although in the past, it never assumed its current prominence. The House of Lords Select Committee report cited above, which drew political attention to the problem, concluded that:

> The huge sums which are being lost due to fraud and irregularity against the Community are losses borne by all the taxpayers and traders of Europe. This strikes at the roots of democratic societies, based on the rule of law and its enforcement, and is a public scandal. (House of Lords, 1989, para. 205)

In a follow-up report in March 1994, the House of Lords continued to focus on the mismanagement of EU finances (House of Lords, 6th Report, 1994). Fraud is becoming a major preoccupation of a number of member states, notably the UK, Germany, Denmark and the Netherlands. Fraud is very controversial especially for *le grand public* at a time when integration is more contested in public opinion than ever before. The usually restrained *Financial Times*, in a leader entitled 'Controlling Euro-fraud' spoke of fraudsters 'frolicking through Europe's complex rules for disbursing funds, particularly those for agriculture and infrastructure. Large sums have been paid for non-existent wheat and for sub-standard olive oil. Car loads of sugar, cattle and sheep have been smuggled across borders and re-imported to earn subsidies' (*Financial Times*, 17 November 1994). It is difficult, if not impossible, to get a true picture about the nature and extent of fraud against the EU budget. It is unclear if fraud is a more extensive problem for the EU than for the member-state public finances, or if it is more extensive in some member states than in others. Growing evidence suggests that EU public finances are particularly vulnerable in a number of respects:

- Agricultural levies and customs duties are particularly open to abuse because of the complexities of the common commercial tariff and the ease with which transit documents can be forged;

- The collapse of communism and the unification of Germany meant that with the opening of borders to the east, Poland and the Czech Republic became bases for the manipulation of imports and exports;
- The transit system is particularly vulnerable because some 18 million transit documents are issued annually. Millions of pounds worth of goods never reach their designated destination and are sold without paying taxes or duties;
- The rules of the EAGGF allow fraudsters to take advantage of loopholes and exploit complexity. A director of an agricultural consultancy suggests that 'it is such a labyrinthine muddle of regulations that anyone with a keen mind can quite easily work out how to exploit the system legally or illegally with little risk (*Financial Times*, 21 March 1994);
- The structural funds, which were thought to be relatively free of fraud, are the cause of increasing concern since 1992 because of growing evidence of abuses;
- A weakness of internal control in the Commission led to two serious cases of fraud – tobacco and tourism – masterminded from within the Commission.

The level of fraud against the financial interests of the Community is usually estimated to lie somewhere between 2 and 10 per cent of the budget. The figure 10 per cent, which was bandied around for many years, is based on the calculations of a German fraud specialist, Professor Tiedemann, in evidence to the House of Lords in 1989. This figure, even if derived from considerable experience in this field, can only be a guess. As it stands, the problem of fraud against the EU budget is a question of dark numbers and a black hole, the depth of which is unknown (Ruimschotel, 1993; Mendrinou, 1994; Sherlock and Harding, 1991).

A wide variety of different types of fraud perpetuated against the 'own resources' side of the budget (that is, monies owed to the EU) and against the expenditure side have been unearthed. The multi-leveled nature of the delivery systems and the complex legal framework of many EU funds makes it difficult to detect fraud, and clearly assists those who are intent on misappropriating EU monies. The following cases, outlined in the Commission's annual reports on *Fighting EU Fraud*, illustrate the many and varied techniques used by the fraudsters.

- *Refined sugar* The Commission received a tip-off that refined sugar purchased in Rotterdam and officially bound for Croatia and Slovenia, would be diverted to Italy. The lorries were tailed though France to Italy where the sugar was disposed of in an illegal manner which undermined the local sugar market. The financial impact of the fraud was estimated at ECU 1.6 million in unpaid levies for imported sugar.
- *Meat carrousels* Frozen meat can be shipped between several different countries (fraudulently imported into the Community and re-exported to collect refunds). The fraud report gives details of one shipment of Eastern European beef (including bags of bones) that went from Italy to Malta and was reimported to Austria via Italy, collecting refunds twice.
- *Milk powder* Some 10 000 tonnes of skimmed milk powder, produced in various countries and destined for export to Algeria, was loaded on to seven ships in the Netherlands, went to the German port of Emden and never left it. The exporter, a Dutch company, claimed ECU 15 million in export subsidies.
- *Production aid to cotton* As many as 10 000 Greek farmers are thought to have inflated their production figures by 10 per cent in 1991 and 1992, gaining about ECU 50 million in subsidies to which they were not entitled. Cotton-processing plants entered incorrect weights on production records or engaged in 'double weighing' the same cotton bales.
- *Non-existent produce* A major investigation of durum wheat stocks in Italy revealed non-existent stocks (some 250 000 tonnes) in some warehouses, and discrepancies in the quality of the produce being stored elsewhere.
- *Non-existent training courses* The Commission has discovered a large number of cases of fraud in Social Fund

expenditure. The most common fraud is to seek funding
for training activities that never take place. These frauds
have included airlines, research institutes, public training
agencies and private consultants.

- *Tourism*   Networks were organised in all member states to
  take advantage of Community funds by over-invoicing and
  by using fictitious subcontractors. A number of
  Commission officials have been suspended from their jobs
  and are the subject of a criminal investigation by Belgian
  police.

                        (European Commission, 1990b, 1994f, 1995n)

The strategy for combating fraud is multifaceted and includes
a strengthening of legal sanctions and obligations, the establishment of an anti-fraud unit in the Commission, and more effective
financial management in the Commission and the member
states. Although those combating fraud face many obstacles,
since the late 1980s there has been a definite enhancement of
measures designed to protect the Community's financial interests. Successive reports from the Court of Auditors detailing
problems in the management of EU finances found a resonance
in the EU institutions and in a number of member states. The
Commission and Parliament began to treat the issue seriously,
which in turn put pressure on the Council of Ministers and on
the European Council to make the issue a priority. The
European Council added its authority to the fight against fraud
with a declaration in the Conclusions of the Copenhagen
Summit (June 1993) which underlined 'the importance of fully
implementing the provisions of the Maastricht Treaty according
to which Member States are to take the same measures to
counter fraud affecting the financial interests of the Community
as they take to counter fraud against their own financial interests' (European Council, June 1993). The need to persevere in
the battle against fraud is a recurring theme in the communiqués
of European Council meetings. The European Parliament is
using its right under Article 138c of the TEU to set up the
Temporary Committee of Inquiry to investigate transit fraud.
This gives the EP the power to question not just EU officials but
national officials as well.

The Court of Justice affirms the loyalty clause

A case of fraud involving the importation of corn from Yugoslavia into Greece which was subsequently re-exported to Belgium without paying the required agricultural levies, led to an important judgement in the Court of Justice concerning the obligation on the member states to protect the financial interests of the Community. The Commission, in a series of 'on the spot' investigations in Greece, ran into serious problems with the Greek authorities so that it took the Greek government to the Court. The Court in its judgement delivered in September 1989, ruled that:

> Article 5 of the Treaty requires the Member States to take all measures necessary to guarantee the application and effectiveness of Community law. For that purpose, whilst the choice of penalties remains within their discretion, they must ensure in particular that infringements of Community law are penalised under conditions to those applicable to infringements of national law of a similar nature and importance and which, in any event, make the penalty effective, proportionate and dissuasive. (European Court of Justice, 1989)

Thus although the Court found that criminal law was a *domain reservée* of the member states, they are obliged to use that law in an effective, proportionate and dissuasive manner to protect EU finances. As a consequence of this case, the TEU specifically obliges them to take 'the same measures to counter fraud affecting the financial interests of the Community as they take to counter fraud affecting their own financial interests' (Article 209a, TEU). All EU pronouncements on fraud – whether by the Court of Auditors, the European Parliament or the anti-fraud unit in the Commission – maintain that action to combat fraud affecting the Community's financial interests is primarily the responsibility of the member states, since it is *they* that have the means at their disposal through their police authorities for detecting, monitoring and penalising fraud.

Providing adequate legal protection of Community finances is very complex because of sensitivities regarding national criminal law and the diversity of definitions of fraud in national legal systems. Lawyers are divided about the relationship between national criminal law and Community law. See Box 7.5 for a list of measures to strengthen the legal framework for combating fraud, which includes an obligation on the member states to notify the Commission of cases of fraud and irregularity. A resolution from the European Parliament in October 1991, followed by a request from the Council to the Commission, led to a cross-national comparative study on the concept of fraud and the sanctions applicable in the member states (Delmas-Marty, 1994). In June 1994 the Commission adopted two proposals:

1. A proposal for a Council Regulation on the protection of the Community's financial interests, which advocates a common legal framework for measures to combat fraud and outlines a system of administrative penalties that could be imposed depending on the seriousness of the irregularity (European Commission, 1995c, p. 400).

BOX 7.5
The Community's legal framework to protect its financial interests

- Statutory obligation of member states to notify the Commission about fraud and irregularity.
- Council Regulation (EEC) no. 1552/89 re. 'own resources', Council Regulation (EEC) no. 595/91 re. EAGGF guarantee, Council Regulation (EEC) no. 4253/88 re. Structural Funds.
- Council Regulation (EC, EURATOM) no. 2988/95 on the protection of the Community's financial interests.
- Treaty Obligation (Article 209a, TEU) that the member states must protect the financial interests of the Community as they would their own public finances. Report on measures taken by the member states to fulfil this requirement.
- Administrative co-operation between the EU and the member states.
- Improvement of transit arrangements and advance warning for sensitive products.
- Strengthening of regulations on export refunds.
- Mutual assistance provisions with non-member countries.
- Administrative penalties for all sectors, with a common definition of fraud and irregularity.
- Convention on the approximation of criminal law regarding frauds against the EU budget adopted 27 November 1995.

---

2. A proposal for an international convention under Pillar 3 of the TEU aimed at harmonising the criminal law of the member states.

Attempts to get agreement in the Council on the Commission's proposals were fraught with difficulty because the member states were conscious that this was entering the high politics of criminal law. The draft regulation was processed by the ECOFIN Council and the Ministers for Justice and Home Affairs handled the draft convention. In December 1994, the Essen European Council, concerned about the delays in Council, requested the Ministers to speed up their considerations so that the proposals could be agreed in the first half of 1995. In November 1994, just before the Essen Council, the UK submitted the text of a proposal for a joint action to protect the financial interests of the Community. Negotiations on the two texts continued during 1995 when the ECOFIN reached agreement on a Regulation on the protection of the Community's financial interests, and the Justice Ministers agreed the accompanying convention which is intended to improve the compatibility of national criminal laws (European Commission, 1996a, p. 412). The importance of the Regulation is that for the first time a common definition of irregularities is in place. It is legally binding on the member states and covers all sectors of EU policy.

The establishment of UCLAF

The Commission established UCLAF (*Unité de Coordination pour la Lutte Antifraude*) in 1988 when President Delors needed to seriously address the issue of financial irregularity, and in response to repeated requests from the European Parliament. The unit was part of the Secretariat General and was not under the auspices of DG 20 Financial Control. For many years UCLAF was regarded as a largely symbolic gesture and not as a serious anti-fraud unit. With an initial staff of 17, and temporary agents from the member states, UCLAF could do little more than co-ordinate the work of the anti-fraud units in the main DGs, notably agriculture, the customs union and structural funds. UCLAF grew gradually, but there was continuing tension with the anti-fraud units in the operating DGs.

The unit assumed a heightened profile within the Commission when, in 1993, Commissioner Schmidhuber was given direct responsibility for combating fraud and when Per Brix Knudsen was made director of UCLAF. In 1993 the European Parliament insisted in its discharge procedure that all anti-fraud divisions in the Commission should be integrated in UCLAF so that they were no longer reporting to the Directors General of their respective DGs. The integration of existing units is underway, which gives UCLAF a complement of 130 staff, a significant increase since its establishment.

UCLAF produces an annual report which gives an overview of its investigative activities and its annual work programme. The reports provide details of developments in the legal framework, co-operation with member states including training activities, the main investigations that are being conducted, and the level of reported fraud. UCLAF has acted as a catalyst within the Commission for increased activity in this field, and it has led to far higher levels of detection. For example, reported fraud in 1994 was more than ECU 1 billion, twice as much as in 1993 (European Commission, 1993n). There are, however, many obstacles facing those fighting fraud, notwithstanding the increased priority it has received in recent times. The main obstacles are:

1. Getting adequate co-operation from the member states, which are still resistant to external involvement in what they consider to be police matters. The Commission has no police investigative powers and must rely on co-operation with local police bodies. National police forces and customs authorities have the local knowledge and manpower to pursue cases of fraud. However, there is also the fact that member states display different levels of enthusiasm in pursuing allegations of fraud against their own nationals and companies. The gradual tightening of the legislative web and the clear Treaty obligation on the member states to protect the Community's financial interests may in time establish and embed the norm of co-operation with regard to the Union's finances. The formalisation of the Advisory Committee for the Co-ordination of Fraud Prevention in 1994 provides an institutional device for dialogue with and between the member states. In addition, a programme of

seminars, held each year in the member states, may socialise national actors into taking the issue of EU fraud seriously.

2. The process of simplifying EU legislation, blocking-off loopholes and codifying administrative penalties takes a considerable amount of time. For example, the 1994 proposals on administrative penalties required a unanimous vote in the Council.

3. Many frauds are perpetuated on a cross-national basis by highly-organised and sophisticated organisations, operating on a Union-wide basis but based in those member states whose legislation is vague and whose administrative capacity is less-capable of detecting fraud. Many investigations involve police forces in a number of states. Legal procedures can be very tortuous with long delays in getting evidence released for a court case in another country.

4. Even when the EU or the member states discover irregularies in the use of European public finance, they have considerable difficulty in recovering the money. The member states alone have the legal and administrative capacity to recover monies paid out wrongly, or outstanding 'own resources'. The Commission's role is to monitor the recovery activity; the 1994 Report on *The Fight Against Fraud* shows that member states have notified the Commission of outstanding money amounting to ECU 411 million in EAGGF irregularities only, ECU 21 million of which has been recovered (European Commission, 1995n, p. 87). The Commission is attempting to strengthen the legal requirements on the member states to recover lost money.

Conclusions

The main conclusion of this chapter is that the management of EU finances has become a central item on the EU agenda, and not just a preoccupation of UK Ministers as it was in the late 1980s. The growing size of the budget and the realisation that there are endemic weaknesses in the management of Brussels money has given renewed impetus to those forces wishing to ensure that the financial interests of the Union are protected. Three major preoccupation's animate the debate. First is the need to reduce the budget's exposure to fraud. Second is the need to enhance the control and accountability of national and European institutions in the budgetary domain. Third is a growing emphasis on evaluation and 'value for money'.

The development of a more stringent approach to the management of EU finances may be seen in the Commission's reform programme, spearheaded by Commissioner Liikanen. The promotion of the Court of Auditors to the rank of a full institution, the establishment of UCLAF, the negotiation of regulations on the protection of the Union's financial interests, and new provisions in the TEU are part of a concerted effort to improve the management of EU finances. The European Council has placed its political authority behind the fight against fraud, with continuous support for a comprehensive strategy to combat the perpetrators. An effective strategy depends not only on a concerted effort by EU institutions, but fundamental change in the attitudes of the member states.

8

The Second Financial Arm of the Union: Borrowing and Lending

A very significant but relatively obscure dimension of EU finances consists of the extensive borrowing and lending activities of the Union. The inexorable but quiet growth of this facet of EU finances stands in stark contrast to the fierce battles about the size, distribution and objectives of the Community budget. Conflict and controversy, so characteristic of the Community's budget, are not found in the more sombre confines of the Community's financial institution, the European Investment Bank, which accounts for 90 per cent of all loan activity in the Community. The Bank traditionally eschews publicity, unobtrusively going about its business from its Luxembourg headquarters. The growth of spending programmes in the budget has been matched by an equally impressive expansion and diversification of the Community's lending instruments since the 1970s. The establishment of a new lending institution, the European Investment Fund (EIF), in 1994 added significantly to the range of financial instruments in the Union. In addition, the Community is an important shareholder in the European Bank for Reconstruction and Development (EBRD), set up in 1990 to assist in the reconstruction of the former communist bloc. The volume of borrowing and lending activity in the Union grew from ECU 7.7 billion in 1985 to ECU 22 billion in 1994 (European Commission, 1995c).

The purpose of this chapter is to analyse the Union's lending institutions and the policy instruments at their disposal. The

217

Union's borrowing and lending activities are characterised by the pragmatic development of different instruments arising from varied political and legal contexts without any unifying rationale. The proliferation of lending instruments led inevitably to overlap (Kuhlmann, 1993, p. 587). See Box 8.1 for an overview of the lending and borrowing activities of the Community. Apart from macroeconomic financial assistance for those states that have balance-of-payments difficulties, the other loan instruments – ECSC, EIB, Euratom and NIC – are designed to fulfil micro-economc goals (Costello, 1995, p. 20). Loans are used for internal Community objectives and increasingly as instruments of external policy. The Commission borrows on the international capital markets for all loan instruments, except those supplied by the EIB from its 'own resources'.

Loan-related activities affect the Union's finances in three ways. First, some loans attract interest subsidies which are paid for out of the Community budget. Second, loans complement grants and subsidies in many policy domains making co-ordination between the two types of financial instrument highly desirable, if not always attained. Third, with the expansion of the lending activities of the Community in third countries, the provision of guarantees to the lending institutions from the Community budget is be-

---

BOX 8.1
Borrowing and lending instruments of the Union

European Coal and Steel Community: high authority can borrow to grant loans for:

1. Investments in the coal and steel sector;
2. Conversion programmes in the coal and steel sector;
3. Subsidised housing for workers in coal and steel.

Euratom: authorised to provide loans to nuclear power stations.

Macro-economic instruments: financial assistance for balance-of-payments difficulties for member and non-member states.

Microeconomic instruments: the *New Community Instrument* 1978.

European Investment Bank: loans.

European Investment Fund: guaranteeing private sector loans.

coming increasingly prevalent. This clearly implies a growing risk and exposure, which stood at ECU 13 billion in 1994. As a consequence, the European Parliament and the Court of Auditors are paying increasing attention to the second financial arm of the Union.

Economists provide two main justifications for the use of Community loan instruments for investment. The most significant justification is to correct market imperfections when private lending institutions will not lend for projects that involve a high initial cost with returns spread over a long period. This is usually the case for large-scale infrastructure projects. The Community enjoys an excellent credit rating – 'AAA' – on the financial markets, and thus can borrow at very attractive rates which can then be passed on to the member states or private sector enterprise. There is also an additional political consideration. Given the small size of the Community budget, borrowing and lending allows the Union to increase its financial muscle without having to enter into tortuous negotiations about revenue. Borrowing and lending is one way of evading the constraints of predetermined budget limits and the need for a balanced budget. Ministers find borrowing and lending attractive instruments of public policy because this financial mechanism allows for a degree of 'fiscal illusion' – loans are a costless substitute for grants (Costello, 1995, p. 20).

The European Investment Bank (EIB)

Nature of the institution

Provision for a European Investment Bank (EIB) is found in the original EEC Rome Treaty. A proposal for a European Investment Fund, as an instrument of economic development, was floated at the 1955 Messina Conference. The Bank was not financially as well-endowed as its original proponents would have wished, nor was it a classical investment fund. Instead of a Fund with an initial paid-in capital of 1000 million units of account, the member states opted for a public banking institution to which they committed from 100 million units of account up to a maximum of 400 million units of account, in case the Bank could not raise adequate funds from borrowing on the international capital markets (Dunnett, 1994). The decision not to create an investment fund owed something to the underlying conflict in the dynamic of integration between those member states that traditionally pursued *dirigiste* economic policies, and those that relied on the market. For those states interested in a European industrial policy the establishment of an investment fund was attractive, whereas others feared the interventionist character of such a fund.

The legal framework of the Bank was established by the EEC Treaty, which specified that:

> A European Investment Bank is hereby established which shall act within the limits of the powers conferred upon it by this Treaty and the Statute annexed hereto [Article 4b of the Treaty on European Union, former Article 3, EEC Treaty].

The Treaty provided the EIB with a legal personality, stipulated that its members would be the member states, and that the Statutes annexed to the Treaty would constitute its legal framework (Article 198d TEU, former Article 129 EEC Treaty). The Statutes were adopted as a Protocol to the EEC Treaty and carry the same legal authenticity (Preface, EIB Statutes 1991, p. 5). The essential character of the Bank is its *autonomous* and *separate* legal status from the EC. The legal properties of the EIB and its relationship to the Community has been fleshed out in a number of actions taken before the Court of Justice, the most notable of which was a case as to whether tax levied on the salaries of the staff of the Bank could be retained by the Bank or should be paid to the EC budget. The arguments deployed in the case concerned the legal personality of the Bank and its relations with the EC. The Court concluded that the Bank's 'operational and institutional autonomy does not mean that it is totally separated from the Communities and exempt from every rule of Community law' (Quoted in Dunnett, 1994). The Advocate General in this case, M. Manchini, went much further than the Court in arguing that the Bank's autonomy was in fact merely a technical device and that it should be treated as an EC institution (Dunnett, 1994). Notwithstanding the Bank's autonomous legal personality, its existence rests on the EC because membership of the Bank is tied to membership of the Union.

The internal organisation of the bank

The Bank has independent decision-making organs established by its statutes which provide for:

- A board of governors – 15 members;
- A board of directors – 25 directors and 13 alternates;
- A management committee (European Investment Bank Statute, Article 8).

The board of governors, which sits at the apex of the Bank's hierarchy, consists of one representative per member state, usually national Finance Ministers, who meet once a year. The board of directors is appointed by the board of governors from national nominees, with one from the Commission, for a renewable term of five years. The board of directors is the central decision-making body of the Bank concerning banking matters. Its role is to ensure that the Bank is managed within the provisions of the Treaty and Statute. It has 'sole power' to take decisions about borrowing and lending, it fixes interest rates on loans and the level of commission on guarantees.

The key internal decision-making body of the Bank is the management committee, which consists of the president of the Bank and six vice-presidents (more if the board of governors so wishes) who form the Bank's management team. The president is more than *primus inter pares* on the management committee; he represents the Bank externally and all employees of the Bank work under his authority. The committee is responsible for the day-to-day work of the Bank and for preparing the work of the board of directors.

The expanded role of the Bank manifests itself in the growth of its staff from 561 in 1982, to 859 in 1994. The Bank's internal organisation displays its character as a financial institution with two lending directorates – one for lending in the Union and one for external lending. The latter has diversified considerably since 1989 when a small unit was set up for operations in East Central Europe. The borrowing activity is managed by the finance directorate. The two technical/advisory departments, one staffed by economists and the other by engineers, were merged in 1995 to improve the quality of project evaluation. The engineers are concerned with the microcosts of projects and the economists assess the potential macroeconomic costs of a proposal. A legal affairs directorate and a secretariat general complete the Bank's organisational profile.

Relations with EU institutions

Because of its legal status and its banking remit, the Bank stands somewhat apart from the Union system. However, its role in supporting Community policy preferences means that it must have particularly close relations with the Commission, as the institution responsible for the implementation of many EU policies. The relationship appears to be complementary, with little of the interinstitutional rivalry which is prevalent in Community decision-making. Two senior Directors from the Commission (DG 2 and DG 16) are members or alternates of the Bank's board of directors and are thus intimately involved in the establishment of the Bank's policy on credit. The new programming approach for structural spending since 1988 has meant that the Bank is involved in the preparations of the Community Support Frameworks and in monitoring their execution. When the Cohesion Fund began operations in 1993, the Bank was for the Commission the ideal institution to assess the technical, economic and financial viability of proposed projects. The EIB's relations with the Commission on Cohesion Fund matters are formalised in an interinstitutional agreement dating from 1993. The expansion of the activities of the EIB, and the desire to enhance the complementarity between loan and grant instruments, have brought the Commission and Bank into a closer policy relationship than hitherto.

Close working relations with the Commission are not matched by easy relations with either the European Parliament (EP) or the Court of Auditors. A recurring theme in Parliamentary resolutions is the need to ensure that there is adequate political monitoring of the lending and borrowing activities of the Union (European Parliament 1981, November). The sense that an important financial arm of the Union was beyond democratic control and accountability led the Budgetary Control Committee to draft a number of reports on the EIB and the Union's borrowing and lending activities. A 1994 report (the Zavvos report) argues that there should be far greater accountability of EIB activity because it manages funds on behalf of the Community, and its lending activity affects the implementation of the structural funds from a budgetary perspective (European Parliament, 1994b). This was followed by the Blak report in March 1995 which called on the European Parliament to be vigilant because of its growing importance of non-budgetary finances in the Union. The report called for:

1. More information on budgetary guarantees;
2. Access to the European Investment Bank;
3. Control of the European Investment Fund. (European Parliament, 1995, 263/263651, March 1995)

The Parliament's Resolution on the 1996 Intergovernmental Conference preparations bluntly states that there should be increased accountability of the EIB, notably judicial review by the Court of Justice, monitoring by the Court of Auditors, and a reporting requirement to the Parliament and the Council (European Parliament, 1995b). The Blak report accuses the Bank's officials of suffering from *hauteur technocratique* because of the specialised nature of their work (European Parliament, 1995, p. 4).

Relations between the Court of Auditors and the EIB, although they share neighbouring buildings on the Plateau Kirchberg, have never been good. The Bank guards its independence jealously and sees itself as a commercial organisation at arms-length from the Union's political process. In fact, it attributes much of its success to its ability to stay above the grubby world of EC politics. Although both the EP and the Court of Auditors acknowledge that the EIB is different and that it must be allowed to run its lending activities as a commercial bank, there are aspects of its work that the Court and the Parliament see as falling within their legitimate domain of interest. First, the Court and Parliament argue strongly that when the Bank manages funds on behalf of the Union, or the Union budget guarantees EIB loans, the Bank must be accountable for this process and the Court should be in a position to audit these funds. Second, the Bank carries out a number of financial transactions for the Union and charges a fee for its services. The Court considers that it has the right to vet the EIB's charges and tends to think that the management charges are too high.

There has been continuing dispute between the Court and the Bank on just what the Court should audit and how it should conduct audit visits. The Bank did not want the Court to have the right to conduct on-the-spot checks of the projects its loans finance, on the grounds that it is competent to assess the validity of a project and that its clients must not be subjected to auditing or monitoring by a range of EU bodies. A tripartite audit agreement between the Commission, the Court and the Bank, signed in 1989, failed to normalise relations, with the result that a second agreement was negotiated and signed in November 1992. The Agreement covers:

- Arrangements for auditing by the Court of operations financed from EIB's 'own resources' but covered by a general budget guarantee;
- The establishment of a basic list of documents which must be available at the Commission for the Court;
- The establishment of a procedure for planning and carrying out on-the-spot audits by the Court and the EIB's Audit Committee. (European Court of Auditors, 1993, *Annual Report 1992*, p. 160)

Although the audit agreement established the procedures to be followed by both the Bank and the Court, there is still considerable tension between the two institutions. The Court has to carry out on-the-spot checks with the Bank's Audit Committee, a committee of three part-time officials who are senior civil servants in their perspective member states and thus not always available for audit visits. The Bank, for its part, thinks that the Court does not carry out sufficient documentary audits before deciding that an on-the-spot visit is necessary.

At a more fundamental level, both institutions have divergent views on their respective roles. The Bank monitors its clients but does not audit them. It requires them to keep adequate records of the development of a project and regards this as sufficient for the purpose of monitoring. A Commission reply, penned with the assistance of the Bank, to an observation in the 1993 Court of Auditors report argued that:

Loans unlike grants are repayable. Viewed in this context, the Bank's monitoring procedures are perfectly adequate to ensure the sound utilisation of Community funds for the purposes for which they were intended. (European Court of Auditors, 1994, *Annual Report 1993*, p. 357)

The tone of the Court's observations on the EIB and Commission's replies suggest that there are deep-rooted issues of principle between the two institutions. The Bank has not been able to use its distinct legal personality and its established independence to keep the Court entirely out of its affairs. It has had to concede on-the-spot visits and the right of the Court to audit activities that are guaranteed by the budget or managed by the Bank on behalf of the Commission. This it has done reluctantly because of its concerns that its independence will be undermined and its commercial nature compromised. Whether the new audit agreement will over time lead to a normalisation of relations between the two institutions remains a matter of conjecture.

What the Bank does

The EIB is the Community's household bank for economic development. The Bank has effectively protected its status as the EU bank when alternative financial structures have been mooted. The Commission's preference for 'Eurobonds' to finance the TENs was shelved, as was the suggestion that the new Mediterranean policy be accompanied by a Med Bank. From a slow start in the early 1960s when it financed about three projects each year, the Bank is now the world's largest development Bank, lending more than the World Bank, with a doubling of its balance sheet since 1989 (Honohan, 1995, p. 315). In 1994 it signed loan contracts worth ECU 20 billion, of which ECU 17.6 billion was for internal Community projects and ECU 2.2 billion for projects outside the European Union. There has been an impressive increase in the level of external lending; which rose from ECU 381 million in 1986 to ECU 1.9 billion in 1994 (see Figure 8.1). The expansion in the lending activity of the EIB in the 1980s and 1990s can be traced to a number of factors, notably enlargement, the enhanced

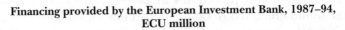

FIGURE 8.1

Financing provided by the European Investment Bank, 1987–94, ECU million

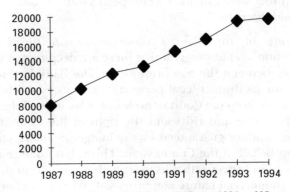

Source: European Investment Bank (1995) *Annual Report 1994*, p. 112.

commitment to cohesion in the Single Act, the collapse of communism and rising external demands on the Union, and new mandates for EIB action. Traditionally, the Bank's lending policy has been characterised by considerable caution. The Bank required guarantees from national governments before it would risk its capital, which greatly reduced the risk of non-payment.

The Bank's remit was originally established by the Treaty (EEC) and was further enhanced by mandates given by the European Council and the by Council of Ministers. Its focus is much narrower and less political than the Commission. The Bank was designed as a development bank, to contribute to 'the balanced and steady development of the common market in the interest of the Community' (Article 198e TEU, former Article 130 EEC). The Bank has interpreted the concept of 'interest of the Community' as support for the policies of the Community as decided by the Community's legislative bodies. In other words, the Bank considers itself as a 'policy taker' rather than a 'policy-maker' in relation to the policies it is committed to support.

To fulfil the objective of 'balanced and steady development', the Bank provides loans and guarantees:

1. For projects in lesser-developed regions;

2. For the modernisation of traditional industry or the establishment of new industries when such projects cannot be entirely financed by the various means available in the member states;
3. For projects of common interest to several member states when such projects cannot be financed by the various means available in the member states. (Article 198e, TEU)

The TEU further stipulates that the Bank should complement the structural funds and other Community financial instruments, thereby enhancing the importance of economic and social cohesion as an objective of EIB lending. The primary role of the Bank relates to redistribution (lagging regions), although allocative objectives are found in points 2 and 3 above (Kuhlmann, 1993, p. 601). However, the role of the EIB is constrained in relation to points 2 and 3 in so far as they may provide finance or guarantees only if alternative sources are not available in the member states.

The statute of the Bank applies the concept of 'subsidiarity' to its lending activity in so far as the Bank grants loans 'to the extent that funds are not available from other sources on reasonable terms' (European Investment Bank, 1991, *Statutes*, Article 18). The Bank's objective is to add to the available pool of investment finance for desirable projects within the terms of Community policy. In judging the quality of a project, the EIB must assess the positive value of the project itself and the 'value added' from EIB financing, by asking how decisive EIB funding is to the project and would the project go ahead without EIB financing? So in addition to the principle of subsidiarity, the Bank is concerned with the additionality of investment funding as a result of its participation, and the complementarity of its funding with other sources of finance.

The EIB has always had the highest credit rating, 'AAA' on the international capital markets. It can thus borrow money on preferential terms, which are then passed on to its borrowers because the EIB is a non-profit making organisation. The advantages of EIB funding are found in the loan terms that it offers, notably longer maturity which may reduce the risk to a project, and in the economic and technical analysis provided by its advisory divisions. The Bank's technical expertise has been built up over a long time in many different countries, which gives its staff a breadth of knowledge not necessarily found in the national technical agencies. Many large projects find that EIB involvement is useful in putting together a financial package. The EIB, from the outset, promoted open public tendering for major contracts, even in those sectors that were excluded from EC public procurement laws. The Bank has thus contributed to the inculcation of the norm of public tendering in the internal market and has always insisted on the highest environmental standards for the projects it finances.

Internal financing

Regional development is the central focus of EIB activity, underpinned by the TEU provision that the EIB 'should continue to devote the majority of its resources to the promotion of economic and social cohesion'. This implies that priority is given to financing projects in Objective 1,2 and 5(b) regions (see pages 128–32). In 1994, the EIB provided loans of over ECU 12 billion for regional development, of which ECU 5.7 billion was directed towards Objective 1 regions (European Investment Bank, 1995, *Annual Report 1994*, p. 116). However, the environment for EIB loans in the Objective 1 regions has been altered somewhat because the reformed structural funds and the Cohesion Fund allow for a very high level of grants for these regions which has led them to scale down their recourse to EIB loans, particularly since 1993.

EIB finance is used to fund projects in many different economic sectors, with a particular emphasis on the provision of infrastructure, environmental protection and industrial development (see Figure 8.2 for a breakdown of financing by sector in 1994). A visitor travelling through any member state is likely to use a road financed by EIB loans, make a telephone call using a communications system modernised by EIB finance, avail of electric light from an EIB-financed power plant, and even experience reduced pollution as a result of EIB-financed environmental improvement schemes.

- Transport is the largest single sector which benefits from EIB support. Motorways, railways, air transport and shipping have all benefited from EIB loan financing. All Europe's

FIGURE 8.2

European Investment Bank loans by sector, 1994

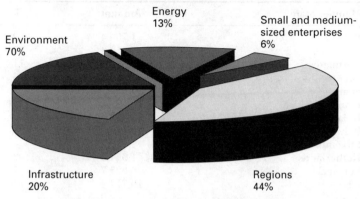

Source: European Investment Bank (1995) *Annual Report 1994*, p. 25.

major infrastructural developments – the Channel Tunnel, the Alpine crossings, the Great Belt link in Denmark, high-speed train networks – have benefited from EIB financing.

- EIB funding contributes to large energy infrastructure projects in all sectors, notably oilfields, power stations, alternative sources of energy, gasline networks.
- The modernisation of telecommunications is a major focus of EIB funding.
- Water and waste disposal.
- Industry

    (see European Investment Bank, *Annual Reports*, 1990–94)

The balance of financing between different sectors tends to fluctuate depending on the priorities of the member states and their investment needs. Because the member states are the shareholders of the Bank, the EIB likes to spread its loans across the EU. Until the 1980s, Italy was the main beneficiary of EIB loans with a very high percentage of loans between 1959 and 1994. Spain joined Italy as a major borrower since its accession in 1986, as did Portugal. A very high proportion of public investment in the two Iberian states involves loan finance from the EIB. Germany also emerged as a more significant borrower from the EIB because of the costs of financing the new *Länder* (see Table 8.1).

TABLE 8.1
Breakdown of European Investment Bank loans by member state,
1990–94 ECU million

Member State	Amount	%
Belgium	1 705.4	2
Denmark	3 519.4	5
Germany	8 332.1	11
Greece	1 966.5	3
Spain	14 321.7	18
France	10 187.1	13
Ireland	1 437.4	2
Italy	18 114.8	23
Luxembourg	88.2	–
Netherlands	1 354.3	2
Portugal	5 625.7	17
UK	10 774.4	14
Austria	162.0	–
Finland	60.2	–
Sweden	15.3	–
Total	77 664.5	100

Source: European Investment Bank (1995) *Annual Report 1994*, p. 112.

External financing

The EIB provides the Union with additional policy instruments
for use in development co-operation and economic development
outside the Union. Article 18 of its Statutes allows the board of
governors to authorise the Bank to provide loans outside the EU.
The Bank's expertise in project financing was brought into play in
the early 1960s as part of the Union's co-operation agreements
with non-member countries. There is little distinction between
what the EIB does within the Union and outside; essentially it
lends money or provides guarantees to projects that it considers
technically sound and economically viable. Its geographical remit
is determined by the association agreements signed by the
Community with third countries. The ACP Lomé states and the
Mediterranean were the focus of the Bank's external activities
until 1989 when the collapse of communism added the countries
of East Central Europe. In 1993 the Bank was given a mandate to
operate in Asia and Latin America. Pressure to add Asia and Latin

America came from Spain, concerned with the increasing concentration of co-operation with Eastern Europe. The growing importance of financing in the CEEC may be seen in the figures for financing outside the Community in 1993 (see Figure 8.3).

EIB financing is an integral component of the financial protocols attached to the Community's Co-operation and Association Agreements with third countries. For example, the Financial Protocol (1991–95) of the 4th Lomé Convention provides for ECU 9.6 billion in grants and ECU 2.3 billion in funds to be managed by the EIB. The latter figure includes loans from the EIB's own resources, risk capital from the European Development Fund, and interest subsidies on loans from the EDF. All the other Financial Protocols are characterised by a similar pattern of EIB activity.

The expansion of the Community's external reach, and financing by the EIB outside the Union, raises the question of how it can protect itself against default by the beneficiaries of its loans. This is an issue for all borrowing and lending activity by the Community and not just EIB loans. The budget has been used as the main instrument to guarantee loans made by the EIB and the Commission. All the borrowing undertaken by the Commission is

FIGURE 8.3

European Investment Bank loan financing outside the Union, 1990–94

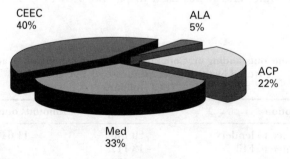

Note:
CEEC   Central and Eastern European Countries
ALA   Asia and Latin America
ACP   African, Caribbean and Pacific states
Med   Mediterranean states
Source: European Investment Bank (1995) *Annual Report 1994*, p. 112.

guaranteed by the budget and EIB loans are guaranteed by the budget for its loans to:

1. Mediterranean states: 75 per cent of loans contracted are covered by Community guarantee, which represented ECU 1.5 billion in non-member Mediterranean countries.
2. CEEC: loans are fully covered by the Community guarantee, with a ceiling of ECU 3 billion up to 1996.
3. Other beneficiaries including Russia and CIS, Latin America and Asia. (European Commission, 1994i, *European Economy*, Supplement no. 10, October 1994)

Because of the growth in lending activities to third countries, the Council and the Parliament called for new warning mechanisms to be put in place to manage the risks against the budget and the growing guarantees provided by the budget. The total risk came to ECU 12.8 billion in June 1993, 14 per cent higher than in December 1992 (European Commission, 1994g, see Table 8.2). The Commission provides the budgetary authority with a report twice a year on the risks for the budgets in future years and the guarantees that have already been activated (ibid.). In 1994, it was decided to create a guarantee fund which would be entered as a reserve in the Community budget and would be activated only if necessary. The budget guarantee was activated in 1994 with respect to loans to a number of CIS states which had failed to pay on schedule, and it was used to pay the EIB ECU 19.7 million

TABLE 8.2
Amounts outstanding on Community borrowing and lending activities covered by the budget guarantee 31 December 1993
(ECU million)

Description	Ceilings	Amounts outstanding
Guarantee to lenders	29 140	11 643
Guarantee to EIB	13 117	2 468
Guarantee on credit to Russia	408	266
Total	42 665	14 377

Source: European Commission (1995) *European Union Public Finance*, p. 146.

when a number of states in the former Yugoslavia failed to make repayments (European Commission, 1995c, p. 408)

New mandates and new challenges

The Bank faces a number of challenges arising from develop-ments in banking and public finance. The growing liquidity and liberalisation of the international capital markets revolutionised banking in the 1980s and forced the EIB to adapt its services and product range. It has to compete in a more competitive and discriminating banking world; its traditional customers can tap other sources of finance with relative ease. More importantly, the trend towards the privatisation of state services and the reduced role of the state in the provision of infrastructure altered the lending environment of the Bank in a fundamental way. Whereas in the past the Bank's customers came predominantly from the public sector, now more and more resources are concentrated in private sector projects, even big infrastructure projects such as the Channel Tunnel and the Canary Wharf project in London. As a result, the Bank's lending portfolio carries a heightened risk. The Bank has had to enhance its credit and monitoring department both in staffing levels and training to cope with the new credit environment. Evaluating risk is not something that the EIB has much experience of because of its traditionally cautious approach (Honohan, 1995, p. 327).

With the economic downturn in 1990/91, the member states looked to the Bank to participate more in what might be loosely called Community economic policy. In many ways the Bank is moving from the role of 'policy taker' to a role in actually shaping policy. The president of the Bank, Sir Brian Urwin, has said that he welcomes new initiatives and mandates, provided that the Bank 'is given an opportunity at an early stage to contribute to the discussion of the policy framework in which it is asked to operate' (European Investment Bank, 1995). The president took part in a number ECOFIN meetings in 1994 and 1995, and repre-sentatives of the Bank participate in all the policy meetings dealing with new mandates. Although the Bank appears willing to take on a growing number of new tasks, it does not intend to expand into fields that carry great risk. For example, the senior management of the Bank let it be known that it would not welcome an invitation from the Council to take charge of the Community's financing of nuclear safety measures in the former Soviet Union. The EIB was willing to accept mandates to manage the European Economic Area (EEA) financial mechanism, to extend its lending activities outside the Community, and to play an increasingly important role in economic policy.

The Edinburgh European Council in December 1992 asked the EIB to establish a new lending facility of ECU 5 billion as part of what was called the *Edinburgh Growth Initiative.* The figure of 5 billion ECUs was subsequently bolstered by decisions of the Copenhagen Summit (June 1993) and the Brussels Summit (October 1993). ECU 1 billion in additional lending would be provided for infrastructure and the same amount in global loans would carry an interest subsidy from the Community budget to foster investment in small and medium-sized firms. The EIB's temporary lending facility was intended for the initial financing of the TENs in transport, telecommunications and energy. The conditions of this lending facility were more generous than normal EIB terms because it could provide up to 75 per cent of the total project cost instead of the usual ceiling of 50 per cent, and if the project involved co-financing with the structural funds the ceiling could go to 90 per cent instead of the normal 70 per cent. The loans under this facility have a maturity of between 15 and 20 years, which was longer than maturities available from other sources.

The Edinburgh Initiative was followed by an intensive analysis and negotiation on the implementation of the TENs programme. The Bank was a full participant in the Christophersen Group, set up to establish the priorities for major capital investment in the EU. The Bank moved from being a 'policy taker' to an important participant in the policy process. The Essen European Council (December 1994) called on the EIB to improve its lending conditions for the TENs, which led it to establish a 'special window' for financing large-scale infrastructure projects. The Bank has conducted economic, technical and financial assessments for the 14 priority projects and is putting together financial packages for many of them. The financial complexity of the TENs projects led to the establishment of a new financial institution – the European Investment Fund, to complement the work of the European Investment Bank.

Institution building: the European Investment Fund (EIF)

The establishment of the European Investment Fund (EIF) in June 1994 as a new financial agency owed its origins to the convergence of a number of distinct trends. The changing nature of EIB lending, with a reduced role for government guarantees, led the Bank to consider ways of strengthening its links with the private banking sector. The Commission, for its part, was searching for a policy instrument that could be used for economic development, particularly for financing large infrastructure projects. Governments would no longer give the guarantees for large-scale investment from their own resources, with the result that the private sector would be called upon to play an enhanced role in providing long-term finance for large-scale undertakings. The Edinburgh European Council proposed that a new financial agency, a guarantee fund with ECU 2 billion capital, should be established. Throughout 1993 the complicated task of establishing a new agency progressed as the legal and financial framework for the new fund was negotiated by the Bank, the member states and the Commission. The statutes of the EIB were supplemented in May 1994 by a new Article 30, which specified that the Bank's board of governors should decide to establish a European Investment Fund under separate statute. Article 30 stipulated that the EC and the EIB could become members of the Fund and contribute to its subscribed capital. The statutes of the Fund were adopted in June 1994 when the EIF was brought into existence.

The Fund is a mixed public/private organisation involving the EC, the EIB and the private banking sector. The EIF, although housed in the EIB's Luxembourg buildings, has a distinct legal framework and separate decision-making organs consisting of a general meeting, a supervisory board, and a financial committee. The financial committee manages the day-to-day operations of the Fund and can decide on projects under ECU 30 million. Above this, the approval of the supervisory board is necessary. The president of the EIB chairs the supervisory board. The financial committee is the Fund's executive organ with three members appointed for a three-year period, one by each category of shareholder.

The mixed nature of the Fund is highlighted by the status of the Bank as the major shareholder with 40 per cent of the paid-up capital, a further 30 per cent from the Commission and 30 per cent from the private banking sector. This ratio underlines the role of the EIB as the major shareholder. The Fund has an initial authorised capital of ECU 2 billion. By the end of 1994, just six months after it began operations, the Fund has reached ECU 1.7 billion in subscribed capital, which enables it to guarantee financing of over ECU 5 billion (EIF, 1994a). The Fund must operate according to sound banking principles and earn an appropriate return on its resources. The Fund operates in two discrete fields that are not closely linked:

- Infrastructure projects in transport, energy and telecommunications (TENs); and
- Small and medium-sized enterprises (SMEs). (EIF, 1994, *Statutes*, Article 2)

The specification of these two distinct areas was a response to what were perceived to be gaps in the EIB's remit. The EIB, because of its statutes, could not take risks of the kind that might be necessary to finance long-term and large-scale infrastructure projects. Nor could the Bank provide the necessary support to small and medium-sized firms that were in need of equity rather than loans. Two years from the establishment of the EIF, the Fund can begin to take equity in small and medium-sized firms. The central objective of the Fund is to draw additional private sector capital into financing long-term infrastructure projects and to enhance the flow of finance to small and medium-sized firms, a critical sector for job creation. In November 1995, a third strand was added to the remit of the EIF. The Commission launched a ECU 200 million fund to bolster film-making in Europe. The purpose of the fund is to enable European film-makers to borrow money to make commercial popular films, a sector which is increasingly dominated by Hollywood. The fund will provide partial guarantees to banks for their lending to film and programme-makers.

The Fund is not a lending agency. Rather it guarantees the loans of private sector banks and financial institutions in the areas specified above. In the first six months of operation, the majority of the Fund's operations involved guaranteeing loans made by the EIB (EIF, 1994a). The Fund still has the appearance of an offshoot of the EIB. The extent to which it will develop its own ethos and activity separate from the Bank remains to be seen. The private banking sector should become more important over time if the Fund is to fulfil its mandate and if the public/private partnership is to succeed.

The borrowing and lending activities of the Community

A range of additional lending instruments has developed at different times under varying legal provisions. The most significant ones are loans from the European Coal and Steel Community (ECSC), Euratom, macro-economic financial assistance for the member states, and the 'New Community Instrument' which was launched in 1978 as part of the agreement on the European Monetary System (European Commission, 1994h). The ECSC Treaty made provision for industrial loans for modernisation of the coal and iron and steel industries. Loans from this source have played a large part in successive efforts to restructure these traditional industries. In 1994 the ECSC made loans of ECU 673 million, although this represents a reduction over previous years. Decisions have already been taken to scale-down the lending activity of the ECSC because the Treaty is due to expire in 2002. Lending via Euratom for financing nuclear power stations began in 1977. A total of ECU 2.8 billion in loans have been signed between 1977 and 1994. In 1994, the Council decided that the Euratom loan facility would be a useful means of channelling finance to the nuclear industry in East Central Europe and in the CIS to improve safety and efficiency.

The rationale behind loans for states with balance-of-payments difficulties is based on the ability of the Commission to take advantage of the Community's 'AAA' rating to raise money on the capital markets at preferential rates, which can then be lent to member states facing financial difficulties. A member state requests financial assistance from the Council, which then authorises the Commission to borrow up to a certain ceiling. The loans under this facility may not exceed ECU 14 billion. Since 1985, the Community has sanctioned two loan facilities for Greece and one for Italy under this heading. A degree of conditionality is attached to these loans since the member states concerned are expected to meet certain economic conditions to draw down the full amount of the loans. With the collapse of communism and the growing demands for external action, macro-economic financial assistance has become a major instrument of policy in East Central Europe, the CIS and in a number of Third World states. Since 1990, the Community has contracted loans with Hungary, the Czech and Slovak republics, Bulgaria, Romania and the Baltic states.

In 1977 the Commissioner for Economic Affairs, M. Ortoli, proposed the creation of a new financial instrument to finance projects in energy, industrial restructuring and regional development. This become known as the 'New Community Instrument' and was intended to complement the lending activities of the EIB and ECSC. The NCI, as it was known, was a response to the recession of the 1970s and part of the package deal that led to the establishment of the European Monetary System (EMS). It was designed to promote investment without fuelling inflation. The original ceiling of ECU 1 billion was raised to ECU 6.8 billion by a number of decisions over the succeeding decade. Interest-rate subsidies were attached to these loans for Ireland and Italy when they decided to join the EMS in 1978. NCI loans are managed by the EIB for the Commission, although no new loans have been contracted under this heading since 1991.

Institution building: the European Bank of Reconstruction and Development

Origins of the EBRD

Although the EBRD is a distinct legal entity and entirely separate from the Union, the EC and the EIB are shareholders of the Bank, and together with the member states hold 51 per cent of the equity in the Bank. Moreover, the Commission channels Phare and Tacis finance through the EBRD. The identity of the EBRD was tied up with the Union from the outset since its Articles contain 'the unprecedented step of making the EC itself and the EIB members of an international financial institution' (Weber, 1994, p. 15). The Bank owes its origins to the collapse of communism in the former Soviet bloc and the need for the West to assist reform and reconstruction in this part of Europe. During this period of extreme political flux, a variety of different proposals were mooted aimed at channelling finance to the former Soviet bloc, including the creation of a special section in the EIB. President Mitterrand was persuaded by one of his senior advisors, Jacques Attali – who went on to become the first president of the EBRD, that a development bank was needed for the East. French policy was part of a deliberate strategy to make the countries of Central and Eastern Europe a 'third concentric circle of the European integration process', so as to dilute German influence and keep the US at arm's length (Weber, 1994, p. 13).

The French President launched the idea in a speech to the European Parliament in October 1989 and received the support of his counterparts in the other member states when the Strasbourg European Council of December 1989 recommended the establishment of a new banking institution. Despite reservations, France's partners felt compelled to support institution-building for the former communist bloc. During 1990 and the first half of 1991, negotiations proceeded on establishing a new multilateral financial institution for Europe. There was considerable disagreement and controversy about many issues such as the amount of equity, the Bank's decision-making organs, location, mode of operation and personnel (Jakobeit, 1992, p. 120). Membership of the Bank was open to European states, non-European members of the Group of 24, the EC and the EIB. The Bank had from the outset a strong European presence and flavour. Controversy about the constitution, role and functions of the Bank centred on disputes between the US and the UK, on the one hand, and France, Germany and Italy on the other (Jakobeit, 1992, p. 120). The US regarded the idea as a French attempt to expand its influence in the former Soviet bloc.

There was considerable disagreement about the extent to which finance from the EBRD should be made conditional on political and economic transformation. The Bank became one of the first multilateral financial institutions to include in its Articles of Agreement explicit reference to multiparty democracy, the strengthening of democratic institutions, the rule of law, respect for human rights and reforms towards market-oriented economies. The conditionality attached to Western aid from Phare was incorporated into the Bank's. A second area of dispute concerned the recipients of EBRD finance. The US and the UK were very insistent that the bulk of finance should go to the private sector. In fact these two countries wanted all finance directed towards the private sector lest the Bank would end up subsidising socialism. The US distrusted the French and felt that France was attempting to promote its statist tradition in the former Soviet bloc. Agreement was reached on a 60:40 ratio between private and public sector lending. The third issue of contention was the status of the Soviet Union in the Bank. France wanted to give it full status and access to the resources of the Bank, whereas the US wanted to restrict Soviet access until it had adopted reformist strategies. The USSR was defined as a recipient state, but with very restrictive terms.

Agreement was finally reached on the legal framework and the technical issues required to establish a new financial institution. In May 1990, 40 states, the EC and the EIB signed the Articles of Agreement. The Bank has authorised capital of ECU 10 billion. The disintegration of the USSR meant that by the end of 1993 the Bank had a membership of 59 states and operated in 25. The Bank makes loans, guarantees debt instruments issued on the capital markets, and may take equity investment. Technical assistance also falls within the remit of the Bank (Dunnett, 1994).

The Attali years

Notwithstanding disputes about the establishment of the Bank, it began operations in April 1991 under the presidency of Jacques Attali, who had first mooted the idea of the Bank to President Mitterrand in 1989. Agreement to Attali as president was part of a package deal which included locating the Bank in London and balancing Attali with a US vice-president. For Jacques Attali, the EBRD was part of the new European order, not just a bank. He described the Bank as 'the first post cold war institution ... totally new in terms of its task and its operational tools' (European Bank for Reconstruction and Development, 1990). He intended the Bank to become the main intermediary between East and West and sought an overtly political role for what was a financial institution. Attali was frustrated with the pace of change in the former communist states and the lack of projects that fell within the Bank's remit. In 1991 the Bank approved 16 projects, and Attali attempted to expand the remit of the Bank but failed to get the support of the shareholders.

Relations between the board of governors and Attali began to deteriorate very quickly when he invited President Gorbachev to visit the Bank without consulting the board in July 1991. In response, the US pressed for a resident board of directors on which it would have a permanent seat. This led all other shareholders to demand similar conditions with the result that the Bank has a bloated board of 23 members which eats up over 12 per cent of the Bank's administrative expenses. The president's position became untenable when, in 1993, newspaper articles claimed that the EBRD had spent more on itself than on loans during its two years in operation. Reports of extravagant expenses, private jets and some $106 million on refurbishing the Bank's headquarters damaged both the credibility of the Bank and its president. Attali was forced to resign in June 1993 when the Bank's internal audit committee concluded that there was mismanagement of the Bank's resources and chronic overspending.

Stability with de Larosière

Jacques de Larosière, a former managing director of the IMF and Governor of the Bank of France, was left to take over the EBRD when, in his own words, 'the life of the Bank was at stake'(*Financial Times*, 29 November 1994). The new president took over at a time of mounting criticism of the performance of the Bank in the former communist bloc and considerable media speculation about its style of operation. M. Larosière set out to improve the Bank's internal management and to refocus its activities. Internally he made a number of significant changes, including a freeze on appointments, a number of redundancies, cost-cutting on all internal administrative services, and changes to the travel policy. This activity was intended to improve the cost efficiency of the Bank. Cost-cutting was accompanied by a major reorganisation of the two banking operations merchant banking and development banking with staff assigned to particular countries.

The new president sought to expand the activity of the Bank beyond the pro-reform states that border the Union to the former CIS. At the beginning of 1994, the Bank's board of directors approved a document dealing with guidelines for the medium term which included:

- A commitment on private sector investment;
- Activity in all countries of operation;
- Importance of financial intermediaries;
- A more active approach towards equity investment;
- Support for projects that are environmentally sound.

(EBRD, 1994, p. 8)

The reorientation of the Bank's activity began to bear fruit in 1994 when it increased the value of its loan portfolio by 74 per cent and signed up for 91 new projects, nearly as many as the first three years of operation. The Bank operates in both the private and public sectors and with international financial institutions. By 1994 there was a pronounced emphasis on private sector funding: 73 per cent of the projects came from the private sector. For the first time, the Bank met the requirements of Article 11.3 of its Agreement which stipulated that no more than 40 per cent of is total committed loans, guarantees and equity investments should go to the public sector (EBRD, 1995). Table 8.3 provides a break-down by country of lending activities of recipient countries between 1990 and 1994.

As a consequence of the performance of the Bank since mid-1993, shareholder confidence has been restored and the Bank is no longer in danger. President de Laroisière received the over-whelming endorsement of the shareholders at the 1994 and 1995 annual meetings. The British Prime Minister, John Major, paid tribute to the new president at the meeting of the board of governors in April 1995 by saying that 'In only 18 months, Mr. de Larosière's clear and strong leadership has transformed the Bank, redirected its activities, and restored confidence in it' (London, 10 April 1995). A *Financial Times* editorial concluded that 'the Bank is no longer wasting its shareholders money. Indeed, its activities now make a positive contribution to the transition to capitalism in eastern Europe' (*Financial Times,* 11 April 1995). The very survival of the Bank depended on the arrival of a new President who had the confidence of the share-holders.

TABLE 8.3
Lending activities of the EBRD, cumulative 1990–94

Country	Amount ECU million
Russia	1074
Poland	901
Hungary	743
Czech Republic	482
Romania	471
Slovenia	309
Slovakia	273
Ukraine	162
Belarus	145
Bulgaria	130
Kazakhstan	112
Uzbekistan	105
Estonia	104
Croatia	95
Lithuania	83
Macedonia	79
Armenia	65
Latvia	59
Albania	49
Azerbaijan	43
Turmenistan	37
Moldova	25
Kyrgyzstan	16
Georgia	15
Regional	195
Total	5772

Source: EBRD (1995) *Annual Report 1994*, p. 13.

Conclusions

Unlike the EU budget, the borrowing and lending activities of the Union appear remarkably free from controversy and conflict. The European Investment Bank goes quietly about its banking business retaining as much autonomy as possible from the Union's political institutions. However, the expansion of its lending activities since the mid-1980s and its involvement in new mandates, particularly in relation to the TENs, has brought the EIB into more sustained co-operation with the Commission and the

ECOFIN Council. The future may hold further challenges of adaptation for the EIB in the event of a single currency, It is likely that the Union will have to develop a capacity for economic and not just monetary management. If so, the Bank is likely to play an important role in the economic domain.

The establishment of the European Investment Fund in 1994 underlines the changing nature of the EIB's financial environment. The EIF enhances the Bank's links with private sector banks which, given the restrictions on public budgets, are increasingly being asked to finance large infrastructural projects. The EIB has also become more involved in the Union's international role as a source of lending finance to countries outside the Union. Its external role complements the Union's external budgetary instruments and increases the flow of EU finance to third countries. Although the EBRD is not a Union institution, both the Commission and the EIB are shareholders and co-operate with the EBRD in Phare and Tacis.

9

An Elusive Budgetary Peace?

The achievement of relative budgetary peace in the 1980s and 1990s is one of the most noteworthy features of the institutional and policy dynamics in the Union since the resurgence of formal integration. Although the budgetary packages have received considerably less scholarly attention than the Single Market, EMU and the intensification of constitution-building in the Union, Delors I and II provided the necessary political and policy cement for these other developments and together represented one of the important achievements of the Delors Commissions. The challenge facing the Union in the future is how to ensure that budgetary peace and a medium-term financial perspective endure beyond 1999 when Delors II runs out.

The future of EU finances is not simply a matter of budgetary peace but affects the nature of the Union as an economic and political space. The budget has implications for the framework of economic policy that emerges and the kind of polity that the Union is becoming. Budgetary issues go to the heart of the relationship between economic and political integration. Two developments, in particular, are set to instil a new dynamic in the process of integration, namely Economic and Monetary Union and enlargement. Enlargement begs questions about the ability of the Union to include many more states without fundamentally weakening its institutions and stretching its policy instruments beyond their capacity.

Although the process leading up to the signing of the TEU reflected the traditional characteristics of EU bargaining and negotiation, the fundamental nature of the 'politics of money' cannot be obscured. Monetary policy is indivisible; responsibility cannot be shared but requires a single institutional framework. EMU begs questions about the political purpose of Union and about the kind of economic governance that is required to make monetary union workable in practice. EMU lies at the borderline between economics and politics because it represents the highest and most advanced level of economic integration and must rest on a deep political commitment to the irreversible nature of the European project. For Chancellor Kohl, monetary union is a necessary step towards an eventual political union, and political union is about 'freedom and peace' (*Financial Times*, 18 December 1995).

The purpose of this chapter is to analyse the unfolding EU agenda and its relationship to budgetary politics in the Union. The Union is facing a multi-faceted and complex political and economic agenda dominated by a series of interrelated issues about which there is considerable friction and argument at the level of the member states, EU institutions and groups representing diverse interests. The first part of the chapter examines the EU agenda in its totality because the outcome on budgetary matters is contingent on agreements in related fields. The second part of the chapter examines the prospects for the future financial perspective after 1999.

The unfolding EU agenda

The EU's agenda between 1996 and 1999 is dominated by four big issues and related negotiating processes:

- An Intergovernmental Conference (IGC) which began in March 1996 designed to further constitution-building in the Union;
- The decision (1998) on which member states will join the EMU in the first phase;
- The opening of accession negotiations with the applicant states six months after the close of the IGC;
- Negotiations on a new financial perspective following Delors II. See Figure 9.1 for an overview of the unfolding agenda.

FIGURE 9.1

European Union: the unfolding agenda

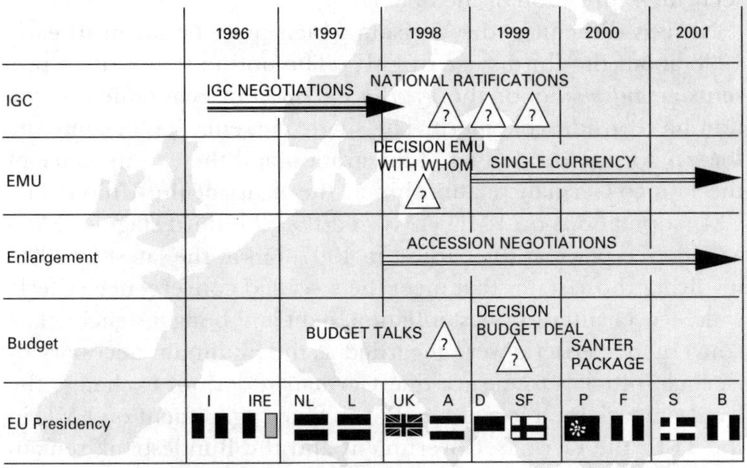

	1996	1997	1998	1999	2000	2001
IGC	IGC NEGOTIATIONS		NATIONAL RATIFICATIONS ⚠? ⚠? ⚠?			
EMU			DECISION EMU WITH WHOM ⚠?	SINGLE CURRENCY ➤		
Enlargement			ACCESSION NEGOTIATIONS ➤			
Budget			BUDGET TALKS ⚠?	DECISION BUDGET DEAL ⚠?	SANTER PACKAGE	
EU Presidency	I IRE	NL L	UK A	D SF	P F	S B

The timing of the different sets of negotiations is far from clear, although a number of key dates are in place. The 1996 IGC opened in March 1996 under the Italian presidency of the Council. The IGC has the two fold task of dealing with the unfinished business of the Treaty on European Union (TEU), and of preparing the Union's constitution and institutions for future enlargements. The core of the 1996 IGC revolves around issues of constitutional design, institutional balance and the Union's international capacity. Economic integration is not a key feature of the negotiations. Preparations for the IGC began in June 1995 with the establishment of a Reflection Group composed of the personal representatives of the member state Foreign Ministers to prepare the agenda for the IGC. The report of the Reflection Group submitted to the Madrid European Council in December 1995 established the outer limits of the negotiations and the areas of agreement and disagreement. The deliberations of the Westerndorp Reflection Group highlight the wide divergence among the member states about the governance structures that they see as desirable and feasible in the Union.

Once the negotiators reach agreement, the new Treaty must pass national ratification procedures, including referenda in a number of member states. The ratification crisis which accompanied the TEU and the Danish 'no' vote underline the potential difficulty of securing ratification of the new Treaty.

No less difficult is the decision which must be taken in early 1998 about the third stage of EMU. The notion that EMU represents a *sauf qualitif* or the *jewel in the crown* of economic integration has considerable merit. The single currency has become the *leitmotif* for the deepening of integration and the maintenance of the Franco-German relationship at the heart of the Union. The TEU stipulations on EMU envisaged that the third stage of EMU would take place at the earliest in 1997, but at the latest by 1999, involving those states that meet the so-called convergence criteria which cover interest rates, inflation, debt and budget deficits. The convergence criteria were regarded as the minimum necessary by German officials to ensure that Germany does not exchange the Deutschmark for a less stable 'Euro'. Since agreement on EMU in the TEU, the German Government and the Bundesbank remain committed to a strict interpretation of the convergence criteria, and have added a demand for a stability council/pact to ensure that those states which join the EMU remain wedded to sound public finances and low inflation.

The provisions on the TEU and developments since then all suggest that if EMU goes ahead in 1999, it will be on the basis of a limited number of states. The TEU already acknowledges that the UK will take a national decision on EMU before the final stage, and that a referendum on the matter may be necessary in Denmark. If the EMU goes ahead with a limited number of states, this raises the prospect of further differentiated integration and the creation of a *de facto* if not a *de jure* core at the heart of the Union. This will have repercussions for the dynamic of the Union both as an economic and political entity. The development of a core has the potential to drive a wedge between the richer and poorer member states and might weaken the commitment of the core states to redistributive mechanisms for the Union as a whole.

The prospect of a continental enlargement of the Union is central to the deliberations on constitution-building in the Union and the next budgetary agreement. The collapse of communism in 1989 ended the artificial division between Eastern and Western

Europe, and meant that the states of Western Europe had to face challenges of continental order and prosperity. For the states of East Central Europe, membership of Western European economic, political and security organisations forms the core of their foreign and domestic policies. The EU accepted at Copenhagen in 1993 that any East Central European state that wished to join the Union could do so. Since Copenhagen the Union has attempted to move towards a pre-accession strategy for these states so that enlargement negotiations can proceed before the end of the 1990s. The timing and duration of enlargement negotiations is far from clear. The Union is committed to opening negotiations with Cyprus and Malta six months after the end of the IGC. At Madrid in December 1995, the European Council instructed the Commission to expedite preparation of its opinions on the applications received so far so that 'the applicant countries are treated on an equal basis' (European Council, 1995, *Conclusions*, Madrid, 15/16 December 1995 p. 23). Moreover, the European Council established the aim of beginning the preliminary stage of negotiations with the CEECs at the same time as with Cyprus and Malta. Enlargement by definition is a process whereby external concerns of the Union become issues of internal Union policy.

The fourth big issue on the Union' agenda is the need to secure a new budgetary package before Delors II runs out at the end of 1999. The Commission submits its proposals on what is already being called Santer I when the IGC deliberations have concluded. This follows the practice in the past when Delors I and II were sold to the member states as part of the process of treaty change. The prospects for a new financial perspective are thus bound up with the outcome of the IGC, EMU and unfolding deliberations on enlargement. Every enlargement in the past changed the dynamic of budgetary politics and this is even more likely this time round.

The unfolding agenda and budgetary politics in the Union

The Intergovernmental Conference

The Union's institutions submitted reports to the Reflection Group, which began its deliberation in June 1995 on the functioning of the TEU as part of the preparatory phase for the IGC. Each institution drew attention to budgetary matters which serve to highlight the central institutional issues surrounding the budget. Not unexpectedly, the European Parliament paid considerable attention to the budget because of its importance in the development of that institution's position in the Union's governance structures. The EP reiterated the demands and procedural prescriptions on budgetary matters that have dominated its thinking in the past. Seven prescriptions were made about budgetary procedures:

1. The unity of the budget should be established;
2. Multi-annual financial planning should be incorporated in the Treaty;
3. The budgetary authority should be responsible for revenue, with the Parliament having a right of assent on revenue matters;
4. The income of the ECB should be deemed a Community 'own resource';
5. The system of revenue should be transparent and reflect the member states' financial capacity;
6. The distinction between compulsory and non-compulsory expenditure should be abolished;
7. The budgetary procedure should be simplified. (European Parliament, 1995b)

This list reflects the Parliament's long-standing demands about budgetary matters which have been echoed in all budgetary debates since it received the 'power of the purse' in 1975.

The Council paid little attention in its report on the TEU to the budget other than to highlight the manner in which the EP established links between budgetary matters and the legislative process. The Council identified the linkage between the co-decision procedure and the insertion of 'amounts deemed necessary' in legislation as one of the teething problems of the TEU. The second problem identified in the Council report was the controversy over the financing of the second Pillar and attempts by the Parliament to use its budgetary powers to increase its presence in Pillar 2 (European Council of Ministers, 1995). Although the Council report is neutral in tone, its underlying message was that the Parliament used its budgetary powers to meddle in issues that were the prerogative of the Council.

The Commission, in its report, draws attention to the divergence between the Union's legislative and budgetary procedures and the need to defuse budgetary conflict. The three problems identified by the Commission were:

- The tendency of the Parliament to use the budget as a means of pushing though measures that should come under the legislative procedure, and the Council's tendency to use legislative channels to adopt financial commitments which should be dealt with under the budget procedure;
- The tension about the financing of Pillars 2 and 3 between the Council and the EP;
- The problem of compulsory and non-compulsory expenditure. (European Commission, 1995m)

The Commission offered no prescriptions on how these conflicts should be resolved other than to underline the benefits of simplifying the budgetary decision-making procedure and smoothing interinstitutional relations.

The Reflection Group identified the renegotiation of the financial perspective for 1999 and beyond as one of the central issues facing the Union, and as part of the broader context of the IGC. The Report's discussion of budgetary matters fell under the rubric of Topic 8 – Instruments Available to the Union. The 1993 Interinstitutional Agreement on budgetary discipline and on the improvement of the budgetary procedure anticipated that budgetary processes would be examined during the 1996 IGC. It is clear from the deliberations of the Reflection Group that most member states oppose addressing the future financial perspective as part of the IGC, because it would extend and complicate the agenda. However, a number of personal representatives drew attention to the connection between the Conference, the Financial Agreement and enlargement. Some delegates clearly signalled that their political masters would want to know 'who will be paying for what' before going ahead not only with enlargement but also with ratification of the Conference itself.

Some of the personal representatives argued that the Conference, although not the appropriate arena in which to discuss budgetary resources, was the appropriate place to lay the treaty foundation for the future of the Union's financial constitution. There was general agreement that the budgetary process should be simplified with the abolition of one of the readings. However, other issues proved more divisive. Only one personal representative signalled support for incorporating multi-annual financial programming in the Treaty. There was disagreement on the removal of the distinction between compulsory and non-compulsory expenditure, on giving the Parliament powers over revenue, and on a new revenue system for the Union. The reform of the Union's financial constitution remains contested.

EMU: the ghost of fiscal federalism

The TEU created a major gap between monetary policy and economic policy. The Treaty established a far more coherent and consistent policy and institutional framework for monetary policy than for economic policy (O'Donnell, 1992, p. 46). The model of economic integration pursued by the Union concentrated on microeconomic policies to do with market creation. Does this provide a sufficient framework for an Economic and Monetary Union? One of the most contested issues about EMU is the implication of a single currency for the EU budget and the Union's financial constitution.

Before the ascendancy of neo-liberal economic thinking in the 1980s, it was assumed that there was a link between the attainment of a single currency and a larger EU budget with a capacity to intervene in stabilisation policy. The MacDougall report, cited in Chapter 2, advocated a larger budget with a capacity for counter-cyclical intervention. The assumption that EMU would require a substantial increase in the budget and a reassessment of its policy instruments was effectively undermined in the run-up to the 1991 IGC on EMU (Laffan and Shackleton, 1996). The previous consensus among economists that monetary union had to be embedded in a strong fiscal capacity to aid adjustment problems and to deal with 'asymmetric shocks' was effectively pushed to one side, despite the fact that in the past all monetary unions have been fiscal unions as well. The absence of a stabilisation capacity is potentially serious as states lose the exchange rate mechanism, are restricted in the use of fiscal instruments, and labour is unlikely to migrate in sufficient numbers to aid adjustment.

The failure to deal with the budgetary consequences of a single currency reflected political realities rather than likely economic ones. Agreement on EMU was difficult to attain and remains fragile. A discussion of the fiscal consequences of an EMU during the IGC would have made the negotiations more controversial and less likely to reach agreement on the goal of a single currency. The major net contributors to the budget were unwilling to accept that a single currency carried budgetary implications. The President of the Bundesbank, Hans Tietmeyer argued rather starkly that:

> In the event of an asymmetric shock, the countries in the monetary union must, on a point of principle, be responsible themselves for achieving the necessary flexibility through internal measures. (Tietmeyer, 1996, p. 8)

The Tietmeyer view is that in monetary union, states must be able to live with low inflation and sound public finances and must not expect to be helped when faced with external shocks.

Notwithstanding the Tietmeyer view, it will be difficult to avoid dealing with the fiscal gap in the Union's financial constitution if a single currency emerges. The Union may be forced, in the interests of political stability, to provide some adjustment mechanism to enable regions and member states to cope with economic shocks that affect some regions more than others. EU finances cannot provide any stabilisation capacity characteristic of the fiscal systems of federal unions. The Commission's report on the future of the Union's financial constitution (1993) represented an attempt to cover the intellectual and economic debate on stabilisation policy. It concluded that regional economic disturbances are to a significant extent absorbed by interregional budgetary flows in federal systems and in unitary states; the regional stabilisation capacity of federal public finance mechanisms amounts to between 20 and 30 per cent (European Commission, 1993b, p. 47). The Commission's report argued for the establishment of a limited financial assistance mechanism (Stabilisation Fund) for regional stabilisation as part of the economic governance capacity in an EMU. The proposals have little political support among the wealthier member states. However, the Union is likely to confront fiscal problems when and if a single currency is established. Stabilisation policy in an EMU raises far more divisive institutional and budgetary questions than the Union has faced in the past.

Enlargement

Central to all discussion on the future of the Union's financial constitution is the question of enlargement and its costs. Enlargement touches key internal bargains in the Union and will affect the budgetary benefits and costs accruing to the present member states. All those internal bargains are the product of highly-contentious and divisive negotiations among the member states about core policy issues. The enlargement debate is fuzzy because the timing, potential membership and transitional arrangements are far from clear. The key questions – of which countries and when – have not not yet been resolved, although the politics of the next enlargement continue to evolve. At present the only predetermined timescale concerning enlargement relates to Cyprus and Malta with whom negotiations will open six months after the conclusion of the 1996 IGC. The Commission has also indicated that it will publish its Opinions on the applications received from the countries of East Central Europe after the conclusion of the IGC.

There are nine applications on the table from East Central Europe – Hungary, Poland, Romania, Slovakia, Latvia, Romania, the Czech Republic, Slovenia, Bulgaria, Estonia and Lithuania. There is no agreement among the member states about the pecking order that should be applied to the applicants. Some states, notably Germany, want to give preferential treatment to the Visegrad four – Poland, the Czech Republic, Hungary and Slovakia – while the Scandinavian states do not want the demands of the Baltic states sidelined. The Madrid European Council (December 1995) concluded that all applicants will be treated equally and on their own merits. Accession negotiations will open at the same time but may be longer for some states than others with varying transitional arrangements.

A continental enlargement of the Union poses policy and budgetary challenges unlike those of the past because the countries of East Central Europe are poorer and more agricultural than the states of Western Europe. The wealth gap between the Mediterranean entrants in the 1980s and the Union, although large, was considerably narrower than the potential gap with the Eastern states. Table 9.1 illustrates the extent of the gap in living standards and the dependency on agriculture, which is as high as 35 per cent of employment in Romania. Average GDP per capita in the ten CEEC countries is about 30 per cent of the EU average with considerable variation. GDP per capita is 50 per cent of the EU average in Slovenia, 40 per cent in the Czech Republic, but less than 20 per cent in Romania and Lithuania. When combined, the ten CEEC countries represent less than 4 per cent of the GDP of the 15 EU countries, an economic weight equivalent to the Netherlands (European Commission, 1995o).

TABLE 9.1
Countries of East Central Europe: basic data

Country	Population (millions)	Area (m. hectares)	GDP (ECU bn)	GDP (per head)	(% EU)	Agriculture (% GDP)	Agriculture (% Employment)
Poland	38.4	31.3	81.8	5029	31.5	6.3	25.6
Hungary	10.3	9.3	35.2	5720	35.8	6.4	10.1
Czech	10.3	7.9	30.8	6738	42.2	3.3	5.6
Slovakia	5.3	4.9	10.6	5365	33.6	5.8	8.4
Slovenia	2.0	2.0	11.3	8076	50.5	4.9	10.7
Romania	22.8	23.8	27.1	2669	15.7	20.2	35.2
Bulgaria	8.5	11.1	8.6	5280	33.0	10.0	21.2
Lithuania	3.7	6.5	2.9	2828	17.7	11.0	22.4
Latvia	2.6	6.5	2.9	4593	28.7	10.6	18.4
Estonia	1.5	4.5	1.9	6136	38.4	10.4	8.2
CEEC-10	105.5	107.7	213.0	4776	29.9	7.8	26.7
EU-15	369.9	323.4	6187.0	15 984	100	2.5	5.7

Note: The data are for 1993 except column 3 which is 1994.
Source: European Commission (1995o), *Interim Report on Enlargement*, sec(95) 605, 6 December 1995, p. 43.

Initial reactions to the costs of enlargement led to newspaper headlines about the dismantling of the CAP, the end of transfers to the cohesion states in Western Europe, and the downgrading of solidarity as a value in the Union. Calculations of the budgetary costs of enlargement are highly-speculative because of the process of economic transformation and internal changes to Union policy. There have been several attempts to calculate the costs of enlargement (see for example CEPR, 1992; Baldwin, 1994; Brenton and Gros, 1993); running though all reports, not un-expectedly given the wealth-gap identified above, is the conclusion that the CEECs would be large net recipients of EU finance if admitted under existing rules and policies (see Table 9.2 for the various budgetary assessments of enlargement). The wealth gap would ensure sizeable flows from the structural funds and their dependency on agriculture would lead to sizeable transfers via the CAP. The potential cost of enlargement led the authors to conclude, in one report, that:

TABLE 9.2
Estimated costs of enlargement (various studies ECU million)

	Net receipts (ECU million) at 1989 output levels[1]	Budgetary effects of membership in 1999 with partial adjustment in agriculture: net receipts[2]	Total budget cost at 1991 income[3]
Poland	5 192		6 500
Hungary	1 458		2 300
Czechoslovakia	1 189		2 900
Visegrad Total	7 839	37.11	11 700
Bulgaria	1 458		2 300
Romania	3 603		9 300
Balkan		16.63	11 600
Baltic		11.41	3 200
Total	12 900		26 500

Source: Adapted from
[1] CEPR (1992), p. 72.
[2] Brenton and Gros (1993), p. 35.
[3] Baldwin (1994).

> the EC faces a stark dilemma: either it must abandon for the foreseeable future any ambition to admit the indisputable European CEECs, or their admission must be accompanied by a change in the budgetary rules. Even though the EFTA countries will be net contributors, their contribution will go only a small way to finance EC enlargement even to a small number of CEEC's. (CEPR, 1992, p. 73)

Not only has the Union not abandoned its ambition to admit the CEECs, but their future membership is now part of stated Union policy, described as a 'political imperative' in the Reflection Group report (European Union, 1995a, p. 3). Although the calculation of the budgetary costs of enlargement are preliminary assessments, they carry political weight in the internal Union debate on enlargement. The budgetary costs of enlargement loom large in the internal Commission debate and in the thinking of the member states.

The Commission approach is to conduct internal and external studies to establish the parameters of the issue, and to begin the slow process of finding policy and budgetary solutions to the dilemmas raised by a larger Union. The Commission's preference is to guard against an erosion of principles such as cohesion and solidarity that it fought hard to embed in the *acquis* in the 1980s. In 1993 the Commission, in the DG 2 study of the Union's finances, examined the budgetary costs of enlargement. The report extrapolated from the flow of EU finance from the structural funds to Portugal and Greece, two of the poorer member states; it calculated that by 1999 the per capita transfer to these two states would be in the order of ECU 400 per capita. On this basis, membership of the four Visegrad countries would imply a prohibitive rise in the structural funds of about ECU 26 billion, with the added inclusion of the Baltics and Balkan states costing ECU 54 billion. Between 1990 and 1992, financial flows to East Central Europe amounted to ECU 3.5 billion (European Commission, 1993b, pp. 112–14).

Given the putative costs involved, the debate on enlargement moved to an assessment of its budgetary consequences for the two main policies – agriculture and structural spending. The internal debate in the Commission and the accompanying bureaucratic politics were fuelled by a series of reports commissioned by Sir

Leon Brittan on the CAP and the CEECs. This followed an earlier
DG 2 report on the future of the CAP which called for radical
reform. Sir Leon asked four agricultural economists to undertake
reports on the options facing the EU and the CEECs in relation to
the CAP. The reports submitted to the Commission in January
1995 took a reformist line on the CAP and argued strongly against
the extension of the present CAP to the CEECs (Buckwell *et al.*,
1994; Tarditi and Marsh, 1994; Tangermann and Josling, 1994).
While DG 6 was highly critical of these reports, it began to assess
the implications of an Eastern enlargement in 1995. The Essen
European Council (December 1994) requested the Commission
to prepare reports on the consequences of enlargement for the
CAP and for structural policy.

The reports, submitted to the Madrid European Council in
December 1995, represent the drift in thinking about these two
sensitive policies in the responsible DGs. The tone of both
reports is that enlargement is costly but *manageable*. The
Commission is intent on avoiding a discussion on the financial
consequences of enlargement before the conclusion of the IGC.
Both reports shy away from very precise costings lest they open a
Pandora's box in the member states on the grounds that 'theoretical estimates based on extrapolation of present arrangements
cannot be a valid basis' (European Commission, 1995m). The
budgetary impact will depend on the Union's level of economic
growth, the timing of enlargements, internal policy changes in
the Union, and the number of states that join at any one time.
The Commission's approach is based on the premise that the
budgetary consequences will be *incremental* and phased since it
does not expect the ten potential CEEC applicants to join at the
same time.

The report on cohesion policy argues that 'the general application of the cohesion policy throughout the Union should be
maintained, even if there is a need for concentration' and that
'Support for least favoured regions should continue to be
the main preoccupation' (European Commission, 1995o, p. 11).
Separately, the Regional Affairs Commissioner, Mrs Wolf-Mathies,
accepts that 'Enlargement eastwards without political guarantees
for the cohesion countries is not socially acceptable or politically
feasible' (*Financial Times*, 30 November, 1995, p. 2). The
Commission is clearly unwilling to antagonise the existing cohe-

sion states at this stage. Concerning the CEECs, the Commission's objective is that the cohesion policy should be fully applied to the new member states with the caveat that 'transitional arrangements after accession will be necessary to integrate them *gradually* into the policy and its financial aspects' (European Commission, 1995, p. 11, italics added). The ability of the new member states to absorb and effectively use financial transfers is a key consideration for the Commission. The report identified 'problems of administrative systems, absorptive capacity and the need for national co-financing' in relation to the level of financial transfers that the CEECs could cope with. This statement is a direct signal that the applicants are unlikely to benefit from the level of per capita transfers achieved by the existing member states, at least in the initial stages of membership.

The Agricultural Strategy paper presented to the Madrid European Council (December 1995) represents the beginning of a process in the Commission whereby DG 6 evolves a plan for dealing with the consequences of enlargement for the CAP. The Commission estimates that if the CAP as presently constituted were to be extended to the CEECs, it would cost ECU 12 billion by 2010, compared to a projected ECU 42 billion for the 15 EU countries. However, the Commission does not envisage the stretching of the existing CAP to incorporate the CEECs. Commissioner Fischler, responsible for agriculture, outlined three possible scenarios of the future evolution of the CAP:

- *Status quo* The paper comes out strongly against attempting to maintain the status quo after 2000 because of the changing external and internal context of agricultural policy. Enlargement is cited as only one of many challenges to the CAP. According to the report, major CAP reform is unavoidable and thus should take place before rather than after enlargement. If reform post-dates enlargement, the Union would have to compensate farmers in the CEECs for higher prices following enlargement.
- *Radical reform* The report discusses the options proposed by many economists for radical reform of the CAP, including the abolition of price support and a total move to income compensation. This option has the advantage that it would lead to a simplification of the CAP and would reduce

agricultural expenditure once compensation payments were phased out. However, the economic and social dislocation could be high and compensation payments would require 'huge sums of additional expenditure' for the first five to ten years of the new system (European Commission, 1995p). Given the agonising negotiations on the MacSharry reforms in 1991 and 1992, such radical solutions are not politically feasible in any event.

- *Developing the 1992 approach* The Commission's report comes out strongly in favour of a continuation of the 1992 MacSharry reforms. Future measures would be designed to make European agriculture more competitive, simpler to run and underpinned by an integrated rural policy. The thrust of future reforms implies a reduced reliance on price support, with compensation where necessary in the form of direct payments to farmers. The report concludes that 'A budgetary margin for such payments would have to be found under the guideline, also in the framework of the new financial perspectives after 1999' (European Commission, 1995p, p. 23).

The further development of the 1992 approach would have the benefit of reducing the costs of an eastwards enlargement. The report argues that CAP compensatory payments were introduced in 1992 as compensation for price cuts, but this was not likely for the CEECs. Instead of making payments to CEEC producers, it would be better to make a significant amount of money available to national and regional authorities for rural development and environmental problems. The message in this report is clear – farmers in the CEECs cannot expect a price and compensation bonzana from membership of the Union.

The prospects for Santer I

The outcome on budgetary matters depends on the evolution of the IGC, the move to stage 3 of EMU, and the timing and conditions of the next enlargement. Failure to secure agreement to or ratify a new Treaty, or subsequent failure to achieve the goal of a single currency, would undermine confidence in the European project and would weaken the political resolve to achieve a significant budgetary agreement. Delors I and II were contingent on the SEA and the TEU in turn. Hence Santer I is heavily contingent on wider developments in integration between 1996 and 1999.

Accession negotiations with the CEECs may be prolonged and membership phased, although developments in the security domain could well force rapid accession. The southern enlargements are instructive on this matter. Council negotiations on Greek membership began in February 1976 and lasted until May 1979 (3 years) when the Treaty of Accession was signed leading to membership two years later (January 1981). Negotiations with Spain and Portugal were even more prolonged and difficult because of Spain's size and Portugal's low level of economic development. Both Spain and Portugal applied for membership in 1977, concluded accession negotiations in 1985 and joined on 1 January 1986. Moreover, the Iberian states did not receive a good budgetary deal; Spain fought hard for a Cohesion Fund to balance what it felt was a bad deal on accession. The Scandinavian states, on the other hand, received significant budgetary compensation to allow them to adjust to the burden of contributing to the EU budget. The CEECs, like the Iberian states, do not come to the table with a strong hand on budgetary matters. Accession negotiations with the CEECs are likely to resemble the Mediterranean pattern. Negotiations may even take longer because of the sheer number of states, their level of economic development and the overcrowded internal EU agenda.

This review of the unfolding EU agenda highlights the possible direction of policy on budgetary matters. The IGC agenda includes the constitutional provisions on financial matters but is unlikely radically to alter decision rules, although some attention will be paid to the Parliament's demands. The simplification of the budgetary process characterised by a reduction to one reading is likely, and the financing of Pillars 2 and 3 must be clarified. However, medium-term planning on budgetary matters is unlikely to become part of the Treaty nor is the distinction between compulsory and non-compulsory expenditure likely to be abolished. The Parliament's desire for powers concerning revenue is highly contentious but might form part of a deal on the powers of the EP.

The budgetary costs of enlargement are the most difficult to assess with any degree of accuracy. Such costs will become clear only when the three questions of 'which countries', 'when' and 'under what conditions' are answered. The budgetary implications of enlargement are likely to be felt on a phased basis as enlargement widens. Debate within the Union on the two most affected policies in the *acquis* – the CAP and structural policy – has only just begun. That said, policy directions are emerging which have the clear purpose of *limiting* the budgetary costs of enlargement. The message from the Commission is that there are increased budgetary costs associated with enlargement, but that these are manageable. The member states have not yet begun to assess the implications of Commission thinking on the level of their existing contributions to, and transfers from, the budget. The level of structural transfers will be influenced by the capacity of the CEECs to absorb EU monies. Suggestions that a ceiling (a percentage of GNP) should be placed on what a state might receive from the structural funds are being examined. On agriculture, a radical dismantling of the CAP is unlikely. Rather, a continuation of the process of incremental reform started in 1992 is the most likely outcome, with long transitional phases for the CEECs.

In 1998 the Commission presents its proposals for the next budgetary agreement. The package will be sold as part of the process of treaty change and the next enlargement. The Commission will look for a larger and better-endowed budget on the grounds that an enlarged Union needs an enhanced financial capacity. The scale of its ambitions will depend on the political climate in the Union and decisions on enlargement. The need for additional resources is likely to manifest itself in proposals for a *fifth resource* which have lurked in the background of previous budgetary rounds. The Commission would like an additional resource (carbon tax, for example) that is not tied to member state contributions but that could be identified as a Union tax. The EP would support the Commission on this. The response of the member states to the Commission proposals is impossible to predict.

The evolution of the negotiations on Santer I will determine just what the member states are prepared to accept in terms of budgetary largesse and additional sources of finance. They succeeded during the negotiations of Delors I and II in reaching agreement on what were very technical, complex and costly financial arrangements. The robustness of the process and the fact that multi-annual financing is part of the *acquis*, although not the Treaty, augers well for agreement on Santer I. However, the dynamic of budgetary politics in the Union altered dramatically after Delors I. On the one hand, the growing number of net contributors and the evident resistance to a larger budget in some member states points to limited, if any, increases in EU funding. On the other hand, the imperative of political stability and prosperity for the continent as a whole may well overcome financial stringency and austerity.

The emergence of many more net contributors makes the Commission's task for Santer I an uphill battle. It may not be able to rely on Germany to provide the final impetus for agreement on a new budgetary deal. Germany has fallen in the prosperity league table, and on equity grounds will expect others to contribute a larger proportion of any budgetary increases. In May 1995, the Bundesrat prefaced its approval of the 1992 own resources decision with the demand that the financial burden of the budget on Germany be corrected post-1999. All net contributors, concerned with the efficiency and effectiveness of transfers, have an interest in attempting to limit the costs to them of a larger budget. The growing emphasis on budgetary management and on combating fraud is set to continue. Evidence of misused or badly-used transfers from Brussels undermines the cohesion states' quest for EU finance and the integration process.

The resistance to sizeable budgetary increases in a number of member states should not be under-estimated. German leaders have increasingly drawn attention to the fact that their contributions to the budget are more than the UK and France combined. The UK is not likely to budge from its traditional stringency on budgetary matters. The Netherlands, once acknowledged as a very *communautaire* state, wants to bring budgetary increases to a halt. For Ireland, the prospect of becoming a net contributor may change attitudes towards budgetary largesse. Yet enlargement to the East is not possible without budgetary costs, however constrained. The EU budget remains a small budget in terms of Western European gross national product, and contributions to the EU budget are a small proportion (2–4 per cent) of public expenditure in the member states. Given the overwhelming differential between the economic weight of EU-15 and the CEEC-10, a relatively small transfer of EU GDP would amount to a significant proportion of the GDPs of the CEECs. A larger EU budget is a small financial and political price to pay for continental stability.

EU finances and the dynamic of integration

The evolution of EU finances tells us much about the dynamic of European integration and the Union's unique model of internationalised governance. It demonstrates one of the great dilemmas when analysing the Union – should we see strength or weakness? EU finances highlight strength in so far as the budgetary policy of the Union and the financial resources at its disposal have grown considerably even at times of austerity in the member states. The decision in 1970 to provide the Union with financial autonomy – own resources – distinguished the Union from other political forms above the level of the state. Grants and loans provide the Union with significant instruments of public policy across a range of policy domains. EU finances are used to foster policy innovation and joint problem-solving throughout the Union. Decisions taken in Brussels affect the material well-being of different social groups, regions and associations throughout Western Europe. The CAP and the structural funds shifted welfare issues above the national level.

EU finances also highlight the limits of integration and the Union as a political space. There has been endemic conflict about the size and purpose of the budget, with every increase the subject of protracted and contentious negotiations. There are clear limits to the willingness of the net contributors to pay for a larger and better-endowed budget. Contributions to the Union budget easily become politicised with resistance from domestic politicians to the distribution of public goods via a supranational budget. Moreover, regulatory instruments remain the dominant form of public power in the system. Even when the Union embarks on an advanced form of economic integration – Economic and Monetary Union – the budgetary consequences are downplayed because the politics of integration are not sufficiently robust to contemplate a significantly larger EU budget, even if such a budget might be warranted.

Bibliography

American Chamber of Commerce (1994) *EU and Wider Europe: Funding Guide* (Brussels: American Chamber of Commerce).

Ardy, B. (1988) 'The National Incidence of the European Community Budget', *Journal of Common Market Studies* 26, pp. 401–29.

Baldwin, R. (1994) *Towards an Integrated Europe* (London: Centre for Economic Policy Research).

Belmont (1995), *Challenge 96*, European Policy Centre, Brussels, Issue 2.

Biehl, D. (1992) 'Fiscal Transfers and Taxation?' in H. Cowie (ed.), *Towards Fiscal Federalism* (London: Federal Trust, conference papers), pp. 17–22.

Biehl, D. (1994) 'The Public Finances of the Union', in A. Duff *et al.* (eds), *Maastricht and Beyond: Building the European Union* (London: Routeledge), pp. 140–56.

Bowles, R. and Jones, P. (1992) 'Equity and the EC Budget; A Pooled Cross Section Time Series Analysis', *Journal of European Social Policy*, 2, pp. 87–106.

Brenton, P. and Gros, D. (1993) *The Budgetary Implications of EC Enlargement* (CEPS: Brussels), Working Paper no. 78.

Brouwer, H. J. (1995) 'A New Budget Deal Means Policy Reform', in H. Brouwer *et al.*, *Do We Need a New EU Budget Deal?* (Brussels: The Philip Morris Institute), June, pp. 16–26.

Buckwell, Allan, S. Hayes, S. Danidova and A. Kwiecinski (1994) *Feasibility of an Agricultural Strategy to Prepare the Countries of Central and Eastern Europe for EU Accession*, Study commissioned by DG 1, EU Commission, 16 December 1994.

Bundesbank (1993) 'The Financial Relations of the Federal Republic of Germany with the European Communities since 1988', Monthly Report of the Deutsche Bundesbank: Frankfurt am Main, 45, November, pp. 62–81.

Centre for Economic Policy Research (CEPR) (1992) *Is Bigger Better? The Economic of EC Enlargement* (CEPR: London), Annual Report.

Coget, G. (1994) 'Les Resources Propres Communautaire', *Revue Française de Finances Publiques*, 45, pp. 51–96.

Collins, D. (1983) The Operation of the European Social Fund (Kent: Croom Healm).

Corbett R. (1994) 'Governance and Institutional Developments', *Journal of Common Market Studies: Annual Review 1993*, pp. 27–44.

Corrie, H. (1994) 'Campaigning to Green the EC Structural Funds', *The European Citizen*, Brussels: Euro Citizen Action Service, pp. 19–20.

265

Costello, D. (1995) 'What Public Functions at the Community level in EMU?', Dublin: unpublished paper for Institute of European Affairs Project 1996.

Cot, Jean-Pierre (1989) 'The Fine Art of Community Budgeting Procedure', *1992 and After: Contemporary European Affairs*, 1, pp. 227–39.

Cova, C. (1990) 'Lomé IV: Une Convention Pour 10 Ans', *Revue Du Marché Commun*, no. 333, pp. 1–2.

Cram, L. (1994) 'The European Commission as a Multi-Organization: Social Policy and IT Policy in the EU', *Journal of European Public Policy*, 1, pp. 195–218.

Deffaa, W. (1992) 'The 1992 Community Budget – A Sound Basis for Community Finances? *Intereconomics* 2, March, pp. 62–9.

Delmas-Marty, M. (1994) *Summary of a Comparative Study on the Protection of the Financial Interests of the Community*, Paper presented to seminar organised by DG 20, Brussels 1994.

Denton, G. (1981) 'How to Prevent the EC Budget Reinforcing Divergence: A British View', in M. Hodges and W. Wallace (eds), *Economic Divergence in the European Community* (London: Allen & Unwin), pp. 80–100.

Denton, G. (1984) 'Restructuring the EC Budget: Implications of the Fontainebleau Agreement', *Journal of Common Market Studies*, 23, pp. 117–40.

Dodsworth, J. (1975) 'European Community Financing: An Analysis of the Dublin Amendment', *Journal of Common Market Studies*, 24, pp. 129–39.

Dunnett, R. (1991) 'The European Bank for Reconstruction and Development: A Legal Survey', *Common Market Law Review*, 28, pp. 571–97.

Dunnett, R. (1994) 'The European Investment Bank: Autonomous Instrument of Common Policy', *Common Market Law Review*, 31, pp. 721–63.

Ehlermann, C. D. (1982) 'The Financing of the Community: The distinction Between Financial Contributions and Own Resources', *Common Market Law Review*, 19, pp. 571–89.

Emerson, M. and T. Scott, (1977) 'The Financial Mechanism in the Budget of the European Community: The Hard Core of the British "Renegotiations" of 1974–1975', *Common Market Law Review*, 14, pp. 209–29.

EBRD (European Bank for Reconstruction and Development) (1990) Speech by Jacques Attali, President of the EBRD to the Bretton Woods Committee, Washington DC, 22 September.

EBRD (1992) *Basic Documents of the European Bank for Reconstruction and Development* (London: EBRD).

EBRD (1994) *Annual Report 1993* (London: EBRD).

EBRD (1994a) *Financing with the EBRD* (London: EBRD).

EBRD (1995) *Annual Report 1994* (London: EBRD).

EBRD (1995a) Proceedings of the Fourth Annual Meeting of the Board of Governors (London: EBRD).

European Citizen Action Service (1993) *A Guide to EC Funding for NGOs – The EC's Most Colourful Flowers* (Brussels: European Citizen Action Service) Guide 1/1993.

European Commission (1978) *Financing the Community Budget: The Way Ahead*, Bulletin European Communities, Supplement 8/78.

European Commission (1987) *The Single European Act: A New Frontier for Europe* (Com (87) 100).

European Commission (1987a) *Report by the Commission to the Council and the Parliament on the Financing of the Community Budget* (Com (87) 101 final).

European Commission (1988) *Research on 'The Cost of Non-Europe' Project: The Cecchini Report* (Luxembourg: Official Publications).

European Commission (1989) *Community Public Finance: The European Budget After the 1988 Reform* (Luxembourg: Official Publications).

European Commission (1990) *One Market: One Money* (Luxembourg: Official Publications).

European Commission (1990a) *The Community and German Unification: Financial Aspect*, Com (90) 400 final, 21 August.

European Commission (1990b) *The Fight Against Fraud: Report on Work Done and Progress Achieved in 1989*, Sec (90) 156 final, 31 January.

European Commission, (1991) *Fourth Periodic Report on the Regions* (Luxembourg: Official Publications).

European Commission, (1991a) 'Communication of the Commission to the Council on the development and future of the CAP', Com (91) 100 final (Luxembourg: Official Publications).

European Commission (1992) 'The System of Own Resources', Com (92) 81 final, 10 March.

European Commission (1992a) *From the Single Act to Maastricht and Beyond: The Means to Match Our Ambitions*, Bulletin European Communities, Supplement 1/92.

European Commission (1992b) *The Community's Finances Between Now and 1997*, Com (92) 2001 final, 10 March.

European Commission (1993) *Overview Preliminary General Budget of the European Communities: 1994*, Sec(93) 800.

European Commission (1993a) *The Economics of Community Public Finance*, Brussels: European Economy, no. 5.

European Commission (1993b) *Stable Money: Sound Finances*, Brussels: European Economy, no. 53.

European Commission, (1993c) *Growth, Competitiveness and Employment*, Brussels: Official Publications.

European Commission (1993d) *Community Structural Funds 1994–99*, Regulations and Commentary (Luxembourg: Official Publications).

European Commission (1993e) 'Promoting Economic Recovery in Europe: The Edinburgh Growth Initiative', Com (93) 164 final, 15 April.

European Commission (1993f) 'G24 take stock of assistance to central and eastern Europe', Press Release, IP (93/341).

European Commission (1993g) *Annual Report 1992: Phare Programme,* (Luxembourg: Official Publications).

European Commission (1994) *The Community Budget: The Facts in Figures,* Sec (94) 1100.

European Commission (1994a) *Overview Preliminary Draft Budget of the European Communities 1995,* Sec (94) 800.

European Commission, (1994b), *Adjustment of the Financial Perspective with a View to Enlargement of the European Union,* Com (94)398.

European Commission (1994c) *Annual Report 1993: Phare Programme* (Luxembourg: Official Publications).

European Commission (1994d) 'The European Union's Relations with the Mediterranean', Internal Memo/94/74.

European Commission (1994e) Press Release on the publication of the 1993 Annual report of the Court of Auditors, 15 November 1994.

European Commission (1994f) *Protecting the Financial Interests of the Community: The Fight Against Fraud: 1993 Annual Report* (Luxembourg: Official Publications).

European Commission (1994g) Commission report on Guarantees Covered by the General Budget-Situation at 30 June 1993, Com (93) 687 final, 26 January.

European Commission (1994h) Report from the Commission to the Council and the European Parliament on the rate of utilisation of the New Community Instrument, Com (94) 494 final, 17, November.

European Commission (1994i) Report on the Borrowing and Lending Activities of the Community in 1993, *European Economy,* Supplement A, no. 10, October

European Commission (1994j), Press Statement by Commissioner Marin, 28 November.

European Commission (1995) *European Union Public Finance* (Luxembourg: Official Publications).

European Commission (1995a) *General Budget of the European Union for the Financial Year 1995,* Sec (95) 10.

European Commission (1995b) *Preliminary Draft Budget of the European Communities 1996,* Volume 4, Com (95) 300.

European Commission (1995c) *General Report on the Activities of the European Union: 1994* (Luxembourg: Official Publications).

European Commission (1995d) *Fifth Annual Report on the Implementation of the Reform of the Structural Funds – 1993,* Com (95), Com (95), 30 final, 20 March.

European Commission (1995e) EU Regional Policies: Fact Sheet 15, February 1995, DG 16, Brussels.

European Commission (1995f) *Protecting the Financial Interest of the Community: The Fight against Fraud: 1994 Annual Report* (Luxembourg: Official Publicatios).

European Commission (1995g) Memo by Commissioner Schmidhuber on Financial Management, Sec 95/26.

European Commission (1995h) *Commission Strategy to Improve Financial Management* approved by the Commission 25 January 1995 at its 1232 meeting.

European Commission (1995i) *2000 – Sound Financial Management,* Information Note from Commissioners Gradin and Liikanen to the Commission, Sec 95, 477, 20 March 1995.

European Commission (1995j) *Report to the Commission on the Improvement of Financial Management: Phase 1,* adopted by the Commision, 21 June 1995, Sec 95, 1013/5.

European Commission (1995k) Press Release IP/95/629, 21 June 1995.

European Commission (1995l) *Sound and Efficient Management,* Brussels, 8 November 1995, Sec (95) 1814 (final)

European Commission (1995m) *Report on the Operation of the Treaty on European Union,* Sec 95, final, 10 May.

European Commission (1995n) *The Fight Against Fraud: Annual Report 1994* Com (95) 98, 29 March.

European Commission (1995o) Interim report to the European Council on the effects on the policies of the EU of enlargements to the associated countries of central and eastern Europe, SEC 95, 605.

European Commission (1995p) Study on alternative strategies for the development of relations in the field of agriculture between the EU and the associated countries with a view to future accession of these countries, CSE 95, 607.

European Commission (1996) *The Fight Against Fraud: Annual Report 1995,* Com 96 173 final, 8 May.

European Commission (1996a) General Report on the Activities of the European Union 1995 (Luxembourg: Official Publications).

European Communities (1970) Council Decision of April 21 1970 on the replacement of financial contributions from member states by the communities' own resources, *Official Journal* L94, 28 April.

European Communities (1988) Council Regulation No. 2052/88 on the tasks of the structural funds, *Official Journal* L 185/9, 15 July.

European Communities (1988a) Interinstitutional Agreement on Budgetary Discipline, *Official Journal* L 185/33, 15 July.

European Communities (1990) Financial Regulation applicable to the general budget of the European Communities (revised and consolidated text), DG 19, Internal Document.

European Communities (1990a) Text of IV Lomé Convention (Luxembourg: Official Publications).

European Communities (1993) Interinstitutional Agreement on Budgetary Discipline, *Official Journal* C 331, 12 December.

European Communities (1993a) Council Regulation no. 2081/93, *Official Journal* L 193/5, 31 July.

European Communities (1994) Council Decision 94/729 on budgetary discipline, *Official Journal* L 293/14, 12 November.

European Communities (1994a) Council decision on the system of the European Communities' own resources, *Official Journal* L 293/9, 12 November.

European Communities (1994b) Commission tender for technical support for the Leonardo Programme, *Official Journal,* C 245/10, 10 September.

European Community Humanitarian Office (ECHO) (1994) *Humanitarian Aid of the European Union: Annual Report 1993* (Luxembourg: Official Publications).

European Council (1978) *Conclusions*, Brussels, December 1978.

European Council (1979) *Conclusions*, March 1979.

European Council (1987) *Conclusions*, Brussels, June 1987.

European Council (1989) *Conclusions*, Strasbourg, December 1989.

European Council (1992) *Conclusions*, Lisbon, June 1992.

European Council (1993) *Conclusions*, Copenhagen, June 1993.

European Council (1994) *Conclusions*, Essen, December 1994.

European Council (1995) *Conclusions*, Madrid, December 1995.

European Council (1996) *Conclusions*, Florence, June 1996.

European Council of Ministers (1995) Report of the Council of Ministers on the Functioning of the TEU, reproduced in *European Report*, no. 2032, 12 April.

European Court of Auditors (1981) Study of the Financial Systems of the European Communities, *Official Journal* C 342, 31 December.

European Court of Auditors (1983) Report in response to the conclusions of the European Council (Stuttgart) *Official Journal* C 287, 24 October.

European Court of Auditors (1992) *Opinion no. 2/92 on EU Financial Management* (Luxembourg: Court of Auditors).

European Court of Auditors (1993) *Annual Report 1992, Official Journal* C 309, 16 November.

European Court of Auditors (1994) *Annual Report 1993, Official Journal* C 327, 24 November.

European Court of Auditors (1994a) Information Note on the 1993 Annual Report (Luxembourg: Court of Auditors) November 1994.

European Court of Auditors (1994b) *Auditing the Community's Finances* (Luxembourg: Official Publications).

European Court of Auditors (1995) *Annual Report 1994, Official Journal* C 303, 14 November.

European Court of Auditors (1995a) *Statement of Assurance: Financial Year 1994*, Luxembourg, 14 November.

European Court of Justice (1989) *Commission Against Greece*, Case 68/88, ECR 2965.

European Investment Bank (1991) *EIB Statutes* (Luxembourg: EIB, updated version).

European Investment Bank (1994) *Annual Report 1993* (Luxembourg: EIB).

European Investment Bank (1995) *Annual Report 1994* (Luxembourg: EIB).

European Investment Bank, *EIB Information: Newsletter*, various issues.

European Investment Bank, *Information Booklets* on lending in non-member countries – Mediterranean, Central and Eastern Europe, Asia and Latin America.

European Investment Fund (1994) *EIF Statutes* (Luxembourg: EIF).

European Investment Fund (1994a) *Annual Report 1994* (Luxembourg: EIF).

European Parliament (1973) *The Case for a European Audit Office*, Aiger Report, Luxembourg: EP.

European Parliament (1977) *The Budgetary Powers of the EP*, PE 49.730 (Luxembourg: EP).

European Parliament (1981) Resolutions on the borrowing an lending activities of the European Community, *Official Journal C 287*, 9 November.

European Parliament (1989) *The Powers of the European Parliament*, Political Series No. 15 (Luxembourg: EP).

European Parliament (Each Year) *Report on the Budgetary Procedure* (Luxembourg: EP).

European Parliament (1993) *Report on Relations Between Bodies Responsible for Control of the Community Budget*, Tomlinson Report, A3-0320/93.

European Parliament (1993a) Discharge for 1991 Budget and Resolution accompanying the discharge, *Official Journal* C 150/102, 31 June.

European Parliament (1993b) EP Debate *Official Journal*, C 437/47, 26 November.

European Parliament (1994) *Report on the Draft General Budget of the European Communities*, 1995, Wynn Report, A 4–0105/94, 12 December.

European Parliament (1994a) Resolution on the delay of the discharge for the 1992 financial year, *Official Journal*, C128/322, 9 May.

European Parliament (1994b) Report of the Committee on Budgetary Control on the democratic control of the financial policy of the EIB and the EBRD, Zavvos Report, EP doc A3–107/94.

European Parliament (1995) Working Document on Borrowing and Lending, Blak Report, EP 211.586, 7 March.

European Parliament (1995a) *Report on Giving Discharge for the 1992 Financial Year*, Cornelisen Report, A4–000/95, 21 March.

European Parliament (1995b) Bourlanges and Martin Report on the 1996 Intergovernmental Conference, EP A4.0102/95, 17 May.

European Parliament (1995c) *Summary of Phare Financial Performance*, Committee on Budgets, 12 April.

European Parliament (1995d), *Summary of Tacis Financial Performance*, Committee on Budgets, 12 April.

European Report (1994) no. 1954, June, p. 2.

European Research Office (1993), 'Understanding the Lomé Convention', Brussels.

Fernandez-Fabregas, F. and Lentz, J. (1994) 'Le Budget 1994: Le Déroulement de la Procédure Budgétaire: Ses Incidentes et son Aboutissement', *Revue du Marché commun et de l'Union Européenne*, no. 381, September, pp. 505–27.

Fortescue, J. A. (1994) 'First Experiences with the Implementation of the Third Pillar Provisions', paper delivered to a conference on Pillar 3, College of Europe, December 1994.

Friedman, B. (1995) 'A German View of Budgetary Reform' in Brouwer *et al.*, pp. 49–58.

Goodhart, C. A. E. (1989) *Money, Information and Uncertainty*, 2nd edition (London: Macmillan).

Grahl, J. and Teague, P. (1990) *1992 – The Big Market* (London: Lawrence & Wishart).

Grant, W. (1995) 'The Limits of Common Agricultural Policy Reform and the Option of Denationalisation', *European Journal of Public Policy*, 2, pp. 1–18.

Groutage, C. and Zangel, P. (1992) 'Next Steps in EC Budgetary Policy' in H. Cowie (ed.) *Towards Fiscal Federalism* (London: Federal Trust, conference papers), pp. 1–9.

Harding, C. (1994) '*The Relationship of Community and State on the Enforcement of Community Law and Policy*', paper presented to a conference on The Single Market, University of Exeter, September 1994.

Havel, V. (1994) Address to the European Parliament, 8 March 1994.

Helm, D. and Smith, S. (1989) 'The Assessment: Economic Integration and the Role of the European Community', *Oxford Review of Economic Policy*, 5, pp. 1–19.

Hewitt, A. (1993) 'Crisis or Transition in Foreign Aid', report prepared by the ODI Institute, London.

Hill, C. (1993) 'The Capability–Expectations Gap, or Conceptualising Europe's International Role', *Journal of Common Market Studies*, 31, pp. 305–28.

Hodges, M. (1981) 'Liberty, Equality, Divergency: The Legacy of the Treaty of Rome?', in M. Hodges and W. Wallace (eds), *Economic Divergence in the European Community* (London: Allen & Unwin), pp. 1–15.

Holland, M. (1994) 'Plus ça change? The European Union "Joint Action" and South Africa' (Brussels: CEPS) paper no. 57.

Honohan, P. (1995) 'The Public Policy Role of the European Investment Bank within the EU, *Journal of Common Market Studies*, September, no. 3, pp. 315–330.

Hooghe, L. L. (ed.) (1996) *Cohesion Policy, the European Union and Subnational Mobilization* (Oxford: Oxford University Press).

House of Lords (1987) *Report on the Court of Auditors*, 1986–87, HL Paper 102.

House of Lords (1989) *Fraud Against the Community*, 1988–89, HL Paper 27.

House of Lords (1993) *The Fight Against Fraud*, 1992–93, HL Paper 44.

House of Lords (1994) *Fraud and Mismanagement in the Community's Finances*, 1993–94, HL Paper 34.

Hungary (1994) Statement by Hungarian Government at the Entry into Force of the Europe Agreement, 31 January, Press Release.

Irish Business Bureau (1995) *EU Structural Funds: A Practical Guide* (Brussels: IBB).

Jachenfuchs, M. and Kohler-Koch, B. (1995) 'The Transformation of Governance in the European Union', paper presented at the Fourth

Biennial International Conference of the European Community Studies Association, Charleston, South Carolina, May 1995.

Jakbobeit, C. (1992) 'The EBRD: Redunant or an Important Actor in the Transformation of Eastern Europe?', *Intereconomics*, May/June, pp. 119–23.

Jenkins, M. (1980) 'Britain and the Community Budget: The End of a Chapter', *Common Market Law Review*, 17, pp. 493–507.

Keemer, P. (1985) *State Audit in Western Europe: A Comparative Study*, University of Bath.

Kok, C. (1989) 'The Court of Auditors of the European Communities: "The Other European Court in Luxembourg"', *Common Market Law Review*, 26, pp. 345–67.

Kuhlmann, M. J. (1993) 'Community Loan and Loan Related Instruments', in *The Economics of Community Public Finance* (Brussels: Commission, no. 5), pp. 585–605.

Laffan, B. (1995) 'Knowledge and Expertise in the EU Policy Process: A Research Brief', HCM Research Network, University of Essex.

Laffan, B. and Shackleton, M. (1996) 'The Budget' in H. Wallace and W. Wallace (eds), *Policy Making in the European Union* (Oxford: Oxford University Press), pp. 71–96.

Leeson, C. (1995) 'Through the Grants Maze', paper presented to a Conference on EU Funding Opportunities, Dublin 23 June.

Ludlow, P. (1989) *Beyond 1992: Europe and its Western Partners* (Brussels: CEPS), paper no. 38.

McAleavey, P. and Mitchell, J. (1994) 'Industrial Regions and Lobbying in the Structural Funds Reform Process', *Journal of Common Market Studies*, 32, pp. 237–48.

MacDougall, D. (1977) *Report of the Study Group on the Role of Public Finance in European Integration*, Vols. 1 and 2 (Brussels: EU Commission).

McMath, J. (1995) 'The EBRD: An Emerging Determinant of EU Policy?', paper presented to the fourth Biennial Conference ECSA, Charleston, USA, 11–14 May.

Majone, G. (1993) 'The European Community between Social Policy and Social Regulation', *Journal of Common Market Studies*, 31, pp. 153–70.

Matthews, D. and Mayes, D. (1992) 'The 1992 UK Presidency of the Council of Ministers', *National Institute Economic Review*, August, pp. 71–80.

Mazey, S. and Richardson, J. (1993) *Lobbying in the European Community* (Oxford: Oxford University Press).

Mendrinou, M. (1994) 'European Community Fraud and the Politics of Institutional Development', *European Journal of Political Research*, 26(1), pp. 81–102.

Metcalfe, L. (1992) 'Can the Commission Manage Europe', *Australian Journal of Public Administration*, 51, pp. 117–30.

Munk, K. J. (1993) 'The Rationale for the Common Agricultural Policy and other EC Sectoral Policies', in *The Economics of Community Public Finance* (Luxembourg: European Economy, no. 5), pp. 295–314.

Musgrave, R. A. and Musgrave, P. B. (1980), 3rd edition *Public Finance in Theory and Practice* (Tokyo: McGraw Hill).

Netherlands (1995) Memorandum to Dutch States General on 'The Net Position of the Netherlands *vis-à-vis* the EU Budget', Produced by Ministry of Finance. 14 February.

Nicoll, W. (1984) 'The Battles of the European Budget', *Policy Studies*, 5 July, pp. 4–20.

Nicoll, W. (1988) 'The Long March of the EC's 1988 Budget', *Journal of Common Market Studies*, 27 December, pp. 161–9.

Nicoll, W. (1988a) 'L' Accord Interinstituionnel sur la Discipline Budgétaire et l'amélioration de la Procédure Budgétaire', *Revue Du Marché Commun*, no. 319, July, pp. 373–80.

Nicoll, W. (1995) 'The Budget Council', in M. Westlake *The Council of the European Union* (London: Cartermill Publishing), pp. 179–91.

Nicora, F. (1990), 'Lomé IV: Processus, Phases et Structures de la Négociation', *Revue Du Marché Commun*, no. 337, pp. 395–403.

Oates, W. E. (ed.) (1977) *The Political Economy of Fiscal Federalism*, (Toronto: Lexington Books).

O'Donnell, R. (ed.) (1991) *Economic and Monetary Union* (Dublin: Institute of European Affairs).

Ó Halpin, E. (1988) 'The European Court of Auditors and National Audit Practice: Prospects for a Common Approach to Public Audit in the European Communities', monograph (Dublin: Dublin City University).

Ostrom, M. J. (1982) *Member States and the European Community Budget*, (Copenhagen: Samfundsvidenskabeligt Forlag).

Padoa-Schioppa, T. (1987) *Efficiency, Stability and Equity: A Strategy for the Evolution of the Economic System of the European Community* (Oxford: Oxford University Press).

Pelkmans, J. (1982) 'The Assignment of Public Functions in Economic Integration', *Journal of Common Market Studies*, 31, no. 1–2, pp. 97–121.

Peter, J. (1995) *A Base in Brussels* (London: Local Government International Bureau), Special Report, no. 2.

Peters, G. B. (1994) 'Agenda-setting in the European Community', *European Journal of Public Policy*, 1, pp. 9–26.

Peterson, J. (1995) 'Decision-Making in the European Union: Towards a Framework for Analysis', *Journal of European Public Policy*, 2, pp. 69–94.

Pinder, J. (1972) 'Positive Integration and Negative Integration: Some Problems of Economic Union in the EEC', in M. Hodges (ed.), *European Integration* (Middlesex: Penguin), pp. 124–50.

Pinder, J. (1991) *European Community: The Building of a Union* (Oxford: Oxford University Press).

Planas, J. and Casal, J. (1994) 'The complexities of assessing ESF performance: some specific examples', *European Journal of Vocational Training*, 3, pp. 32–8.

Reichenbach, H. (1994) 'The Implications of Cohesion Policy for the Community's Budget', in J. Mortensen (ed.), *Improving Economic and Social Cohesion in the European Community* (New York: St. Martin's Press), pp. 195–210.

Revue du Marché Commun: each year the Revue publishes a detailed commentary on the elaboration of the annual budget usually written by officials from the Council Secretariat who have witnessed the process at close hand.

Rey, V. (1993) 'La Dimension Financière des Relations Extérieure de la Communauté Européenne', *Revue du Marché Commun et de l'Union Européenne*, no. 368, May, pp. 3–9.

Riddell, R. C. (1990) 'European Aid to Sub-Saharan Africa: Performance in the 1980s and Future Prospects', *The European Journal of Development Research*, 4, pp. 59–80.

Robins, N. (1994) 'Upgrading EU Foreign Aid: Last Chance for Lomé?', *Economist Intelligence Unit*, May, pp. 65–71.

Ross, G. (1995) *Jacques Delors and European Integration* (Cambridge: Polity Press).

Ruimschotel, D. (1993) *The EC Budget: Ten Per Cent Fraud? – A Policy Analysis* (Florence: European University Institute), working paper EPU, no. 93/8.

Sabatier, P. A. and Jenkins-Smith, H. C. (1993) *Policy Change and Learning: An Advocacy Coalition Approach* (Boulder: Westview Press).

Sandholtz, W. (1992) 'ESPRIT and the Politics of International Collective Action', *Journal of Common Market Studies*, 30, pp. 1–22.

Shanks, M. (1977) *European Social Policy: Today and Tomorrow* (Brussels: Pergamon).

Scharp, M. and Pavitt, K. 'Technology Policy in the 1990s: Old Trends and New Realities, *Journal of Common Market Studies*, 31, pp. 129–52.

Sedelmeier, U. and Wallace, H. (1996) 'Policies Towards Central and Eastern Europe', in H. Wallace and W. Wallace (eds), *Policy-Making in the European Union* (Oxford: Oxford University Press), pp. 353–88.

Shackleton, M. (1990) *Financing the European Community* (London: Printer).

Shackleton, M. (1993) 'Keynote Article: The Delors II Budget Package', *The European Community 1992, Journal of Common Market Studies*, pp. 11–26.

Sherlock, A. and Harding, C. (1991), 'Controlling Fraud within the European Community', *European Law Review*, 16, pp. 20–36.

Simmonds, K. R. (1980) 'The Second Lomé Convention: The Innovative Features', *Common Market Law Review*, 17, pp. 415–35.

Simmonds, K. R. (1985) 'The Third Lomé Convention', *Common Market Law Review*, 22, pp. 389–420.

Simmonds, K. R. (1991) 'The Fourth Lomé Convention', *Common Market Law Review*, 28, pp. 521–47.

Smith, M. (1994) 'The European Union, Foreign Economic Policy and the Changing World Arena', *Journal of European Public Policy*, 1, pp. 283–302.

Smith, M. (1996) 'The European Union and a Changing Europe: Establishing the Boundaries of Order', *Journal of Common Market Studies*, 34, pp. 5–28.

Smith, S. (1992) 'Financing the European Community: A Review of Options for the Future', *Fiscal Studies*, 13, pp. 98–127.

Spahn, B. P. (1994) 'Fiscal Federalism: A Survey of the Literature', in J. Mortensen (ed.), *Improving Economic and Social Cohesion in the European Community* (New York: St Martin's Press), pp. 145–54.

Strasser, D. (1992) *The Finances of Europe*, 7th edition (Luxembourg: Office of Official Publications).

Sutherland, P. (1992) 'Progress to European Union – A Challenge for the Public Service, *European Institute of Public Administration Newsletter*, no. 992/3.

Tabary, P. (1990) 'Le Nouvel Instrument Communautaire, une Cooperation Efficace au Service d'investissements Prioritaires pour L'Europe', *Revue du Marché Commun*, 355, pp. 203–7.

Tangermann, S. and Josling, T. E. (1994) *Pre-accession Agricultural Policies for Central Europe and the European Union*, internal study prepared for DG 1, Commission, 12 December.

Tarditi, S. and Marsh, J. (1994) *Agricultural Strategies for the Enlargement of the European Union to Central and Eastern European Countries*, DG1 study, 19 December 1994.

Tietmeyer, H. (1996) 'European Monetary Union: A Challenge for Europe', Address to the Institute of European Affairs, Dublin, March 13.

Tommel, I. (1993) 'The European Community's Strategy for System Transformation in Eastern Europe', paper presented to ECPR workshop, University of Leiden, The Netherlands, 2–8 April 1993.

Tsebelis, G. (1990) *Nested Games: Rational Choice in Comparative Politics* (Berkeley: University of California Press).

United Kingdom (1982) *Britain and the European Community: The Budget Problem*, Pamphlet prepared for the Foreign and Commonwealth Office by the Central Office of Information, 27 September.

University College Dublin (1995) *Research Bulletin*, no. 59.

Vibert, F. (1994) 'The Future Role of the European Commission', London: European Policy Forum, Discussion Paper, May.

Vuylsteke, C. (1995) 'The EBRD: Its Mandate, Instruments, Challenges and Responses', *MOCT-MOST*, no. 5, pp. 129–55. Journal Published by Kluwer in NLS.

Wallace, H. (1980) *Budgetary Politics: The Finances of the European Communities* (London: Allan & Unwin).

Wallace, H. and Wallace, W. (eds) (1996) *Policy-Making in the European Union*, 3rd edition (Oxford: Oxford University Press).

Wallace, W. (1995) 'Germany as Europe's Leading Power', *World Today*, July, pp. 162–4.

Weber, S. (1994) 'The European Bank for Reconstruction and Development', *International Organization*, 48, pp. 1–38.

Weiss, C. (1970) 'The Politicisation of Evaluation Research', *Journal of Social Issues*, 26, pp. 50–62.

Wynn, T. (1994) 'Europe's Budget: The Italians Fooling the Council, the Council Making Fools of the Germans', *European Brief*, October, pp. 5–6.

Wynn, T. (1994a) 'A Good Budget for Europe', *European Brief*, November, pp. 36–7.

Zangel, P. (1989) 'The Interinstitutional Agreement on Budgetary Discipline and Improvement of the Budgetary Procedure', *Common Market Law Review*, 26, pp. 675–85.

Zangel, P. (1993) 'The Financing of the Community after the Edinburgh European Council', *Intereconomics*, 3, pp. 1–17.

Index